*Michelangelo once broke out in indignant protest against his
fellow artists who were for ever depicting Christ in his death
on the cross. 'Paint him instead the Lord of life. Paint him with his
kingly feet planted on the stone that held him in the tomb.'*

*But Michelangelo continued to isolate the death of Christ,
from the* Pietà *of his youth in St. Peter's to the unfinished* Pietà
*in Florence. . . . So did the theologians and the preachers.*

## THE JESUS LIBRARY
### edited by Michael Green

The Hard Sayings of Jesus
*F. F. Bruce*

The Teaching of Jesus
*Norman Anderson*

The Empty Cross of Jesus
*Michael Green*

The Counselling of Jesus
*Duncan Buchanan*

Jesus: Lord & Savior
*F. F. Bruce*

The Evidence for Jesus
*R. T. France*

The Healings of Jesus
*Michael Harper*

Jesus, Man of Prayer
*Margaret Magdalen*

Jesus and Power
*David Prior*

The Parables of Jesus
*David Wenham*

THE JESUS LIBRARY
*Michael Green, series editor*

# The Empty Cross of Jesus

## Michael Green

*InterVarsity Press*
*Downers Grove*
*Illinois 60515*

Published in the United States of America by InterVarsity Press, Downers Grove, Illinois, with permission from Hodder and Stoughton Limited, England.

InterVarsity Press is the book-publishing division of Inter-Varsity Christian Fellowship, a student movement active on campus at hundreds of universities, colleges and schools of nursing. For information about local and regional activities, write IVCF, 233 Langdon St., Madison, WI 53703.

Cover illustration: Janice Skivington

ISBN 0-87784-930-7
ISBN 0-87784-933-1 (The Jesus Library set)

Printed in the United States of America

Library of Congress Cataloging in Publication Data

Green, Michael, 1930-
    The empty cross of Jesus.

    (The Jesus library)
    Bibliography: p.
    1. Jesus Christ—crucifixion.  2. Jesus
Christ—Resurrection.   I. Title.   II. Series.
BT453.G68              1984              232              84-19312
ISBN 0-87784-930-7

17   16   15   14   13   12   11   10   9   8   7   6   5   4   3
96   95   94   93   92   91

*For Duncan and Di Buchanan
and the community of St. Paul's, Grahamstown,
where this book was written.*

# Editor's Preface

In recent years much New Testament scholarship has once again become concentrated on the person of Jesus of Nazareth. The church and the Holy Spirit had dominated much study in the seventies, and it is healthy to return to the founder of Christianity.

*The Jesus Library* is designed to take a fresh look at some of the controversial issues about Jesus, and to explore some neglected aspects. Every volume in the series is written by a theologian who is concerned with the practical life of preaching, teaching and living the Christian faith. It is hoped, therefore, that they will each address issues which are in dispute among scholars, but do so in a way which will engage with the questionings and impinge on the discipleship of Christians who may lack technical knowledge of the subject. Accordingly, as in the *I Believe* series to which *The Jesus Library* is a sequel, footnotes and the apparatus of scholarship are eschewed so far as possible. Emphasis is laid on the academic competence of the author, on his concern for the living church, and on his ability to communicate clearly and relevantly.

It has been a privilege to attempt this book on the empty cross of Jesus. It has made me realise afresh how little I have pierced into the central mystery of the Christian faith. I offer it in the hope that, for all its inadequacies, it may help some Christians in a deeper awareness of what Calvary cost our Lord, and what Easter can mean for the individual, the church and the world. Much of the book was written in the home of the Venerable Duncan and Mrs. Di Buchanan, the Warden's House, Grahamstown, South Africa. They were hosts to my wife and myself for nearly two months of sabbatical leave from the parish, which we spent with them in February and March, 1983. It is a pleasure to dedicate this book to them along with the staff and students of their Theological College, from whom we learnt much.

I also want to thank my wife Rosemary for her help with chapter 13 on counselling: she knows more on this subject than I ever shall. Professor Howard Marshall of Aberdeen gave me helpful initial advice. I am very grateful to St. Aldate's for granting me a sabbatical, to Jane Holloway, my colleague, for retyping the manuscript, and to Rob Warner and Carolyn Armitage at Hodder's for the unfailing courtesy and encouragement they have afforded me. Most of all, I want to thank God for the empty cross.

Michael Green

# Chapter 1

## What God Has Joined

Jesus of Nazareth is without doubt the most celebrated person who has ever lived. And the most famous event in his whole life was the way it ended. He was executed in agony on a cross in *c.* A.D. 30. Ever since, that death has cast its spell on mankind. No death has been so talked about, so depicted in art and music, as the death of Jesus, and none has had so many books written about it. Why, then, write another on a subject which has, surely, been exhausted?

*Why should the cross and resurrection require further examination?*
There are several reasons. In the first place, the cross of Jesus is the very core of the gospel, and it needs to be re-examined in every generation. The human heart shrinks from the cross. It is too painful, too bloody, too humiliating for proud modern man. And so we prefer to concentrate on the absence of God, or man come of age, or the church, or the Holy Spirit. The cross remains for us, as it did in the first century, both 'folly' and a 'stumbling-block' and yet it is the power of God and the wisdom of God. The cross is the central symbol in Christian churches. The cross lies at the heart of the Holy Communion, the only service Jesus left behind him. The cross is the key to the ultimate problem of how a holy God can accept sinners into his company. So fundamental is the cross of Jesus to Christianity that no apology needs to be made for a further examination of this central mystery of the faith.

There is a second reason for undertaking this study. I have found during many years as a university and theological college teacher that the subject of the cross of Christ is often a matter of debate and argument. It is interpreted in different and often contradictory categories. It is treated as an item in dogmatic theology. But what has the cross to say to the man in despair, to the heartbroken and the guilty? How does it relate to human situations such as loneliness and bereavement, to struggles between races or power blocks? What has it to say in the face of terrible natural disasters like Aberfan or ghastly expressions of human wickedness like Auschwitz? It is one of the merits of Jürgen Moltmann's *The Crucified God* that he does seek to make precisely that application. But that is very rare. All too often the cross of Jesus is boxed away in a theological compartment, and books are written by professional theologians for and against one another on the subject. But Jesus died for human beings, not only for theologians. Accordingly, the cross is too important a matter to be left to the theologians. If it is true that God Almighty was in Christ redeeming the world on Calvary, which is certainly part of the New Testament claim about the death of Jesus, then we need to understand what that cross can mean for ordinary individuals and communities. This book will attempt some application of the wonder and achievement of Christ's death to our everyday situations. And if it succeeds, to however small an extent, in doing that, it will not be wasted. For the cross was *for us*: it was meant to meet our varied human needs.

But I had a third reason for undertaking this study in *The Jesus Library*. Part of the purpose of the series is to take a fresh look at current theological assumptions or emphases which appear to be at variance with the New Testament. And one of the most marked differences is the way in which the first Christians did not lay a great deal of emphasis on the cross, *tout simple*. They did not isolate it, as Bultmann has done, and regard it as *the* saving event, with the resurrection being a mythical way of stressing its saving nature. On the contrary, the overall emphasis of the New Testament proclamation is preserved very typically in the account of Peter's sermon on the Day of Pentecost.

> This Jesus, delivered up according to the definite plan and foreknowledge of God, you crucified and killed... This Jesus God raised up, and of that we are all witnesses. Being therefore exalted at the right hand of God, and having received from the Father the promise of the Holy Spirit, he has poured out this which you see and hear (Acts 2: 23, 32f).

The cross was not generally proclaimed by itself, but in union with the resurrection and in the power given by the Holy Spirit. The cross and resurrection of Jesus belong together. They should never have been divorced into separate and all-but hermetically-sealed compartments of dogmatic theology. It is not the cross which saves. It is Jesus, crucified and risen. 'Jesus was put to death for our offences and raised for our justification' (Rom. 4: 25). And because this link has been so often lost sight of, our grasp on both cross and resurrection has been weakened. How could the death of a self-styled messianic figure avail for anyone – if God had not raised him from the dead? And what is the resurrection but God's vindication of that suffering figure who died in ignominy on the public gallows? It is for this reason that I am attempting to hold together these two great aspects of the central drama of salvation. They belong together.

*Why does the isolation of cross from resurrection matter?*
Does the separation matter? After all, the cross and resurrection are both mighty themes; surely each deserves a treatise on its own? I think that the separation does matter, and that the isolated treatment of these two vital aspects of God's action for the human race has had a number of unfortunate consequences. Here are some of them. The list is far from exhaustive.

Take first exemplarism. This is a way of looking at the cross as if it were simply and solely an example of self-sacrifice. Jesus had taught that 'greater love has no man than this, that a man should lay down his life for his friends'. And on the cross we find him practising what he preached. But is that all there is to it? There is a hymn often sung on Remembrance Sunday which refers to the deaths of those who perished in two world wars as 'their lesser Calvaries'. But surely that will never do. Their deaths were sometimes involuntary, sometimes willing; sometimes cowardly, sometimes brave; sometimes on purpose, sometimes by accident. Often they were for an ideal, such as freedom or duty to country. But in no way were they identical or even comparable to the purposive, voluntary, self-sacrificial surrender of his life by the Son of God for sinful men and women the world over. Of none of those deaths in warfare could it be said that 'God so loved the world that he gave his only Son, that whosoever believes in him should not perish but have everlasting life.' Nobody could have said of one of those heroic mariners, airmen or soldiers 'he bore our sins in his own body on the tree, that we, being dead to sin, might live to righteousness'. Yet that is what they said about the death of Jesus, and it is precisely this difference that exemplarist teaching about his cross obscures. To be sure, his death was the supreme example of total self-sacrifice, not just for his friends, but for his enemies. But that is one of the lesser heights of the Everest of Calvary. Exemplarism springs from failing to grasp that the cross and resurrection belong together. Nobody could have seriously put forward an exemplarist doctrine of the cross if they had held it together with the resurrection of Jesus. For his rising from the tomb – if it be true – is just what did *not* happen to other heroes and martyrs for a thousand causes.

At the opposite extreme from exemplarism lies another doctrine of the atonement which also fails to grasp the significance of the resurrection. I mean, of course, that doctrine of satisfaction which has been found in some parts of Christendom since Anselm. Christ's death on the cross was the means whereby satisfaction was made for sin, and harmony restored in a world which had clearly run amok. A variation on this view can be found in many evangelical circles which see a crude substitution as lying at the heart of the cross. God's affronted justice required payment in redress by somebody: on the cross Jesus paid it instead of sinners. I would not deny for a moment that there is a substitutionary element in the cross, but it cannot be expressed fittingly by claiming that God arbitrarily substituted Jesus for the sins of all the world. That would be a bookkeeping transaction, and would give us a very strange doctrine of the justice of God who was happy for the wrong person to suffer; it would also give a very subpersonal understanding of Jesus, almost as if he were some commodity to be exchanged. But once the cross and resurrection are held together, a very different picture emerges. It is the picture the New Testament itself gives us, of a living Christ who died for us and rose again. The one who entered into our alienation and estrangement at the most profound level is alive to welcome us back, 'ransomed, healed, restored, forgiven' into the Father's home of love.

A third weakness which springs from separating the cross and resurrection can be seen in the popular Roman Catholicism of Latin America. Everywhere there are images of the Virgin Mary, at times no more than a mild Christianisation of the feminine fertility principle endemic in animism. Where Jesus is recognised at all, he appears in one of three guises. Either he is the helpless baby held in the arms of his Mother; or he is the dying hero, his pains depicted with a very gruesome realism in the Stations of the Cross; or else he is the awesome future Judge. At no time while visiting a number of Latin American countries did I get any sense that Jesus was risen and alive, except in circles that had been revived by the Catholic charismatic movement. Everywhere else it seemed to be a powerless Jesus, a dead Jesus, or a threatening Jesus that was presented. The balance was only put right when the cross and resurrection were held together.

Rationalism has also had a hand in the separation of the cross and resurrection in Christian thought. Since the rise of the Enlightenment the miraculous has been greatly at a discount. It has therefore seemed naive and credulous to believe the greatest of all miracles associated with Christianity, the resurrection of Jesus Christ from the dead. The cross presents no such difficulties. There is nothing supernatural about it, particularly if it is separated from associated dogmatic theories, and it is perfectly possible to continue discussing and writing about it without having any real Christian faith whatsoever. This is not possible with the resurrection. And the New Testament makes it very plain that both stand or fall together as acts of God, the God who gives Christ for our offences and vindicates him by the resurrection.

What is more, if the cross and resurrection are separated in our thoughts and in our writings, the way is paved for a powerless orthodoxy. Doctrines are neatly tabulated in the mind of the Christian and filed away. They do not spring to life: they did not with me, until I came to see that the resurrection, if it is true, changes not one branch of Christian doctrine, but everything. It gives us a living Christ not a dead one; a contemporary one, not a figure in a history book. It is not a part of the Christian landscape. It is the light by which we discern that there is a landscape at all, and what lies behind it.

A sixth consequence of this disastrous separation of cross and resurrection is the silence of much of the Christian church in the face of disaster and tragedy. The early Christians went to their funerals with a real measure of joy over their departed loved ones; they saw death through the lens of the resurrection hope. They dated the deaths of their martyrs by the appropriate year and added, *regnante Jesu Christo*, 'in the reign of Jesus Christ'. They were able to hold disaster in perspective because they saw the cross, the central mystery of faith, through the light of the resurrection. Well, is that early Christian resilient faith apparent in Christian circles today? Do clergy normally enable their congregations to face agony with at least one eye on the empty tomb? Is there in the average Christian funeral anything distinctively different in attitude from atheist funerals? I fear there is often no difference at all. And part of the reason is that we have separated the cross and resurrection in our minds, have lightly said to a suffering friend

'It's your cross, dear' and have failed to set tragedy and pain in the light of the resurrection. Instead of a robust faith which can face suffering with quiet confidence in God who raises the dead, we have degenerated into a selfish eudaemonism which regards pleasure and good times as our right, and complains that the first touch of adversity destroys our faith. 'Why does God allow it?' would not be stilled, but it would be heard a lot less often in church circles if we had not separated cross and resurrection.

Finally, if you separate cross from resurrection you are prone to yet another distortion. It is strongly attacked in Ernst Käsemann's *Jesus Means Freedom*. It is a form of enthusiastic religion which is very strong on the resurrection and very weak on the cross. Like the Corinthians there is the implication that we are already filled, already rich, already entered into our reign (1 Cor. 4:8). So real are the powers of the age to come, to Christians of this ilk, that they forget we are still children of this age, subject to its limitations and frailties. A religion of the resurrection separated from the cross is a dangerous and an unlovely thing. It breeds arrogance. It writes other Christians off. It assumes we may have anything we ask without qualifications – if only we ask in faith. This is a current danger in one wing of the charismatic movement, represented by large and growing churches such as Rhema in America and South Africa which are strong on the healing and prosperity principles. In other words, so clear are they that Christians are sons of God and therefore heirs to all his riches, that we can rightly expect full prosperity in this life, provided we trust God and pay our tithes. And because God is a God of wholeness and salvation we can expect full health here and now in this life; healing is always available if we believe God sufficiently. It may be that I have oversimplified; but that is certainly the impression given in considerable circles of the Renewal Movement, and it is just as dangerous as when Käsemann attacked it with such gusto half a generation ago in Germany. It was to counter this sort of emphasis at Corinth that Paul was determined to know nothing among them but Jesus Christ and

him crucified. They were so strong on the resurrection that they
had forgotten the cross. They were so strong on the age to come
and its power that they had forgotten that they were also still
heirs to this age and its weakness. They revelled in the
resurrection of Jesus, but did not want to share his cross. But
the two inevitably hang together, and any Christianity which
stresses the one at the expense of the other is a perversion of the
truth. The way for Jesus and for his followers alike is *per ardua
ad astra*. No thorns, no crown.

I have perhaps said enough to justify taking the cross and
resurrection of Jesus together as a single theme in this book.
Theological apartheid is a dangerous policy. It has disastrous
consequences for Christian faith and Christian life alike.
Martin Hengel is the modern theologian who has seen this
most clearly. After a fascinating exploration into the origins of
the New Testament teaching about the death of Christ and his
resurrection he concludes:

> The death of the Messiah and his resurrection or exaltation
> from the dead was understood, in terms of the salvation thus
> given, as an indissoluble unity... There is no clear way of
> pointing to a pure resurrection kerygma without a
> soteriological interpretation of the death of Jesus. Con-
> versely it was also impossible to refer only to the death of
> Jesus without confessing his resurrection: 'if Christ has not
> been raised, your faith is futile and you are still in your sins'
> (1 Cor. 15: 17). The content of this statement of Paul's
> essentially applied from the beginning: through the
> resurrection the death of the Messiah Jesus was manifested
> as valid and effective representative atonement by God
> himself.
>
> In this way the kerygma of the death and resurrection of
> Jesus for our salvation prove to be a unity which cannot be
> separated (*The Atonement*, p. 70).

That is why we shall treat them together.

# Part A

## The Cross

# Chapter
# 2

The Most Famous Death in History

*The death of Jesus by crucifixion*
He was a travelling teacher, a jobbing builder by trade, and he had fallen foul of the authorities. After a burlesque of a trial he was led out to die outside the city walls of Jerusalem, the main town of one of the most insignificant provinces on the edge of the Roman map. The year was about A.D. 30. The date, Easter. The time, nine o'clock in the morning. They crucified him. Not at all pleasant, but it happened to a great many people in those days. No worse than what takes place in the torture chambers of more than seventy countries in the modern world. And yet it has become the most famous death in history.

It was a messy business. The Romans, who seem to have got hold of the idea of crucifixion from the Phoenicians in the Punic Wars, became expert at this most grisly method of execution. They reserved it, however, for the *humiliores*, the lower classes in the Empire. And in particular it was what Cicero called a *servile supplicium*. It was the penalty for slaves. Apart from them you might find a deserting soldier being crucified, or someone who had interfered with the Vestal Virgins. This 'most cruel and most terrible punishment' (Cicero, *In Verrem*, 2.5.165) was a death reserved for the lowest of the low. Cicero maintained that it ought not even to be discussed by Romans: it was too degrading. Yet this was the death that became the most famous in history.

There were various ways of doing it. The most basic was to hang the man or impale him on a stake (*crux simplex*). More frequently there was a crossbeam (*patibulum*) across the *stipes*, or upright. It could be fixed to the top of the upright, making the shape of a capital T (*crux commissa*), and the Christian writers of the second century made considerable play with that fact. More often it was fixed a third of the way from the top, thus forming the Latin cross (*crux inmissa*), and it is widely believed that Jesus was executed on a cross of this shape. The third variety was what we know as the St. Andrew's cross, shaped like a capital X (*crux decussata*) on which the victim could be stretched either the right way up or upside down.

The condemned man was invariably scourged, and men were known to die under that punishment alone, so severe were the wounds inflicted by this cruel cat-o'-nine-tails inset with pieces of metal. It is possible that Jesus suffered this punishment both from the Jewish and from the Roman authorities (Matthew 26: 67f; John 19: 1). Thereafter, he had to carry the *patibulum* of his cross, and was led out under armed guard to die. There was a variety of ways of fixing the condemned man on the cross. He might have his wrists tied or nailed to the *patibulum* and then be hauled by ropes up on to the *stipes* which was already firmly fixed in the ground. More commonly the cross was put together on the ground, the condemned man bound or nailed to it, and the whole thing then erected and dropped into a pit that had been prepared to receive it. The degradation of the criminal was completed by his very clothes being taken from him. He was exposed naked on the cross. The cause of his being there was written above his head and fixed to the cross; and he was left there to die slowly in intense agony from exhaustion, thirst, and wounds. The criminal had, of course, no recourse but to curse, spit and urinate on his tormentors. Often the kindlier execution squads would offer a draught of drugged wine before nailing the man up. This went some small way towards dulling the pain. And sometimes a rough *sedile* or saddle was fixed to the cross. This offered support to the crucified man, and often prolonged his life. By raising himself up on his lacerated feet and the saddle he could give some respite to heart and lungs which were put under immense strain by the position of crucifixion. When the torture was deemed to have gone on long enough, or in order to ensure that the man was dead, the soldiers would perform the *crurifragium*, or breaking of the legs. This meant that the man, if still alive, could no longer hoist himself and would soon expire.

The physical effects of crucifixion were appalling. Of all deaths it is the most lingering and agonising. The unnatural position of the body made every movement a pain. The suspension of the whole body on jagged iron nails (one dating from A.D. 50 has recently been discovered in Jerusalem) driven through the most sensitive nerve centres of the wrists and ankles, ensured constant exquisite torture. The wounds of the nails and the weals from the lash soon became inflamed and even gangrenous. The body's position hindered circulation and caused indescribable pain in the chest. A raging thirst set in, brought on by the burning sun. The flies were thick around the victim. The agony of crucifixion was terrible beyond words. But it was not uncommon. In the unrest that had followed the death of Herod the Great in 4 B.C. Varus, the Roman general, had crucified 2,000 men and lined the road from Sepphoris in Galilee with them. Jesus had certainly heard of this. He had probably seen crucifixions. His execution was one among many, in that barbarous age. Why, then, was his death so special?

## The death of Socrates by hemlock

It might be useful at this point to contrast the end of Jesus with the only other death which could possibly rival it as the most famous in history. Just over 400 years earlier Socrates had died from drinking hemlock, while discoursing about immortality with his friends. This was an Athenian method of execution, and the immensely moving story of that death is told by Plato in the *Phaedo*. Socrates had been a courageous soldier at Plataea; thereafter, shunning public office, he had given his time to pursuing the true wisdom. He was the wisest man among the Athenians, but maintained that he knew nothing.

He lived an exemplary life, but in 399 B.C. he was indicted by

Anytus on two counts: corruption of the young and neglect of the traditional gods while setting forth new deities. Socrates in his defence poured scorn on the charges and in response to the prosecution's demand for the death penalty proposed that he should be fed at the public table as a benefactor of the city! This did not go down very well, and the comparatively small majority which had deemed him guilty of the charges brought against him (280 to 220) were furious at his puckish arrogance and condemned him to death by a much larger majority. Had Socrates proposed a small punishment instead of the prosecution's death penalty, he would have got off: they wanted him silenced, not killed. But he refused to take that way out. The issue was plain. The prosecution regarded him as a traitor to the state, and probably believed he was involved, with his friend Alcibiades, in the profanation of the Mysteries which caused such a stir in Athens just before the Sicilian Expedition in 416 B.C.. Socrates maintained he was an envoy from God, or 'the divine' as he called it. So he chose to die on principle, even though he had no need to. While he was awaiting death an escape plan was mounted for him, but he refused to take it. He maintained that the sentence, being passed by a properly constituted court, must stand – even though it was unjust. And so he talked of immortality as man's inalienable possession, of death as the great liberator, drank the hemlock, and died.

*The two deaths contrasted*
The similarities in these two famous deaths are obvious. Both were good men wrongly condemned. Both were men of high courage prepared to put principle before personal safety. Both believed they had a divine commission to bear testimony to the truth. Both believed in life after death. Both taught a small group of followers.

But the contrasts are no less striking. Socrates was aged 70 and Jesus a little over 30. Socrates claimed that he did not know the truth, Jesus that he was the truth. Socrates spoke whimsically of being an emissary of the divine: Jesus categorically claimed to be the Son of God. Socrates died easily from increasing paralysis: Jesus in utmost agony. Socrates saw death as a friend, liberating his spirit from the prison of the body, and releasing it back to its eternal home. Jesus saw death as the last and most horrible enemy from whose jaws he had come to rescue mankind. Socrates died for principle, Jesus for sinners. Socrates had human failings, Jesus had none. Socrates believed all men to be immortal, Jesus believed all men lost without his death. The followers of Jesus had a badge – the cross: the followers of Socrates did not sport hemlock. There was indeed a great difference between these two deaths.

*The appeal of the cross*
What an astonishing way for a religion to start – founded on a cross! Imagine the incongruity these days of starting a religious movement based on a hangman's noose. And yet think of the amazing spread of that cross, all because Jesus died on one nearly 2,000 years ago. No subject has had such attention paid to it in art or sculpture. No subject has been the inspiration of such wonderful music. No subject has so dominated the literature of the world. No subject has been such eloquent shorthand for the acme of heroism and self-sacrifice, as the cross of Jesus Christ. It was the cross and resurrection which set the new faith apart from Judaism. It was the cross and resurrection which seemed to the early Christians so to encapsulate the central truth of God that they would tolerate no other gods, even if it meant courting execution for their narrow-mindedness. It was the empty cross which founded a missionary religion which has spread into every country and tribe in the world, and which has attracted more followers than any other religion. Every revival of Christianity has had that empty cross very near its core. The cross has had a profound effect on education, medicine and the relief of social injustice wherever the Christian gospel has been given a chance to spread. The cross has been the official mark of Christianity since the days of Constantine. He is reputed to have seen a vision of it in the sky on the eve of his famous victory over

Maxentius in A.D. 312. But long before that it had been at the
very heart of Christian devotion. The apologist Justin Martyr
is full of it. So is Aristides. And Tertullian, always prone to
exaggeration, shows how central the cross was in his day for
ordinary Christians.

> At each journey and progress, at each coming in and going
> out, at the putting on of shoes, at the bath, at meals, at the
> kindling of lights, at bedtime, at sitting down, whatsoever
> occupation engages us, we mark the brow with the sign of the
> cross (Tertullian, *de Cor. Mil.,* 3).

## The scandal of the cross

And yet, for all its rapid spread, the centrality of the cross of
Jesus is very remarkable and surprising. After all, there is
nothing specially Christian about the cross. Almost every
culture from stone age times onward has made use of the
symbol. It is found widely from China to Egypt. It has a variety
of forms, including the swastika, as used in India and China.
Why should this particular cross of Jesus have had such
enormous impact and made it such a universal emblem? After
all, one could scarcely have chosen anything more offensive to
Roman, Greek and Jew alike, than a cross.

As we have seen, the Romans regarded the cross with
loathing – though they continued using it! It was not a death
designed for Roman citizens; only for subject peoples, as a
vicious and exemplary deterrent. It spoke of shame, of guilt, of
pain, but above all of failure. If a man ended up on a cross he
was an undoubted failure. Romans were practical empiricists.
Impatient of theory, they were a nation in search of what
worked. Well, the Christian religion manifestly could not
work. It was based on a complete failure: a man who had
claimed divine honours and who had not vindicated the claim.
It is hard to imagine any more difficult way of launching a new
religion in Rome than the triple combination which Christianity offered. It was, in the first place, of oriental origin, and
the Romans despised that. *In Tiberim defluxit Orontes,* as

Juvenal complained with distaste: the East had deposited its sewage in the heart of Rome. Second, this new faith was a Jewish offshoot, and that made it instantly unsavoury. One has only to read the Latin authors of the first century A.D. to see how very unpopular the Jews were; for their financial success, for their strange beliefs, for their mutilation of the body in circumcision, for their political and social inscrutability and for their special privileges. A faith from Judaea was not a good recommendation. And thirdly, the presentation of a central figure in this new religion who had been put to death on a cross as a failed pretender after kingship – why, this was the kiss of death. And yet the faith of an empty cross spread fast in Rome and eventually captured the Empire.

It was no less unattractive to Greek ears. As Paul remarks in 1 Corinthians, 'the Greeks seek wisdom, but we preach Christ crucified' (1: 22). It was very plain to civilised Greeks, the sophisticated élite of the ancient world, that wisdom resided in universals; beauty, truth, goodness, freedom and the like. These had universal validity and applicability. But here were these followers of Jesus maintaining that the wisdom of God was to be found in a particular; and a very disgusting particular at that, the mangled body of a crucified man. What an unlikely message to capture the heart of leading intellectuals. Yet that is precisely what it did; for not only did the church make a speedy home in all the main centres of Greek learning, but, in the decades which followed, it brought some of the brightest minds in the whole of antiquity in humility to that sordid cross.

And to the Jews, of course, the cross was the ultimate insult. It was bad enough to tell them that their Messiah had come and they had not recognised him. It was bad enough to tell them that he had suffered and died. That was most unwelcome news, because a dead Messiah could never deliver the nation from Roman occupation (and that was one of their main expectations, as the 17th *Psalm of Solomon*, written a few decades before the birth of Jesus, makes so clear). But, worst of all, the Christian claim was blasphemy. Every good Jew knew that someone hanged upon a stake lay under the curse of God.

Deuteronomy 21: 22–3 made this very plain.

> And if a man has committed a crime punishable by death,
> and you hang him on a tree, his body shall not remain all
> night upon the tree, but you shall bury him the same day, for
> a hanged man is accursed by God: you shall not defile your
> land which the Lord your God gives you for an inheritance.

How could Jesus be other than an imposter? He was a guilty
man, executed on a 'tree'. He had defiled the land, and so he
rested under the curse of God. That is how it seemed to a Jew,
and Christians had to work very hard to overcome this most
understandable prejudice. Justin's *Dialogue with Trypho*
rehearses the arguments on both sides. But the Christians did
not draw back from the full implications of the Deuteronomy
passage. They often called the cross by the name of *xulon*, 'the
stake', using the very word from this passage in Deuteronomy.
And they absorbed the language about the curse of God:
'Christ delivered us from the curse of the law, having become a
curse for us – for it is written, "Cursed is every one who hangs
on a tree"' (Gal. 3: 13). Yes, they said, the cross is indeed the
place of cursing. Jesus died there, and took upon himself the
curse occasioned by men's sins with which he identified himself
(3: 10). He was certainly subject to the curse. But the curse he
bore was our curse, not his own. That has been demonstrated
by the fact that God raised him from the dead. The empty cross
has changed from the place of bane to the place of blessing.

Thus the gospel began to make headway among Romans,
Greeks and Jews. But the cross was undeniably a disadvantage
rather than an asset. Why did they stress it so much? Why did
they find it 'the power of God to save men' (Rom. 1: 16; 1 Cor.
1: 18)? What made the empty cross of Jesus so special?

*Why was Jesus' crucifixion so special?*
There are several reasons. Taken together they make it
abundantly plain why the cross is the most famous symbol in

the world, and the death of Jesus the most famous death in history.

The cross of Jesus was so special because of the one who was suffering there. On any showing his was the best and greatest life the world has ever witnessed. He should never have been put on that terrible cross. More, he was the fulfilment of the hopes of the Old Testament. Here was the 'prophet like Moses'. Here was 'Elijah returned'. Here was the Son of David's line. Here was the Son of Man whom Daniel had predicted. Here was Isaiah's Suffering Servant. Never in all history had all these threads from centuries ago converged into a single knot: and that knot was Jesus Christ on the cross. Here was the fulfilment of the prophetic, priestly and kingly expectations of the Old Testament. This is indeed why the name 'Christ' was applied to him, and why it stuck to him so closely that within a few years it acted as surname. It means 'Anointed One' and Jesus was seen as fulfilling the three figures in Old Testament days who received anointing – the prophet, priest and king. All three converge in *the* anointed one, Jesus: and the cross is the supreme prophetic act, the complete sacrifice, and the ultimate demonstration of his royalty. But even that does not exhaust the person of that silent sufferer. The New Testament roundly asserts, and Christians have always believed, that 'God was in Christ, reconciling the world unto himself' on that awesome cross (2 Cor. 5: 18). No mere man; no third party, no angel, but God himself was present in a unique way in the person and the sufferings of Jesus on Calvary. 'The Son of God loved me, and gave himself for me,' wrote Paul (Gal. 2: 20). That is what makes the cross so special: the identity of the sufferer. There never has been and never will be a parallel to that. No wonder it is the most famous death in history. The very name Jesus, given him at his birth, means 'Yahweh saves'. Yahweh was doing just that as Jesus hung on the cross.

A second reason for the very special nature of Calvary flows out of the first. His death is unique because the love which activated it is unique. A mother might die for her child; a man might die for his friend. But who would die for his enemy? Yet that is what Jesus did. 'God shows his love for us in that while we were yet sinners Christ died for us. While we were enemies we were reconciled to God by the death of his Son' (Rom. 5: 8, 10). Many have done something like it since, in the power that the crucified and risen Jesus gives. Father Damien, giving his life to a leper colony for Jesus' sake, and eventually contracting leprosy and dying; Toyohiko Kagawa, a Japanese college student, who identified himself with the lowest and neediest of his own people in the degraded slums of Shinkawa. Men like these have given embodiment, in their day and generation, to the infectious love of Jesus who gave himself for sinners. But men have not learned it from anyone else. His love was unprecedented. It was for those who opposed him, had no time for him, and hated him. That is what makes Calvary so special. It shows us that God is not alienated by the mess we have got the world into: he is not against us. Rather, he loves us so much that there is nothing, literally nothing he will not endure for us. God so loved the world, that he gave his only Son. On Calvary we see it, and it nerves the heart to face whatever comes, in the confidence that nothing can separate us from a God who loves that much.

There is a third reason which sets the suffering of Jesus apart from all others. Given who he was, he could at any time have ended the whole business. He could have walked out of Pilate's courtroom as he had walked through a murderous mob (John 8: 59). He could have asked the Father and been given twelve legions of angels. He could have done as his enemies taunted and come down from the cross at any moment during that appalling Good Friday. Unlike any sufferer before or since, Jesus' suffering remained entirely voluntary for every moment it lasted. He was totally in charge of circumstance. As K. C. Thompson puts it in *Once For All* (p. 37):

No man's sufferings ever have been, or ever can be, as voluntary as were the sufferings of Christ . . . It is the divinity of Christ that sets his human heroism on a pinnacle beyond the reach of any rivals in heroic martyrdom ... He only had complete and absolute power to save himself all through his Passion, and all through it at every second he actively refused to do so. This magnified beyond conception the intensity of his ordeal. The crucifixion is the unique example of an entirely and totally voluntary acceptance of extreme suffering and of agonising death in the presence of total ability to escape them at any moment.

Finally, the uniqueness of that death lies in what it achieved. Luke puts it well in his account of the transfiguration. 'Moses and Elijah appeared in glory and spoke of the Exodus which he was to accomplish at Jerusalem' (Luke 9: 31). That was it. His dying and rising again was the main film to which the historic Exodus was only the trailer. That had brought a limited and temporary deliverance from servitude and death in Egypt for the Israelites. It had been inaugurated by the death of a Passover lamb in every Jewish household. This Exodus would free mankind from the final death of the soul in irreversible alienation from God, the source of life. It would break the power of evil in the characters not of Israelites only, but of all men everywhere throughout all generations who would make his death their passing over into new life. There has never been another death like that. It broke the entail of human sin. It broke the ultimate grip of death. It meant hope for the hopeless, pardon for the guilty, a future for the dying. His death was not for himself: all the rest of us die for and by ourselves. He died for the sake of others, of the whole world of men and women. And he rose again. There has never been anything like it. That is why, no doubt, the death of Jesus remains the most celebrated in the history of the world, and always will.

# Chapter
# 3

Why Did Jesus Think He Had to Die?

At first sight this is a foolish question. If Jesus was human, then of course he had to die. But there is something very odd about the emphasis on his death in the Gospels. In any ordinary biography of a great man the account of his last days and death would normally form only a short chapter in a longish book. But with Jesus it is very different. The account of his last few days, his death and resurrection occupies very nearly half of the Gospels. What accounts for this remarkable imbalance? Well, there are many theories, and many of them are partial in the evidence they adduce, or tendentious in the illustrations on which they lay the greatest weight. In order, therefore, to get a preliminary answer to this vital question, I propose in this chapter to examine what, according to our sources in the Gospels, Jesus himself regarded as the causes of his death. Why did Jesus think he had to die?

The Gospels pay a lot of attention to the teaching of Jesus on this rather surprising matter. It is most unusual for men to teach about their death. But Jesus clearly referred to it many times.

*His death was inevitable*
First, we find him teaching that his death is inevitable. It *must* be so. Early in Mark's Gospel he says that he, the Bridegroom, will be taken away from the party (Mark 2: 19, 20). In the next chapter we find him seeing to the heart of the Pharisees, who were complaining at his healing on the sabbath. He asked

them, 'Is it lawful on the sabbath day to save life or to kill?' And immediately a plot was hatched to kill him (3: 6). No sooner does Peter confess him as the Messiah than Jesus tells him 'the Son of Man must suffer many things and be rejected by the elders and the chief priests and the scribes, and be killed, and after three days rise again' (Mark 8: 31). That statement is remarkable for identifying the Son of Man, that most glorious figure (to whom was given dominion, glory and kingdom and whose destiny was to ascend to the Ancient of Days, cf. Daniel 7: 14) with the fate of the Suffering Servant of Isaiah 53. That I take to be the most probable meaning of the verse; but if, with Vermes, we take 'the Son of Man' to be merely a circumlocution for 'I', the fate described is no less certain. He knew he had to die. And the theme is repeated time and again in the central portion of the oldest Gospel. He gives the prediction of his fate in almost the same words in Mark 9: 31 and 10: 33, culminating in the ransom saying of 10: 45 to which we will return.

*His death was a fulfilment of scripture*
Second, his death was necessary in order to fulfil the scriptures. Jesus clearly believed that the scriptures had much to say about himself, and that they predicted his death. All the evangelists mention this. Luke represents Jesus after the resurrection as saying:

> O fools, and slow of heart to believe all that the prophets have spoken! Was it not necessary that the Christ should suffer these things and enter into his glory? And beginning at Moses and all the prophets he interpreted to them in all the scriptures the things concerning himself (Luke 24: 25f).

That is the most comprehensive passage, but in Mark 9: 12 we find Jesus musing on the fate of Elijah, 'Is Elijah to come first to restore all things? Then how is it written of the Son of Man that he should suffer many things and be treated with contempt?' As the passion drew near we find Jesus saying 'I tell you that this scripture must be fulfilled in me "And he was reckoned with transgressors"; for what is written about me has its fulfilment' (Luke 22: 37). In St. John's account of the end of Jesus' life, the theme of the fulfilment of scripture is a major one: the betrayal by Judas, the loss of Judas, the thirst of Jesus and his final cry, are all in fulfilment of scripture (John 13: 18; 17: 12; 19: 28, 37). The evangelist clearly shared this view, and attributed the fact that Jesus' robe was not torn and his clothes shared out among the executioners, the fact that his legs were not broken, and the piercing of his side to the fulfilment of the scriptures (John 19: 23f, 36, 37). It would be hard to exaggerate the importance of this sense of necessity for Jesus' death coming through the Old Testament scriptures, and influencing the main actors in the drama of the cross.

*His death was entirely voluntary*
Third, Jesus sees his death as totally voluntary. He said 'I lay down my life, that I may take it again. No one takes it from me, but I lay it down of my own accord' (John 10: 18). That is why he 'steadfastly set his face to go to Jerusalem' (Luke 9: 51), knowing he was going to his death. In St. John's Gospel Jesus repeatedly taught that nobody could touch him because his hour was not yet come. But when it did come, he was to be found making his way to Jerusalem and to his death. It would be hard to make the point more strongly that his death was voluntary. 'The Son of Man came to give his life' he said (Mark 10: 45). And that is what he did. Unlike any other person on this earth, it can be fairly said of Jesus that he came into this world to die. Death was no accidental ending to a fine life. It was what he was born for.

*His death was the Father's will*
Fourth, Jesus makes it plain that this voluntary death of his was the Father's will. 'For this reason the Father loves me, because I lay down my life, that I may take it again' (John 10: 17). The sublimest words in the whole Gospel make this plain: 'For God so loved the world that he gave his only Son...'

(John 3: 16). And when the sunshine of those words changes to the night of Jesus' agony in Gethsemane it is the same message that comes through. 'Abba, Father, all things are possible to thee; remove this cup from me; yet not what I will but what thou wilt' (Mark 14: 36). Jesus deliberately chose Calvary, it would seem, much though his human emotions revolted from it. He did so knowing it was the Father's will. As ever, he and the Father were in perfect harmony: 'I and the Father are one' (John 10: 30).

### By his death Jesus identified with sinners

A fifth point Jesus makes about his death is that in it he identifies with sinners. This was totally unlike any rabbi, who despised the 'people of the land' as sinners who could never attain to the law of God. But Jesus received such; he ate with them. And at the very outset of his ministry he unambiguously asserted his identity with them. John the Baptist was baptising 'a baptism of repentance for the remission of sins' (Mark 1: 4), and men and women who felt the burden of their sins came to be baptised by him. So did Jesus, though his relationship with his Father was unclouded by any awareness of sin. But he wanted to throw in his lot with sinners, to identify with them, as Matthew's account makes plain (Matt. 3: 14ff). It was then that he received assurance of his Sonship and the empowering of the Spirit for service as the Saviour of the world. And when he spoke about his death he saw it as the fulfilment of that baptism of his. 'I have a baptism to be baptised with, and how I am constrained until it is accomplished' (Luke 12: 50). In the further teaching that he gives about his death, Jesus shows how that identification with sinners was worked out.

### His death was God's judgment on the world

Sixth, then, his death is God's judgment on the world. Jesus made this plain in direct statements like the following: 'Now is the judgment of this world . . . and I, when I am lifted up from the earth, will draw all men to myself . . . This he said to show by what death he was to die' (John 12: 31ff). The theme recurs

many times in St. John, but it also comes in more pictorial ways
in other Gospels. One of the starkest is the parable of the
wicked husbandmen (Mark 12: 1-9), based as that is upon the
famous parable of Isaiah about the vineyard of God's people
Israel (Isa. 5: 1-7). God, like the vineyard owner, looks for
some return from his tenants, but gets none. He sends one
servant after another for the fruit, but they get misused or
killed. Last of all he decides to send 'his beloved son, saying
"They will respect my son". But those tenants said "This is the
heir; come, let us kill him and the inheritance will be ours". And
they took him and killed him and cast him out of the vineyard.
What will the owner of the vineyard do? He will come and
destroy the tenants'. And to rub in the theme of judgment Jesus
puns on the word *ben* 'son' and *eben* 'stone' and continues,
'Have you not read this scripture "The very stone which the
builders rejected has become the head of the corner; this was
the Lord's doing, and it is marvellous in our eyes"?' The Jews
saw the point, were furious, and tried ineffectually to arrest
him. His time had not yet come, but he had made very plain
that one purpose of his death was to demonstrate God's
judgment on the sinfulness of a rebel world.

*His death was a sacrifice*
Seventh, Jesus saw his death as a sacrifice. This is very plain
from the Last Supper, a meal laden with Passover imagery.
Instead of referring to the lamb or the 'bread of affliction' eaten
by their forefathers in the Exodus, Jesus says 'This is my body'
and 'This is my blood of the covenant'. As Jeremias has
demonstrated so conclusively in *The Eucharistic Words of
Jesus*, body broken and blood poured out could only mean one
thing: violent death. And Jesus forsees that death of his as
fulfilling the pattern of the Exodus when the blood of the lamb
sprinkled on the doorpost spelt safety for the Israelites, while
its body brought them nourishment for the journey into the
promised land. His death was about to initiate a new covenant
between God and man, necessitated not because God had
changed but because man had proved unequal to the task of

keeping his side of the covenant. Jeremiah and Ezekiel had looked forward to the day when this new covenant would come about; it would mean the interiorisation of God's law within the heart, personal knowledge of him, and forgiveness of sins, together with the indwelling of his Spirit (Jer. 31: 31-4; Ezek. 36: 26-8). But curiously enough neither prophet had said anything about the sacrifice that would accompany this new covenant – and, as Hebrews 9: 22 observes, 'under the law almost everything is purified by blood, and without the shedding of blood there is no forgiveness of sins'. The old covenant on Sinai had been inaugurated with blood sacrifices. Part of the blood was sprinkled on the altar and part on the people; and thereafter Moses and the elders were admitted to communion fellowship with God. Now Jesus inaugurates the new covenant with *his own blood*, the sacrifice that takes away sins once and for all. 'Drink of it, all of you, for this is my blood of the covenant which is poured out for many for the forgiveness of sins' (Matt. 26: 27). The vital missing link to the new covenant is thus supplied – by the blood of Jesus offered in sacrifice. That is why he was content to be betrayed and die: in order to make it possible for men and women to have their sins forgiven and eat and drink in the presence of his Father in the Kingdom of God. And lest they should ever misunderstand, lest they should ever forget this supreme purpose of his death, he instituted a meal, the Communion, to be celebrated 'often' in remembrance of him, thus replacing the annual reminder of the Exodus in the Passover feast of the Jews. This was the ultimate Passover, the ultimate Exodus. It was to achieve this that he came to die (Luke 9: 31 – 'they spoke of the *exodus* which he was to accomplish at Jerusalem').

### His death was a ransom

An eighth word which Jesus seems to have spoken about his forthcoming death was also heavy with meanings from the Old Testament. It was the word 'ransom'. 'The Son of man came ... to give his life as a ransom for many (*lutron anti pollōn*)' (Mark 10: 45). In the Psalms it says 'No one can by any means redeem

his brother, nor give to God a ransom for him' (Ps. 49: 7f).
What no man can do for another, this man proposes to do for
many (a Hebraism for 'all'). What can he mean? It can only be
that our lives are forfeit, but that they can be liberated by the
surrender of his own. The word 'ransom' was widely used in the
ancient world. It applied to the release of prisoners of war and
the manumission of slaves. In the Old Testament the word
always means redemption through payment of a price. It is as if
man is a prisoner of war, in the power of the enemy: Jesus has
released him. Or as if he is a slave: Jesus has given him his
freedom. Or as if his life is forfeit: Jesus delivers man from that
terrible predicament, but only by surrendering his own. That is
the supreme service which the Son of man came to do – to give
his life as a ransom for many. The whole idea is so staggering
that it has received a lot of attention among scholars. One of the
best treatments remains that by Leon Morris in *The Apostolic
Preaching of the Cross*. This is not the place to go into the
deeper nuances of the saying, but one thing is noteworthy, and
had a lot of influence on later New Testament teaching. Jesus'
life is not only offered 'for us': *huper* is the Greek word for that,
and it is significantly not used at this point. Jesus says *anti*, and
that means 'in place of'. Jesus makes it very plain that he came
to give his life as a ransom in the place of the lives of men which
are forfeit.

*His death was representative*
But lest this should seem to be cheap grace, Jesus has a ninth
word for us. As soon as he began to speak about his death Jesus
also told his disciples that they must take up their cross and
follow him (Mark 8: 34). The principle of costly self-giving
must mark the disciple as it does the master. When asked by the
sons of Zebedee about the position of honour in the Kingdom
of God, Jesus asked them if they were able to drink the cup he
was to drink, or be baptised with the baptism which was to
overwhelm him (10: 38f). The cross is not merely *extra nos*. It
has to become a way of life for every disciple of Jesus. If the
ransom saying speaks of Christ the substitute, the baptism

saying speaks of Christ the representative, two aspects of the atonement which we shall consider later.

*His death was a victory*
There was another claim Jesus made about his death, though the basis of it had begun long before. St. Mark's Gospel lays particular stress on his overcoming the demonic forces which so assailed his ministry. As early as Mark 1: 21-7 we read of the power of Jesus over an unclean spirit: 'are you come to destroy us?' it asked. That is precisely what he had come to do, and the Gospels are full of his victory over 'the strong man', being himself 'the stronger than the strong' (Matt. 12:29). The culmination of this victory of Jesus is to be found at the cross. During the Last Supper he said he would no more drink of the fruit of the vine until he drank it new in the Kingdom of God (Mark 14: 25). As he faced the cross he said 'The ruler of this world is coming. He has no power over me. The ruler of this world is judged' (John 14: 30; 16: 11). This stress on Jesus the victor is drawn out very much in the fourth Gospel and in some of the Epistles. It has been carefully explored by Gustaf Aulén in *Christus Victor*, and we shall return to it. But it is all part of the reason why Jesus went to the cross.

*His death was total darkness*
There remain two other aspects of the cross which Jesus himself speaks about. They complement one another. The one is all darkness. It springs from the uncanny darkness which fell on the world during the crucifixion, out of which came that terrible cry of inner dereliction 'My God, my God, why has thou forsaken me?' (Mark 15: 34). Nobody has pierced to the full depths of that cry, drawn from Psalm 22. It has been pointed out that the psalm, on which Jesus was perhaps meditating as he hung on the cross, ends in confidence and victory ('men shall tell of the Lord to the coming generation, and proclaim his deliverance to a people yet unborn, that he has wrought it'), but that cannot take away from the horror of desolation which is the content of most of the psalm, nor

detract from the real suffering of Jesus as he felt – and was – Godforsaken. It is very fashionable to say that he only felt that: never had God been closer to him than on Calvary. We cannot probe the inner realities of the suffering Saviour, but if he cried out that he was Godforsaken I believe him. So did St. Paul (2 Cor. 5: 21). He had told them that he was going to give his life in exchange for the lives of many: on that cross it was taking place. Time and again in the Qumran psalms the Teacher of Righteousness confesses, 'Thou has not forsaken me, *lo asabthani*.' What an amazing thing: no Qumran heretic was ever so Godforsaken as the crucified heretic on Golgotha!

### His death was total vindication

But that was not the end, and if the first words of Psalm 22 are not meant to give indication of the triumphant conclusion to that psalm, there are many other occasions on which Jesus predicted a wonderful outcome of his sufferings. This must have helped him to face them as he did. In each of the passion predictions in St. Mark Jesus says that after his cruel torture he will rise again the third day (Mark 8: 31; 9: 31; 10: 34). In St. John's account he had said that he was God's bread which, when broken, would give life to the world (John 6: 33, 51). He said that he laid down his life so that he might take it again (John 10: 17). He said to his detractors (and it was brought up in a garbled form at his trial: they had not forgotten it) 'Destroy this temple and in three days I will raise it up' (John 2: 19). He was referring, John tells us, to the temple of his body. In flash after flash Jesus looks through the calamity of the cross to God's vindication of him. As he taught the couple on the Emmaus Road, in the light of all the scriptures (particularly Isa. 53 and Ps. 110: 1) 'was it not necessary that Christ should suffer these things and enter into his glory?' (Luke 24: 26). In passages such as these we see Jesus doing precisely what this book is attempting to do. He is holding together his death and vindication. The cross without the resurrection is utterly disastrous: the sad end of a great man. The resurrection without the cross is utterly banal: the traditional happy ending.

Jesus held both together in at least some snatches of his recorded teaching.

This evidence has been drawn from all four Gospels. Although each evangelist contributes his unique perspective, the overall picture is clear, and abundantly substantiated. Jesus had no illusions. He knew that a life and ministry like his could only end in death. It had to be. That was the clear indication of scripture. It was his own willing determination. It was the plan of his heavenly Father. He knew it would mean total identification with the lot of sinners, though he himself was sinless. He was drawn to that cross to express God's judgment on the world, and at the same time to offer his life as a sacrifice, a ransom, in which he would be Godforsaken as he bore the sins of the world. Yet he seems to have perceived that his death would not be the end. God would raise him from the dead, and by going to Calvary he would open a gate through death for believers. And all this would spell God's victory over evil in all its forms, together with its satanic fount.

That is a powerful combination of answers to the question with which this chapter began, Why did Jesus think he had to die? Nor must we forget that the disciple is called to the same path of self-sacrifice. As Bishop Stephen Neill is fond of observing, 'We all have some dying to do: Jesus showed us how it should be done.'

# Chapter
# 4

Why Did the Disciples Think He Had to Die?

As we saw in the last chapter, there is a great deal of material in the sayings attributed to Jesus himself which enables us to see the uniqueness and the significance of that death. In this chapter I shall attempt a brief survey of the rest of the New Testament testimony to the death of Christ and its meaning. This cannot be exhaustive, but I hope it will at least be representative of the various strands which go to make up the New Testament, and will show us some of the major categories in which the early disciples sought to interpret the death of their master – in the light of his resurrection.

## The Synoptic Gospels

Mark is in all probability the earliest evangelist, and had links with both Paul and Peter in the early Church. How did he understand the climax of 'the gospel of Jesus Christ the Son of God' (1: 1)? Clearly he sees Jesus' death as inevitable: a dark shadow lies upon his Gospel from the opening series of controversy stories (2:1–3:6) onward, reinforced by the three passion predictions, and spelt out in the last two chapters. Given who Jesus was and what man is like, there could be no other outcome. Mark sees that outcome not only as inevitable but as God's will. Jesus is the one destined by scripture and the purposes of God to be betrayed, die and rise again (8: 31; 9: 31; 10: 33). His life will be a ransom for many (10: 45). It will result in the forging of a new covenant (14: 22ff) at the cost of his sacrificial death. The shepherd will be smitten, the sheep scattered; but after the resurrection Jesus will lead his people into Galilee – probably not merely the geographical area, but with the wider meaning, as Lohmeyer perceived, of the Gentile mission (14: 27; 16: 7). Mark knows that in dying on the cross there is a profound sense in which Jesus was saving others while unable to save himself (15: 30, 31). He knows that Calvary brought terrible darkness and separation into the heart of Jesus, and yet that the achievement of his death was sufficient to bring his executioner to admit that Jesus was the Son of God. Whatever the centurion meant by it, his words very soon became an important part of the Christian baptismal confession, and Mark's readers would not be slow to catch the allusion. For the most tremendous thing had happened. The 'veil of the temple', a great curtain keeping people out of the Holy of Holies in the temple, was split from top to bottom when Jesus died, Mark tells us, as if God were showing that the way into his holy presence was no longer confined to one high priest, once a year, after due sacrifice for his own sins and those of the people. No, the way into God's presence was now available for all who would confess Jesus as the Son of God: even for the most brutal of murderers, even for the person who nailed him to the cross! Finally, we must notice the strong emphasis in Mark on Jesus' victory over the forces of Satan. Throughout his ministry he is depicted as the strong one who ravages Satan's kingdom and sets free his captives (e.g. 1: 23–7, 39; 3: 20–7). That victory is completed through the cross and resurrection, where he suffers with dignity, where in dying he wins over his executioners, and where he is raised in power to go before his disciples into the Gentile mission.

Matthew has many of the same emphases as Mark. But he has a more explicit beginning and end to his story. The names accorded Jesus at his birth are highly significant. He is 'Emmanuel' (God is with us) and 'Jesus' (the Lord saves). The role of saving God's people, attributed to God himself in Ps. 130: 9, is applied from the outset to Jesus. He is brought before us by the evangelist as no less than God, saving his people from their sins. Accordingly there is a great stress on the royalty of

Jesus, particularly in his trial and passion. Jesus is King (Matt. 21: 5; 27: 11, 29, 37, 42). His innocence is stressed (27: 24) and so is the fact that his death was designed to procure for us the forgiveness of sins (26: 28). There is more than a hint of substitution in the way Jesus dies on Barabbas' cross in Barabbas' place, particularly if the reading 'Jesus Barabbas' is correct in 27: 16, 17. The true 'Son of the Father' dies for the bogus; the innocent in the place and on the cross of the guilty, so that the guilty may go free. In addition Matthew stresses the victory of Jesus: nothing – no guard, no stone, can hold him in the tomb. He is the conqueror over death, and as the Risen One has all power in heaven and earth, which he entrusts to his followers as he accompanies them on their mission of evangelising the world (28: 18–20). Matthew adds a unique and mysterious verse, 27: 53, which emphasises his belief that the death of Jesus burst the bars of death for mankind. There is a cosmic significance in what happened on Calvary. His passion avails not only for the living but for the departed.

Luke has an advantage in presenting a rounded interpretation of the passion, because he writes a two-volume account which includes the early history of the church. He gives no explicit doctrine of the atonement, perhaps because of his *imitatio Christi* theme: Christian suffering is suffering with Jesus (Acts 9: 4); the fate of Jesus is parallel to that of his innocent first martyr, Stephen (6: 11–15; 7: 55–60); and the way of the suffering servant (13: 47) is the way to glory for the disciple and his Lord alike (14: 22, cf. Luke 12: 1–12).

Nevertheless the Acts shows that Luke had some very clear ideas on what the cross and resurrection indicated. He knows that the cross was both the responsibility of wicked men and the agelong plan of God (2: 23; 3: 18). He identifies Jesus with the Servant of the Lord – and always in a context of suffering and vindication (8: 22f; 3: 13, 26; 4: 27–30). His shed blood constitutes a ransom (20: 28). Indeed, he took the place of cursing for us, being exposed on the 'tree' of Calvary (5: 30; 10: 39; 13: 29, cf. Deut. 21: 22f). Consequently Luke makes a frequent juxtaposition of forgiveness and the passion of Jesus

(2: 26, 38; 5: 30f; 3: 18f), though he never attempts to give a rationale of the atonement. Unlike many later theologians, who have often presented us with a theory of the cross, Luke presents us with a living Saviour, the crucified who has been raised by God and offers to the penitent both forgiveness of sins and his Holy Spirit (13: 38; 2: 23f, 38). Thus Luke makes plain that it is not the cross that saves; rather it is the crucified and risen Jesus.

*The Pauline Letters*
Paul makes the largest contribution of any writer in the New Testament to our understanding of the cross and resurrection. His range of imagery is amazing. Perhaps his best known picture is that of the lawcourt, where we all have to plead guilty before God; and, by an astonishing act of grace, God is able to declare us 'justified', acquitted, on account of what Jesus achieved on Calvary. Though 'all have sinned and come short of the glory of God' they are 'justified by his grace as a gift, through the redemption that is in Christ Jesus' (Rom. 3: 23f). It is universally agreed nowadays that 'justify' does not mean 'to make righteous' as used to be argued by Roman Catholic theologians; it is almost certainly a forensic term, and means 'to account righteous'. Possibly it may have the overtones, as T. W. Manson has suggested, not so much of the lawcourt as the throne room, where the sovereign can say to the commoner 'Arise, Sir John' and that word not only *declares* something but *does* something. Thereafter he is not merely accounted a knight; he *is* one. And God does not merely account us in the right with him; he makes us so. And how does he do that? Through what Jesus achieved by his death on the cross and resurrection. For 'he was delivered to death for our offences, and was raised for our justification' (Rom. 4: 25).

Sometimes Paul speaks of Christ's death as a sacrifice, after Old Testament analogies, particularly the Passover-sacrifice (Eph. 5: 2; 1 Cor. 5: 7). He asserts that what Jesus did was *huper* us, 'on our behalf', or, more sharply, *anti* us, 'in our place'. So Jesus on the cross can be seen as an *antilutron huper pantōn*, 'a substitutionary ransom for all' (1 Tim. 2: 6). In this way he has become a mediator between God and man, being firmly in touch with both sides (2: 6). Paul speaks of the tremendous love of God the Father and of Jesus for sinful men as the deep underlying cause of the cross and resurrection (Rom. 5: 8; Eph. 5: 2). It led Christ to suffer unthinkable torments for us. We rightly lay under a curse, having broken God's laws time and again (Gal. 3: 10); but he delivered us from that terrible predicament 'by becoming a curse for us' (3: 13). What that cost him we can barely begin to imagine, but Paul does not shrink from attributing to Christ a double exchange of places. It is his deepest understanding of the agony of Calvary. He writes 'For our sakes he (i.e. God the Father) made him (i.e. Jesus) to be sin, Jesus who knew no sin; so that in him we might become the righteousness of God' (2 Cor. 5: 21). We shall return to this verse: it is one pole of a paradox. The other is that 'God was in Christ reconciling the world to himself', and Paul maintains this too in the very same context (5: 18).

Separate those two assertions, and all understanding of the profundity of Calvary is dissipated. But if we hold them together, we realise that the passion delivered us from the righteous wrath, *orgē*, of God. There is nothing capricious or vindictive about this divine wrath. It is his settled attitude of total opposition to all evil. On the cross he showed that by his own intervention he has delivered us from the consequences of breaking his laws (Rom. 5: 9; 1 Thess. 5: 9). The wrath of God against evil is a terrible thing, and Paul shows how every one of us, Jew and Gentile, good and bad, merits it richly. That is the whole thrust of the first three chapters of Romans. He makes this uncomfortable fact crystal clear 'so that every mouth may be stopped and all the world may be held accountable to God... For there is no distinction, for all have sinned and come short of the glory of God' (Rom. 3: 19, 23). Yet God found a way to 'justify the ungodly' (4: 5), and now Paul uses a remarkable word to explain how it came about. God set forth Jesus, he tells us, as 'a *hilastērion* by his blood' (3: 25).

There have been three main interpretations of this word,

which Paul does not use elsewhere, but which has a rich history in the Old Testament. It may mean 'propitiation'. It may mean 'expiation'. It may mean 'mercy seat'. We shall be looking at this again in chapter 12, but it is at least clear that Jesus' death on the cross is seen as the means for cancelling out human sin. If 'mercy seat' is the meaning (as it is in the only other New Testament occurrence of the word, Heb. 9: 5) it makes little difference, for the 'mercy seat' of the ark was the place where the sacrificial blood was offered on the Day of Atonement (Lev. 16: 1–22). It was the place where God met with Israel's leader and showed himself to be gracious (Num. 7: 89). To put it another way, the very nails which held Jesus' *titulus* (charge sheet) in place on the cross could be seen to hold our sins there, and his death dealt with them for good and all (Col. 2: 14). Thus the crucified and risen Jesus can offer us reconciliation with God (2 Cor. 5: 18); deliverance from the old age dominated by such tyrants as wrath, sin, law and death (Rom. 5–8); and the emancipation which was the lifetime's goal of a slave (1 Cor. 6: 20; 7: 23). Indeed, we are brought into a share of that death and resurrection of his: baptism means no less. We go down into the water and are 'buried'. We rise from the water 'to newness of life'. That is the sacrament of our incorporation into Christ, so that we can henceforth be described as 'in Christ' (constantly in Paul's letters). Christ, the one who repairs the ruin Adam wrought, involves us in his risen life, having first dealt with our accusing past (Rom. 5: 21). No wonder Paul exclaims in wonder at the victory which Jesus achieved on Calvary, and in which we share. 'He disarmed the principalities and powers and made a public example of them, triumphing over them in him (or, more probably 'in it' – the cross, Col. 2: 15). And therefore 'thanks be to God who in Christ always leads us in triumph' (2 Cor. 2: 14). Not even death itself will be able to take that victory away from him and those who are 'in him'. Is he not the risen one? Therefore 'I am persuaded that neither death nor life . . . nor anything else in all creation, will be able to separate us from the love of God in Christ Jesus our Lord' (Rom. 8: 39).

That is not all Paul has to say about the cross and resurrection of Jesus. Far from it. But it is enough to show the central importance he attached to it, the varied imagery in which he thought of it, his conviction that somehow it has for ever shattered the sin barrier, and his confidence that it is not external to us but involves us profoundly both in suffering and in triumph.

### *The Epistle to the Hebrews*

Hebrews is the letter in the New Testament which has most to say about the sacrificial aspect of the death of Christ. The author is at pains to point out that the whole sacrificial system of the Old Testament is merely educative: its fulfilment comes through the Son of God who offered himself, personally and willingly for the sins of men down the ages. This is not the place to attempt to summarise his brilliant teaching: merely to isolate several strands in it. He sees Jesus as the perfect priest. All others have serious shortcomings – such as their personal sinfulness and the fact that they are carried off by death. Jesus had no sins of his own to atone for, and he 'is able for all time to save those who draw near to God through him, since he always lives to make intercession for them' (7: 25). If it be objected that he was not a member of the Aaronic priestly line, so much the better. His endless life, his royal lineage and his superiority over the Aaronic priesthood were all presaged by that shadowy Old Testament Christophany, Melchizedek (ch. 7).

But not only is Jesus the perfect priest. He has made the ultimate sacrifice. Old Testament sacrifices could not actually atone for sins; they merely acted as a painful reminder of them (10: 1–4). The blood of bulls and goats could never remove sin: they, too, acted as a *praeparatio evangelica*, and pointed forward to the fully voluntary and fully personal offering of Jesus the ultimate sacrifice. We have been sanctified by the offering of the body of Christ once for all. Where there is forgiveness of sin, there no longer needs to be any offering for sin (10: 11–18).

The third great insight into the achievement of Christ which the author of this Epistle gives us is the idea of the covenant. The old covenant was ineffective because man failed to keep his part of it. But the Old Testament itself had looked for the day when God would give a new covenant, which would include a personal knowledge of God, an interiorising of his commands and the forgiveness of sins. This is what he has brought about through the death and resurrection of Jesus (chs. 8, 9 and 10). The ambivalence of the Greek word *diathēkē* allows the writer to make a further point. It can mean either 'covenant' or 'will'. Now no will is effective without the death of the testator. But that is precisely what has happened on Calvary. So in Christ crucified and risen, we have the ultimate sacrifice, the ultimate priest and the ultimate covenant between God and man. Rightly can Campbell Morgan call the Epistle to the Hebrews *God's Last Word to Man*. There is a great deal more in this Epistle about the passion and its achievement. Notably, his dying and rising have drawn the teeth of death, smashed the power of Satan, and 'delivered those who through fear of death were subject to lifelong bondage' (2: 12). Another great theme springing from the atonement is confidence: 'we have a great high priest who has passed through the heavens, Jesus the Son of God ... Let us then with confidence draw near' (4: 14f). But it is the finality of the covenant, the priesthood and the sacrifice of Christ which stand out as the major contribution of Hebrews to our understanding of Calvary.

*The Catholic Epistles*
The Catholic Epistles have their own contribution to make. 1 Peter has an astonishing amount to say on the subject for so short an Epistle. Peter is deeply gripped by the example of Jesus, the innocent sufferer, and the call to discipleship which that imposes (1 Pet. 2: 18-25; 3: 17-22; 4: 14-19). He sees the death of Jesus on the cross as vividly as if it had happened but yesterday: for ever it is etched on his mind. 'He himself bore our sins in his own body up to the tree,' writes the one who describes himself as 'witness of the sufferings of Christ and

partaker in the glory that is to be revealed' (2: 24; 5: 1). That death is a fulfilment of the Old Testament prophecies (1: 11), particularly the ones concerning the Suffering Servant: there are at least five references to Isaiah 53 in 1 Peter 2: 21–5. Jesus in his death was the fulfilment of the death of the Passover lamb, which spelt freedom and life for the beleaguered Israelites who lay under threat of death in Egypt (1: 18, 19). His death was planned from all eternity: there was no accident about it (1: 20). Essentially, the meaning of the cross is very simple and clear. 'For Christ died for sins once for all, the righteous for the unrighteous, that he might bring us to God, being put to death in the flesh but made alive in the Spirit' (3: 18). That death was the harrowing of hell: it proclaimed his cosmic victory to the most notorious of sinners in Jewish thought, the men of Genesis 6: 1–8 (1 Pet. 3: 19). It was accompanied by the glorious resurrection that Peter had witnessed, and that had made a new man of him (5: 1; 1: 3). It was the pledge of glory (5: 4), and the assurance of final salvation (1: 4–9). And baptism incorporates us in this saving event, as we offer the pledge of allegiance to the living Saviour (3: 21f) who is even now in God's place of power. But the death and resurrection of Jesus must have their counterpart in our own lives (4: 1, 2, 6; 2: 24). We may well be exposed to extensive suffering as he was (1: 6; 3: 17; 4: 12; 5: 9). But we shall certainly share the glory assured by his resurrection to the place of all authority and power (1: 4, 5, 9; 4: 13; 5: 9–11). No wonder this constant harping on the cross and resurrection of the Saviour, in whose benefits and example believers share, makes the author cry out time and again in sheer wonder at the grace and generosity of God (1: 3, 8; 5: 10; 11).

2 Peter adds only a couple of facets: the subject matter of his letter is entirely different. But in 2: 2 he talks of the false teachers as 'denying the Master who bought them', again alluding to that remarkable image of purchase through a costly price which began with Jesus' ransom saying and pervades the New Testament. The man who does not respond to the divine

initiative by growing in discipleship 'is blind and shortsighted
and has forgotten that he was cleansed from his old sins' (1: 9).
Cleansing and purchase: two central aspects of the atonement.

## The Johannine writings

It will be convenient to take the Letters, the Gospel and the
Revelation of John together. The Gospel has a very broad
understanding of the cross and resurrection. It is the judgment
of God on a rebel world (3: 18f; 12: 31). It is the broken bread
that becomes the food of men (6: 51). It is the lamb which takes
away sin (1: 29). It is the death of the one in the place of the
people (11: 50). It is the grain of wheat that falls into the ground
and dies in order to produce a harvest (12: 24). It is the
powerful force that draws men of all sorts to him (12: 32). It
means the defeat of Satan (16: 11). It was the building of the
new temple, the Christian community, resulting from the
destruction of his human body (2: 19). It was the precondition
of the release of the Spirit (16: 7). It was the way to life and
freedom for the world (3: 16; 8: 36). It shows him as the Saviour
of the world (4: 42). His self-giving would unify his people (ch.
17) and bring together 'his sheep' and his 'other sheep, not of
this fold', moulded into one by the laying down of his life (10:
15, 16). In common with so much of the New Testament John
stresses the themes of the fulfilment of scripture, Jesus'
voluntary death, and the harmony of his will with the Father's.
He knows that Calvary is the supreme expression of the love of
God the Father and of Jesus (3: 16; 10: 18). But with his stress
on 'the hour' of Jesus he insists that Jesus was invulnerable
until the moment selected by the Father for his self-offering for
the salvation of the world (2: 4; 7: 30; 12: 23; 13: 1; 16: 32). In
chapter 12 he shows, by brilliant counterpoint, that new life for
Lazarus was only achieved by means of the Saviour's journey
to his death. And perhaps the greatest paradox in the Gospel,
assisted by the ambiguity in the word 'lift up', is the repeated
assertion that the lifting up of the Son of Man on the cross is
not the precursor to his being raised in glory but actually *is* his

exaltation. It would be hard to make the point more clearly that the supreme glory of the deity is the stoop to Calvary (3: 14; 12: 32; 8: 28).

The Epistles of John concentrate on a small number of crucial themes. One of these is light: 'God is light, and in him is no darkness at all' (1 John 1: 5). But the same cannot be said of us (1: 8). Therefore there is a problem. How is a holy God to accept sinners? 'God loved us and sent his Son to be the expiation for our sins' (4: 10). This means 'we have an advocate with the Father, Jesus Christ the righteous, and he is the expiation for our sins' (2: 2). On Calvary he did for us what we could not do for ourselves. He dealt with the sins of mankind: 'not our sins only, but the sins of the whole world' (2: 2). And all this arises from the supreme love of God, stressed time and again in these Epistles. 'Not that we loved God, but that he loved us, and sent his Son . . .' (4: 10). In fact, 'God is love' (4: 8). It is worth pausing on this word. There were several words for 'love' in Greek, among them *storgē*, *erōs* and *philia*. The New Testament uses none of them. They are all determined by the worthiness of the recipient. But that is not so with the love of God. It is something entirely different, so the New Testament writers are driven to an entirely new word which is almost unknown in classical writers. The word is *agape*, and it is not qualified and determined by the worthiness of the recipients but by the nature of the donor. God loves us for the simple reason that he is like that. He is the supremely generous giver, even though it costs him everything. 'God so loved that he gave'. And the only way we know that God is like that is because Jesus Christ his Son went to the cross for us. There was nothing he would not do to prove to us that God loves us passionately, unworthy though we are. There are modern theologians who say 'God loves, and therefore he can dispense with atonement.' The apostles say 'God is love, and therefore he provides the atonement'. That is the difference. There is nothing shallow or soft about the love of God. He is light as well as love. He can by no means clear the guilty, for his is a moral universe. But such is his love that there is nothing to prevent his standing in for the guilty at their place of greatest need. That is precisely what he has done, and John celebrates the fact.

Intertwined with light and love is the theme of life. John believes that only the man in Christ has real, eternal life. 'He who has the Son has life, and he who has not the Son of God has not life' (1 John 5: 12). It is as clear a division as that. And it is only possible to share the divine life because he has come and shared his life with us, first by the incarnation (1: 11f) and then by the cross (4: 9). He surrendered his life that we might live it. 'We are in him who is true, in his Son Jesus Christ', he concludes. 'This is the true God and eternal life' (5: 20).

Finally, the Johannine school provide, in the Book of Revelation, an amazingly powerful interpretation of the passion. At the outset we are reminded that the cross and resurrection stand together. John is given a vision on Patmos of Jesus Christ. He says 'I am the first and the last, and the living one; I died, and behold, I am alive for evermore, and I have the keys of Death and Hades' (Rev. 1: 18). That says it all. The Jesus who died, who is the conqueror of death, confronts John as his very life. The victory theme is continued from the Johannine Epistles, which come from the same circle though probably not from the same pen. 'The reason the Son of God appeared was to destroy the works of the devil' (1 John 3: 8), and this theme of victory over evil in all its forms is a major cause for celebration in the Apocalypse. The writer can face all the horrors of persecution under Domitian, all the prospect of the final Armageddon, because he is sure that the crucial victory has been won on Calvary, and that the future will show the gradual unfolding of that central battle.

Nowhere does the author make the point more strongly than in the vision of Revelation 5. He is bewailing the inscrutability of history, and the inability of anyone to pierce its inner secrets. Then in his vision he hears one of the heavenly elders saying 'Weep not; lo, the Lion of the tribe of Judah, the Root of David, has conquered, so that he can open the scroll' (*sc.* of human destiny, 5: 5). And to his amazement he saw not a Lion but a Lamb, with all the marks of slaughter upon him. He 'went and took the scroll from the right hand of him who sat on the throne' and he unravelled the secrets of human destiny. This is the ultimate mystery of God. The Lion of God's strength is the Lamb of God's sacrifice. Self-sacrificing love is actually on the throne of the universe, and is the key to the understanding of human history and destiny. If we could get to the very heart of God we would find there that the Lamb has been slain since the foundation of the world (13: 8). Calvary displays in time God's attitude to sinners from all eternity. There is nothing more fundamental in the whole universe than the self-sacrificing love of God. This is the ground for Christian hope.

No wonder, then, that this writer makes much of the blood of the Lamb which makes the sinner's clothes white before a holy God (7: 14), releases him from the sins which held him fast (1: 5), ransoms him for God (5: 9), and makes him an overcomer in spiritual battle (12: 11). No wonder the redeemed are written in the Lamb's book of life: they owe their place in heaven entirely to his sacrifice, and under his tutelage they are safe from the second death (20: 12, 15). No wonder the host of heaven cry out in praise to the Saviour who died and rose for them:

> Worthy is the Lamb who was slain, to receive power and wealth and wisdom and might and honour and glory and blessing... for thou wast slain and by thy blood didst ransom men for God, from every tribe and tongue and people and nation, and hast made them a kingdom and priests to our God, and they shall reign on earth (5: 12, 9f).

It should be plain from this cursory survey of what the New Testament writers have to say about the significance of Calvary, that it is a many-splendoured thing. There is a remarkable harmony in the central thesis, and remarkable diversity in the ways the different writers look at the cross. Here we see supremely the love of God for sinful men who are lost, alienated from him by sin, and are in a plight from which they could never extricate themselves. Salvation depends on what God has done for us in the Christ who is both human and divine. He silenced sin's accusing voice. He removed sin's guilt. He broke sin's power. He made satisfaction where we could not. He reversed Adam's fall. He defeated Satan. He rose as conqueror over the Last Enemy. He makes us partners of his life. He calls us to a share in his cross as well as in his triumph. And he teaches us that all eternity will be too short to understand the profundity of the salvation wrought by the incarnation, death and resurrection of the Saviour of the world.

# Chapter 5

## Why Did Later Centuries Think He Had to Die?

Given the variety of ways in which the New Testament writers sought to understand the cross of Jesus, it is hardly surprising that there has been a great spate of books on the subject throughout the centuries. Nor is it surprising that the interpretations are very different. This is due partly to the great richness of the New Testament material, partly to the inexhaustible depth of the subject, partly to the fallenness of men and the influence of the cultural scene from which they wrote, and partly to neglect of major emphases in the teaching of Jesus and his followers on the matter. In this chapter we shall attempt a brief survey of some of the more influential interpretations of the cross and resurrection, and make some comments on their strengths and weaknesses, remembering that we, too, are children of our age, with limited vision and understanding.

### Example

The simplest and most obvious understanding of the cross is to see it as the supreme example. At Calvary Jesus showed his obedience to his heavenly Father to the very end. Here was one who lived every moment of his life in dependence on God, and he carried it through to death itself. That perfect life became the illumination of our ignorance. This is a favourite theme in the early Fathers, as H.E.W. Turner showed in *The Patristic Doctrine of Redemption*. Thus we read 'Let us then be imitators of his endurance, and if we suffer for his name's sake, let us glorify him. For this is the example which he gave us' (Polycarp, *Ep.*, 8.2). It can scarcely be denied that much of the second century understanding of the cross was frankly exemplarist. And that is only a step away from legalistic moralism. Moreover the stress on the incarnation and cross as 'God's word proceeding from silence' (Ignatius, *Magn.*, 8.2) or 'through him the Master willed that we should taste immortal knowledge' (*1 Clem.*, 36.2) runs another danger: of seeing Christianity as just another philosophy, which was what Paul was so passionately opposed to in 1 Corinthians. Christianity does not primarily offer us an example, and it is not primarily the illumination of our minds. The exemplarist theory is manifestly inadequate.

But two things must be said. First, the second-century writers were seeking to apply the passion of Christ to the prime need of the day, which was holiness of life in the midst of pagan immorality. They were also trying to commend the faith, in terms most readily understood by their contemporaries: and that made the theme of illumination highly attractive to them: it was fashionable talk. We see, therefore, both a necessary process, namely putting the message in terms that will be understood; and also a real danger, namely limiting the Christian message to what will be acceptable or what is deemed immediately relevant. Later generations have regularly made the same mistake as these early Fathers.

Moreover, we must remember that we have only a very limited selection of their works, and that they did not stick rigidly and exclusively to any one aspect of the cross. Thus Ignatius writes 'The eucharist is the flesh of our Saviour Jesus Christ, who suffered for our sins and whom, in his goodness, the Father raised' (*Smyrn.*, 7.1). Again, 'He took pity on us, and in his tenderness he saved us, since he saw our great error and ruin, and that we had no hope of salvation unless it came from him. For he called us when we were nothing, and willed our existence from nothing' (*2 Clem.*, 1). Even in the days of the second century when they had no clear collection of apostolic writings, and were heavily inclined to moralism, they realised

that the atonement was a many-splendoured thing. The saints
and martyrs were indeed called to follow Christ's example, but
in so doing they shared in the sufferings of 'one who died on our
behalf and was raised by God for our sakes' (Polycarp, *Ep.*,
9.2).

What is more, it is important to notice that they had fastened
on, in their exemplarism and illuminationism, to two clear
New Testament emphases. God has shed his light on our
darkness (1 John *passim*; 2 Cor. 4: 4–6; John 1: 9); the life of
Jesus is the light of men (John 1: 9). And we are called to follow
his example, for 'Christ also suffered for you, leaving you an
example, that you should follow his steps' (1 Peter 2: 21).

*Recapitulation*
A second influential and profound understanding of the cross
comes from Irenaeus, perhaps the first writer after the
apostolic age seriously to work out what happened on Calvary.
He does so in Book 5 of *Adversus Haereses*. Taking Ephesians
1: 10 as his starting point, and God's purpose of 'summing up'
all things in Christ, Irenaeus thought of Jesus as recapitulating
the whole of human history. He, the last Adam, stands ranged
against the first Adam, and succeeded where the former had
failed. Irenaeus understood the corporate nature of mankind,
and realised that by his cross and passion Jesus had done
something of cosmic significance. Adam was the type of Christ.
Our bondage to sin had been originated by the fruit of a tree,
and so it was redeemed by the fruit of the cross. Adam had
fallen through the disobedience of a virgin, Eve; therefore it
was fitting that our salvation should come through the
obedience of a virgin, Mary. And so on. The parallelism comes
to its climax in the atonement, where Christ turns the abject
defeat of Adam into his own glorious victory. In a word, he
repeated human history the way it should have gone.

There is something very profound about this understanding,
though it is alien from the individualism of modern Western
man. It is almost ludicrous to read the distaste for it in a liberal
like Hastings Rashdall (*The Idea of the Atonement in*

*Christian Theology* p. 237f). The teaching of our human solidarity, in creation, guilt and salvation, is very strong in scripture. Romans 5 and 1 Corinthians 15: 21f are explicit sources for Irenaeus' teaching, but it is based on the whole biblical view of man. In these days of nuclear power, totalitarian regimes, trades unions, multinational corporations and political and economic constraints, it is abundantly clear that we swim or sink together. Indeed, Barclay in *Crucified and Crowned* goes so far as to say that

> this may well be called the most modern of all conceptions of the work of Christ... Through man's disobedience the process of the evolution of the human race went wrong, and the course of its wrongness could neither be halted nor reversed by any human means. But in Jesus Christ the whole course of human evolution was perfectly carried out and realised in obedience to the purpose of God (p. 100).

An important development of this recapitulation theory of Irenaeus is very startling, and has been highly influential in the Greek Orthodox Church. It is hardly too much to say that it sees the work of Christ as the deification of man. 'He became what we are' wrote Irenaeus in the Preface of Book 5 of the *Adversus Haereses* 'to make us what he is'. This was picked up by many of the Fathers. 'He was made man' said Athanasius, 'that we might become God' (*de Incarnatione*, 54). Augustine says, 'He was made a sharer in our mortality... He has made us sharers in his deity' (*de Trinitate*, 4.8; 2.4), and Clement of Alexandria goes so far as to claim 'The Logos of God became man that from man you might learn how man may become God' (*Stromateis*, 7.16).

Clearly this is very dangerous language despite the various ways the Fathers seek to safeguard themselves. But it is not totally beside the mark. John speaks of the new birth (John 3: 3), Paul of the new creation (2 Cor. 5: 14), and 2 Peter 1: 4 of becoming partakers of the divine nature. We can never become all that Christ is. He is not sinful: we are. We are not divine: he is. But the Fathers were right in seeing that one of the most profound meanings of the atonement was to enable us to share in the Father's home as sons, albeit adopted sons. Needless to say, it was both an attractive and a dangerous model for use in pagan circles. It was all too easy to present Christianity as yet another of the Mystery religions whereby you attained immortality and partnership with the deity through the initiation rite of baptism and the mystery of the eucharist.

*Victory*

A third major category for understanding the achievement of Jesus is that of victory. Christ reigning from the tree (strongly hinted at in St. John's Gospel) became a favourite theme of the writers of the second century. As I have observed in *I Believe in Satan's Downfall*, the ancient world, both Jewish and Greek, was hag-ridden with the sense of demonic forces gripping and ruining men's lives. The Gospels, particularly Mark, show Jesus taking on the forces of evil and winning all along the line, particularly in the final victory of the cross. This was something, as Gustav Aulén has shown, which meant an inestimable release to ancient man. 'Christ has delivered us from ten thousand demons' exulted Tatian (*Orat.*, 29). The cross was the place where the power of the demonic forces was broken for ever.

Had the 'world rulers' not overreached themselves, they would never have driven Jesus to the cross where he sealed their final defeat (1 Cor. 2: 8). His descent to Hades robbed even death of its powers. Cyril puts it powerfully: 'Death was struck with dismay on beholding a new visitant descended into Hades, not bound with the chains of that place' (*Catechetical Lectures*, 14.19), and there is an emotive passage in the apocryphal *Gospel of Nicodemus* (6.22) where the legions in Hades cry out 'We are overcome. Woe to us!' It was not only his life, his death, and descent to Hades which wrought this total victory over the forces of evil. Origen sees the force of the resurrection too. 'Through his resurrection he destroyed the kingdom of death' (*Comm. in Rom.*, 5.1). This is, of course, a powerful New Testament theme, notably in such passages as Colossians 2: 15 and 1 John 3: 8; 4: 4. The Fathers got themselves into many problems in working this theory out in terms of how the devil was tricked, and robbed of his prey. But their central theme of the victory of Christ through the cross and resurrection became the main way of understanding the cross for nine hundred years. It is not the whole truth, but it is a very important aspect of it.

*Ransom*
A fourth interpretation of the cross common in the ancient world was the ransom theory. This derived from Jesus' own ransom saying in Mark 10: 45 but took strange byways after that. In the *Didache* (4.6) it is even suggested that if your salary is high enough you ought 'to pay a ransom for your sins'! This is bizarre, but the main thesis which we find in Irenaeus, Origen and Gregory, is that on the cross Christ paid a ransom for us. This really spoke to an age beset with brigandage and the constant capture of prisoners, just as eloquently as it spoke to those who lived in the midst of slavery from which the only way out was by the payment of a price. So it was a marvellous and contemporary preaching of the cross. Unfortunately it became over-elaborated. Man is seen as in bondage to the devil. Release must mean that mankind is bought back by a ransom to which the devil would consent. And this whole transaction must take place in such a way that even the devil is given his due by the justice of God, and mankind is rescued by the love of God. The theory developed still further: we see a hint of things to come in Ignatius' astonishing comment that 'Mary's virginity, her giving birth and the Lord's death, three secrets crying to be told, escaped the notice of the prince of this world' (Ignatius, *Ephes.* 19.1). Subsequently a variety of strange understandings of the devil's part in all this were developed. Some thought the devil had a just claim on mankind because man had voluntarily fallen. Others thought the devil had deceived himself by engineering the death of Jesus: he had imagined that would be the end of Jesus, but how wrong he

was! This was taken even further in a talk by Gregory of Nyssa who saw God as deceiving the devil in the ransom, and thus paying the deceiver back in his own coin. God saw Satan's jealousy and pride, and so 'in order to make himself easily accessible to him who sought the ransom, veiled himself in our nature. In that way, as it is with a greedy fish, he might swallow the Godhead like a fish-hook along with the humanity, which was the bait' (*Oratio Catechetica* 24).

It is salutary to see how far we move from the New Testament when more weight is put on any particular image of the atonement than it will bear. The main idea of the ransom aspect of the cross is our rescue from a perilous predicament through the very costly self-giving of Jesus. Rescue and costliness are the point. Gregory of Nazianzus cut short the foolish elaborations of this theory trenchantly. 'Was the ransom then paid to the evil one? Monstrous thought! What an outrage, for then the robber receives a ransom' (*Oration* 45.22). He gives equally short shrift, in the same passage, to the idea that it was paid to God, 'for how could God delight in the blood of his Son?'

### Satisfaction

If the ransom theory spoke eloquently to the social conditions of the early centuries, the famous satisfaction theory which Anselm, the eleventh-century Archbishop of Canterbury, developed spoke equally powerfully to the feudal system of his day. He attacks the whole basis of the ransom theory which had assumed that the devil as well as God had acquired rights over us, and therefore required his due. In *Cur Deus Homo?* he shows that man has one allegiance, not two: God is sovereign, and the rights of the devil are not those of a usurper to the throne but of a rebel slave. Man has broken his loyalty to his liege Lord: God's honour is slighted, and satisfaction must be made. Man cannot make it: that Christ undertook to do.

Anselm is strong on the grace of God and on the need for faith, but as a child of his age he sees man's sin in terms of civil rather than criminal law: satisfaction, not punishment was what was required. The legalism of Anselm's Latin mind is very obvious, and while taking both grace and guilt seriously, it is miles away from the joyous, personal and powerful gospel of Jesus and the resurrection which we find in the New Testament. However his wrestling with this mighty theme in the barbaric days of the eleventh century, and his use of contemporary imagery in the attempt to meet the doubts and difficulties of ordinary people are a beacon and a challenge to theologians, and history shows that Anselm's views were seminal for the subsequent development of both Catholic and Protestant theology.[1]

*Moral Influence*
A contemporary of Anselm was Peter Abelard, and his understanding of the moral influence of the cross on hard hearts, bringing them to repentance, has had a great deal of influence in recent years, through such writers as Hastings Rashdall and Mozley. Abelard rejected not only the ransom theory but *any* theory which gave objective significance to the cross and resurrection. He saw them as a supreme exhibition of God's love to kindle our love in return.

He, too, was a child of his age, and more particularly of his circumstances. Love was the dominant theme of his life – though not the pure *agapē* of the love of God, but a very red-blooded *erōs* for Heloise which has made him one of the great romantics of the Middle Ages. Abelard believed, in short, that the ultimate meaning of the death of Jesus on the cross was to show men that God loves them like that. His death did nothing to alter the attitude of God to sinners: it exemplified it. And when men see such love, they will naturally respond to it.

---

[1] Anselm's stress on *sola gratia*, and on faith which both challenges unbelief and rationalism and also grasps the grace proffered by God, is thoroughly Protestant. In his emphasis on the Mass rather than Baptism as the central sacrament, together with his accent on the sinlessness of Mary, Anselm prepared the way for sacrificial theories about the Mass in Roman piety and a Mariolatry which led logically to the idea that she is co-redemptrix.

Both his emphasis on love and his objection to any conception of ransom or atonement in the cross are very modern.

> Indeed, how cruel and wicked it seems that anyone should demand the blood of an innocent person as the price for anything, or that it should in any way please him that an innocent man should be slain – still less that God should consider the death of his Son so agreeable that by it he should be reconciled to the whole world (Abelard, *Exposition on the Epistle to the Romans*, 2).

Attractive though it is, and modern though it is, this emphasis on the love of God as the sole category in which we should understand the atonement is unbearably shallow. Anselm's words, *'Nondum considerasti quanti ponderis sit peccatum'* ('You have not yet considered the weight of sin') are highly applicable to Abelard. He had little influence on the thought of his contemporaries, and only since the rise of liberalism in the nineteenth century have his views been revived.

## Substitution

At the Reformation there was a great flowering in the interpretation of the atonement, as of all Christian doctrine. Freed from the opposing schools of the nominalists and realists in the late Middle Ages, the reformers got back to the scriptures, and for the first time since the early days of the church we see them stressing a wide variety of understandings of the cross and resurrection (though they were not so strong on the latter).

The name of Luther is very much associated with justification by faith in the sheer grace of God. Europe was lit up by the recognition that the living God cared enough for us to become one of us and take on himself the responsibility for all our failures. Justification, acquittal, was possible for all. No longer need men be enslaved by penances and the supposed treasury of merit in the Virgin and the saints. *'Sola gratia, sola fide, soli Deo gloria'* was the cry of the Reformation, as its leaders went back to the scriptures and the earliest Fathers. How was this undreamed-of acquittal possible? Because Christ had borne instead of us the righteous judgment of God's holy wrath against sin. In his *Commentary on Galatians* (3: 13) Luther graphically imagines the Father identifying Jesus with the sins of all the great sinners: 'Be thou Paul, that persecutor. Be thou David, that adulterer!' and so on, and maintaining that 'they are Christ's own sins, as verily as if he himself had done them'. 'If Christ be made responsible for all the sins we have committed, then we are delivered utterly from our sins, not by ourselves nor by our own merits and works, but by him. But if we let him not bear our sins, then we do bear them ourselves, and in them die and be damned.' Calvin holds the penal substitution theory with great stringency. 'The only end which the Scripture uniformly assigns for the Son of God voluntarily assuming our nature is that he might propitiate the Father to us by becoming a victim' (*Institutes*, 2.12.4).

It must not be thought that the Reformers had one-track minds on the subject of substitution. Calvin, Luther and the English Reformers show an astonishing breadth in their understanding of New Testament categories. But they were clear that because of what Christ had done on Calvary there was full and free forgiveness for every sinner. They were sometimes incautious in the language they employed. For example, though the New Testament does speak of the cross as propitiation, it never says that Christ propitiated God the Father. Though the New Testament does speak of Christ's bearing our sins, it does not call this, as Calvin does, 'the penalty which we had incurred' or 'the price of satisfaction to the just judgment of God'. Indeed, the New Testament does not use the word punishment, *kolasis*, of the death of Christ. Though the New Testament is strong on the wrath of God, it does not apply the verb *orgizomai*, 'be wrathful', to God, and certainly does not go so far as the Reformers did in saying 'God in his character as Judge is hostile to us'. Nor does the New Testament talk of the 'merits' of Christ being put to our account: but the Reformers were operating with the imagery of the mediaeval Treasury of Merit, and within the limitations of that category rightly stressed that we are not accepted because of the merits of the saints or our good works, but because of Christ and his one, perfect and sufficient sacrifice.

### Sacrifice

Sacrifice was the other great interpretation of the death of Christ which was given fresh emphasis by the Reformers. Luther and Calvin are both strong in this reviving of the patristic stress on the sacrifice of Christ, a major category of New Testament thought. In Book 2 of the *Institutes* Calvin sees Jesus as fulfilling both the priestly and the sacrificial roles of the Old Testament. Had they not pointed forward to what Jesus would do on Calvary, the ancient animal sacrifices would have been 'a foul odour in the nostrils' and 'a mere mockery'.

Cranmer paid with his life for his clear views on the uniqueness of the sacrifice of Christ; he refused to accept the Roman Catholic doctrine that the sacrifice of Christ was offered in the Mass, but made a memorable distinction between Christ's sacrifice and ours.

> One kind of sacrifice there is which is called a propitiatory or merciful sacrifice, that is to say, such a sacrifice as pacifieth God's wrath and indignation, and obtaineth mercy and forgiveness for all our sins... And although in the Old Testament there were certain sacrifices called by that name, yet in very deed there is but one such sacrifice whereby our sins be pardoned... which is the death of God's Son, our Lord Jesus Christ; nor ever was any other sacrifice propitiatory at any time, nor never shall be. This is the honour of this our high priest, wherein he admitteth neither partner nor successor.
>
> Another kind of sacrifice there is, which doth not reconcile us to God, but is made of them that be reconciled by Christ... to show ourselves thankful to him; and therefore they be called sacrifices of laud, praise and

thanksgiving. The first kind of sacrifice Christ offered to God for us; the second kind we ourselves offer to God by Christ (*The Lord's Supper*, 5: 11).

It would be helpful if subsequent writers had seen this distinction as clearly as Cranmer did. Recently Frances Young has written what is in many ways a helpful and irenic book on *Sacrifice and the Death of Christ*. But in her attempt to broaden the concept of sacrifice to the full range of the biblical sacrifices, and so build a bridge between the subjective and objective understanding of Christ's sacrifice, she confuses what Cranmer and the Reformers had seen so clearly: 'the sacrificial language of the early Church represented not merely response to, but participation in the sacrifice of Christ. Worship, service and atonement were inseparable' (p. 97). We do not, in the eyes of the New Testament writers, partake in Christ's sacrifice except as recipients. Our self-offering, our worship and obedience, are not part of Christ's self-offering, but a grateful response to his prior act. While we may agree with Young that it is in the eucharist that the sacrificial emphasis of scripture most comes alive, we must keep clear Cranmer's distinction. It is true that in the second and third centuries Christians often spoke of the Holy Communion as a sacrifice; just as they did of prayer, evangelism and so forth. But they did not suggest that our sacrifice is incorporated in Christ's. Instead they saw the eucharist as the fulfilment of Malachi 1: 11, the Old Testament meal-offering. It was 'a sacrifice of thanksgiving' which the church 'offers to God for having made the world . . . and also for having set us free from evil' (Justin, *Dialogue*, 41). The Fathers see this as a response to the sacrifice of Christ for sins upon the cross. They take up the image of the meal-offering which was given by the leper once he was cleansed. This is the thanksgiving sacrifice they see in the eucharist: a responsive sacrifice by those who have been cleansed and set free.

*Review of theories*
These are eight of the great categories in which Christians

down the ages have looked at the cross and resurrection. All of them have some anchorage in the New Testament. None of them is adequate by itself. All of them throw the cross into distortion if they are taken to extremes or their imagery developed further than it will stand. Many of them have been weak on the resurrection, and on giving us a person who reconciles rather than a cold doctrine which must be believed. Some of them, such as the doctrine of penal substitution, have gone perilously near to separating the attitude of the Father and the Son in our redemption. Most of them have sought to interpret the central mystery of the faith in terms which made sense to their particular generation, and that is why the doctrine of the cross and resurrection needs to be restated afresh in every age and cultural milieu.

It would be tedious to go further into the attempts to understand the atonement that have been made in more recent years. Moberley saw it as vicarious repentance on the part of Jesus for us. Kirk saw it as reparation. Hicks sought the key to Calvary in the idea of life offered, transformed, and shared. Quick saw it as redemptive suffering inaugurating a new world. Hodgson regarded the pain which follows sin as both the expression of God's wrath and the raw material from which he fashions a higher good. Barth was strong on Christ as our substitute, and Brunner understands the atonement as 'the unveiling of our guilt in its truly fatal character, and the incomprehensible act of grace by which God has taken our part'; while Moltmann sees the immanence of the crucified in horrors like Auschwitz, and draws inferences from this in the areas of political reform and liberation theology.

But despite all this diversity, it would be true to say that there is increasing coming together in understanding the atonement. Thus all thoughtful theologians are agreed that there must be no separating the Father from the Son in our redemption. All are agreed that the perfect human life of Jesus cannot be dissociated from what happened on the cross. Most see that the resurrection is integral to the act of God on Calvary, and that he there dealt with human sins in a way mankind could never have done. All recognise the victory theme of the atonement, and all are agreed on the re-establishment of personal relations with God. Moral influence theories are in most quarters recognised as inadequate by themselves, but the link between the cross and ethics is seen to be strong, and that was one of the main planks in Abelard's position. There is a tendency to stress sacrificial imagery in writers like Whale, Baillie, Vincent Taylor and Forsyth, and to see the eucharist as the place where we are caught up in the drama of redemption, the central expression of the redeeming work of Christ. Finally, particularly since World War Two, there has been a recovery of the social and corporate aspect of the atonement. The cross spelt cosmic redemption, and it is the calling of the Church to work for that tirelessly by its worship, its life and its witness in society.

It is clear, now, why the Church at large has never defined a doctrine of the atonement, though plenty of denominations and Christian societies have done so. The atonement of Christ is as big as the heart of God. We can never get to the bottom of it. There is certainly no one theory of what happened on Calvary which covers the whole mystery. In the chapters which follow we shall see some of the ways in which different aspects of the cross and resurrection speak to different needs of the human heart. In the next chapter we shall look at the cost of forgiveness. Perhaps the most appropriate way to end the present chapter, which has very inadequately attempted to cover a vast field of theories, is to focus on our own response to the personal self-giving of Jesus on the cross:

One thing I know – that because of Jesus Christ and because of what he is and did and does, my whole relationship with God is changed. Because of Jesus Christ I know that God is my father and friend. Daily and hourly I experience the fact that I can enter into his presence with confidence and with boldness. He is no longer my enemy; he is no longer even my judge. There is no longer an unbridgeable gulf between him and me. I am more at home with him than with any human being in the world. And all this is so because of Jesus Christ,

and it could not possibly have happened without him
(William Barclay, *Crucified and Crowned*, p. 130).

Unless you can say something like that, all the atonement
theories in the world will avail you nothing.

# Chapter 6

## The Cost of Forgiveness

'In Christ we have redemption through his blood, the forgiveness of our sins, according to the riches of his grace which he lavished upon us' (Eph. 1: 7). There we have the antinomy in a nutshell. If God is really one who lavishes his love upon us in forgiving us our sins, where do all these heavy concepts like redemption and the blood of Christ fit in?

In this chapter I propose to examine the question of God's forgiveness, which is certainly one of the central strands at the heart of the cross. It has long been the case that conservatives have espoused a doctrine of forgiveness which is based upon a definite transaction on the cross: Jesus bears for sinners the outcome of their sins in order that they may not have to bear it. It is a powerful doctrine, and has a great evangelical appeal. And yet liberals have been repelled by it and have criticised it sharply. It seems to them immoral that God should punish someone else instead of us. They cannot understand why God cannot simply forgive sinners without need for atonement. They maintain that the cross demonstrated God's attitude to sinners and in no way changed it. It seems to them disastrous theology to set the wrathful Father against the loving Son in redemption. In a word it is Anselm versus Abelard all over again – a thousand years later. What are we to make of all this?

It might be a useful way of proceeding if we ask, and try to answer, some common questions on the matter.

*Why do we need forgiveness?*

Because we are sinners. Every single man, woman and child who has ever lived has done things wrong: wrong words, wrong thoughts, wrong actions, wrong attitudes, resulting in warped character. 'The heart of man is deceitful above all things, and desperately wicked' (Jer. 17: 9). 'There is no difference, for all have sinned and come short of the glory of God' (Rom. 3: 23). 'From within, out of the heart of man' said Jesus, the great physician of the soul, 'proceed evil thoughts, fornication, theft, murder, adultery, coveting, wickedness, deceit, licentiousness, envy, slander, pride, foolishness. All these evil things come from within, and they defile a man' (Mark 7: 21ff). The heart of the problem is the human heart. All over the world, it is 'very far gone from original righteousness'. We have broken God's laws, we have come short of his standards, we have rejected his love, we have kept him out of our lives, we have put all our idols before him. And we have the effrontery to wonder why we need forgiveness!

We in our generation are exceedingly smug about ourselves; we are confident that basically we are all right. And yet this generation above all others is raping the earth, squandering non-renewable resources, fouling the environment, and resting very satisfied that one-third of the world is overfed while the other two-thirds are in need, and over 30,000 people across the world starve to death every day. Ours is the generation of genocide and torture unparalleled in the history of the world, and it has largely taken place among the most 'civilised' of nations. Our corroding nationalism, our dishonesty, our social unconcern, our jealousy and pathetic materialism, not to mention our national godlessness, must all rise as a foul odour in the nostrils of Almighty God. We assume that all will be well. We imagine that if God exists he must be as vapid as we are. But the scriptures will not allow us to live with that illusion. He is the God who will by no means clear the guilty. He is the judge of all the earth who will do right. He is the Holy One. He is light, and in him is no darkness at all. That is why we need forgiveness.

*Why cannot God simply forgive us everything?*
Because he is the moral ruler of the universe. God is not a private person, who could pat us on the head and assure us that it does not matter. That is what you can do to me if I offend you. But there would be an outcry if any judge acted like that. The consistent teaching of the Bible is that God is the king of the whole earth. He is the supreme judge, the lawgiver, the ruler of all. His laws are not arbitrary. They are truth. They spring from his own being. To disobey them is not like committing some offence against the property laws of the state: it is self-destructive, because evil is always like that. In rebelling against God the sinner rebels against his own highest interests, and those of others. You only have to universalise failings like lying, stealing, and immorality to see what a chaotic world it would be if everyone acted like that – and yet we make excuses for ourselves when we do. For God just to forgive without any cost to anyone would be sheer indifferentism. It would obliterate any distinction between right and wrong. It would say that right does not matter, and that evil is a matter of indifference.

How can that be before a holy God? All such views regard forgiveness as God's job (*c'est son métier*). It is not his job. It is never anyone's job when they have been wronged. Forgiveness is always a matter of sheer generosity on the part of the wronged party. It can never be demanded as a right. And how much less in God's case. He is no private person. We have not only repudiated relations with him, but have laughed at his standards and pleased ourselves. It perhaps shows the extent of the blindness of our age that we should marvel that God might not forgive everyone at the wave of a hand, whereas previous generations have wrestled with the problem of how a holy God could have any sinners in his company at all. Shall not the Judge of all the earth do right? He will by no means clear the guilty. Paul, in the Epistle to the Romans, wrestled with the problem of how God could be just and at the same time the justifier of him who believes in Jesus (3: 26).

There is a genuine antinomy here. It will not do to subsume

all aspects of God's character under love. He is also light: he is a consuming fire. And the same scriptures that tell us the one aspect of his character reveal the other. The teaching of Jesus is explicit on this matter. Nobody spoke with more love and warmth of the God who welcomes sinners and forgives the penitent, but nobody spoke so much and so fearsomely about the possibility of hell as Jesus. Reflect on some of his sayings. 'Whoever shall say to his brother "you fool" shall be liable to the hell of fire'. 'Enter in at the narrow gate, for the gate is wide and the way is easy that leads to destruction, and those who enter by it are many'. 'Many will say to me in that day "Lord, Lord, did we not prophesy in your name... and do many mighty works in your name?" And then I will declare unto them "I never knew you. Depart from me, you evildoers"' (Matt. 5: 22; 7: 13, 14, 21–3). Those passages all come in Jesus' manifesto, the Sermon on the Mount.

The Gospels are full of much more in the same vein. 'Do not fear those who kill the body but cannot kill the soul; rather fear him who can destroy both body and soul in hell' (Matt. 10: 28). 'Whosoever speaks against the Holy Spirit will not be forgiven, either in this age or in the age to come' (Matt. 12: 32). 'So it will be at the close of the age: the angels shall come out and separate the evil from the righteous, and throw them into the furnace of fire; there men will weep and gnash their teeth' (Matt. 13: 49f). 'And in anger his lord delivered him to the jailers till he should pay all his debt. So also my heavenly Father will do to every one of you, if you do not forgive your brother from your heart' (Matt. 18: 34). Or consider the conclusion of the parable of the wicked husbandmen: 'when the tenants saw the son, they said... "This is the heir; come, let us kill him..." And they took him and cast him out of the vineyard and killed him. When therefore the owner of the vineyard comes, what will he do to those tenants? They said to him "He will put those wretches to a miserable death"' (Matt. 21: 38ff).

In the remaining chapters of this Gospel there are five parables, every one of which contains the note of judgment (Matt. 22: 13; 24: 48–51; 25: 12; 25: 30), and the teaching of the

Gospel ends on the solemn and terrible warning at the end of the parable of the sheep and goats: '"Depart from me, you cursed, into the eternal fire prepared for the devil and his angels" . . . And they will go away into eternal punishment, but the righteous into eternal life' (25: 41, 46).

Now those are some – by no means all – of the words of Jesus *as recorded in a single Gospel* on the subject of God's impending judgment. Nobody could say they are a collection of proof texts. Nobody could say they are not a substantial body of material. They could be greatly extended if we were to look at the other Gospels, but that would be tedious and unnecessary. The plain fact is that Jesus did not see the forgiveness of God as cheap, easy and universal. Men must reckon with his judgment as well as his grace. There is no cheap forgiveness to be had.

*What father would treat his children so hardly?*
This is a common objection, but it will not withstand careful scrutiny. For the Gospels would rebut it on two clear counts.

The first is that the analogy is far from exact. God is not a private person like an earthly Father. He is the source and upholder of the moral universe in which human beings live. And we would never have any idea that he might be called Father were it not for Jesus who gave him the unprecedented title of 'Abba' and in the Lord's Prayer instructed his disciples to do likewise. But if it is Jesus who introduces us to the concept of God as Father, we must pay attention to what he says. And nowhere in the Gospels does he indicate that all men are children of God. Far from it. He says that even punctiliously religious Pharisees are a 'viper's brood' (Matt. 12: 34) that they belong to 'their father the devil' and are by no means children of God (John 8: 41–4). He did indeed attribute sonship of God to his followers: the words 'your Father' in the Gospels are invariably directed to disciples. It is clear from his teaching that there is only one Son of God in the full sense of the word himself: but that it is possible for us to *become* sons of God by 'believing in' him or 'receiving' him (1: 12). So to say

'What Father would treat his children so hardly?' breaks down at once. We are not children of God unless we have come to Jesus, the Son of God, for adoption and grace.

But there is another point to consider. As we have seen in answer to the previous difficulty, the holiness of God is a major theme in the teaching of Jesus, alongside his readiness to welcome the penitent sinner. But there is no suggestion in Jesus' teaching that God's love modifies his justice. Here is one among many remarkable passages in the Gospels which highlights the separate action of God's love and holiness. 'And when he drew near and saw the city, he wept over it saying "Would that even today you knew the things that make for peace! But now they are hid from your eyes. For the days shall come upon you when your enemies shall cast up a bank about you and surround you, and hem you in on every side, and dash you to the ground, you and your children within you, and they will not leave one stone upon another in you; because you did not know the time of your visitation"' (Luke 19: 41ff). Here we have the passionate love of Jesus for Jerusalem. But Jerusalem is adamant against him. What is to be done? Love can only weep while judgment acts. And act it did, with ferocious intensity in the destruction of Jerusalem in A.D. 70. Love does not override either the holiness of God or the free will of men. People sometimes ask how a loving God can send even an Adolf Hitler to hell. The love of God does not send anyone to hell. The love of God, with arms extended on a cross, bars the way to hell. But if that love is ignored, rejected and finally refused, there comes a time when love can only weep while man pushes past into the self-chosen alienation which Christ went to the cross to avert. God sends nobody to hell. But it takes two to make a friendship. If man firmly and repeatedly refuses the proffered hand of God, God will honour and ratify that man's decision to live to himself and die by himself. God respects our free will even in the hell of our own choosing.

*The category of law is inadequate for understanding the forgiveness of God*

That is perfectly true. It is inadequate, but it is one of the major biblical categories which is used to help us understand this tremendous unexpected act of grace on God's part, whereby he welcomes the sinner back to himself. In point of fact, justification, sacrifice, and forgiveness are three quite distinct though collateral concepts. Justification meets the legal claim against those who have offended against the laws of God. Sacrifice brings near those who are unclean and alienated from his life. Forgiveness is the restoration of a personal relationship that has been impaired.

The category of law is, therefore, only one of the ways in which we need to reflect on Calvary and its achievement. But it is an important one. As we have seen, God is no private person, who can shrug his shoulders and say 'It doesn't matter'. Sin does matter. It ruins his world. If God was to accept back into fellowship a fallen world full of sinful men and women, he had to find a way whereby he could do so without being false to his own eternal rectitude. And we need to know that his divine reception back into fellowship is no brushing of sin under the carpet, no condoning of our wickedness, but a completely fair settling of the accounts, a clearing of the charges against us.

The cross of Jesus assures us of that exactly. It tells us that through Calvary God has proved that he remains just and is at the same time the justifier of the believer in Jesus, as Paul puts it in Romans 3: 24-6. How can this be? It all springs from the sheer grace of God as a free gift. But that free gift did not dispense with the expiation of sin. It required it. And it came about through the redemption that is in Christ Jesus, which he wrought by shedding his blood on the cross, and which needs to be appropriated by faith. There is no contradiction between the *gratuito* and the *propter Christum*. The coming and dying of Jesus is the expression of the free grace of the God we have affronted. But because of what he did on that cross we are not only forgiven – a personal act of grace. We are justified, acquitted, and the accusing finger of the law we have broken can no longer be pointed against us. For the sheet has been wiped clean. The bill has been paid. The guilt has been expiated. It will never be raised again. Forgiveness assures us of our relationship with God restored. Justification, the forensic term, assures us of our eternal standing, guaranteed by what Jesus did for us at Calvary.

But while the legal category is indispensable, it is also inadequate, and can be most misleading. It is unduly loved by evangelicals, who sometimes forget that as an interpretation of the death of Jesus it is only to be found in Paul, and even there only in contexts where it is advanced in opposition to those who make human merit the means of restoring relationships with God. A great deal of harm has been done by teaching that God is a wrathful Judge, determined to punish somebody, who takes it out of Jesus rather than us. It cannot be denied that this sort of preaching still exists. It leads to an aversion from God who is felt to be cold and calculating, and to a love for Jesus who is felt to be caring and on our side. Such preaching often includes lawcourt analogies which would be an outrage in any court of law, by which the innocent suffers the punishment of the guilty. We shall return to some of these distortions of the biblical teaching. But it is clear that though necessary, the legal category is too small to embrace the atonement. Its purpose is simply to show us that God was acting with perfect propriety as ruler and judge when he accepted sinners; he himself has dealt with all our outstanding debts at Calvary.

There is an important distinction to bear in mind between crime and sin. We commit crime against society, but we commit sin against a person. That is why people rarely have a deep sense of sin until God becomes real to them. All crimes are sins; but all sins are not crimes. Malice and jealousy, for instance, cannot be touched by law. There are really two different worlds here: crime relates to the impersonal concept of law, where guilt and justice are the relevant considerations and forgiveness is totally inappropriate. What would we think of a judge who forgave a murderer? It is not his prerogative to do so. But there is also another world, the world of personal relationships. Law does not enter here; but sin does. It is the rupture of personal relationships. And it can only be put right by forgiveness. Both worlds are God's worlds. Scripture uses the categories of both. But we should not confuse them.

Forgiveness, then, is all about repairing broken relationships, and if we examine merely human examples of forgiveness, some very interesting considerations emerge.

First, there must be no excuses. The guilty party must admit he is in the wrong. He may be called to make reparations if this is possible: generally it is not.

Second, there can be no condoning. You do not get real forgiveness by saying 'It doesn't matter'. It does matter, and the relationship has been disturbed. Sin, in other words, must be faced.

Third, forgiving involves forgetting. It will not be raked up again later if it has really been forgiven.

What does this mean? It means that *it is only the injured party who is in the position to initiative forgiveness.* The one who has done wrong is not in the position to claim it as a right. It springs from grace, sheer unmerited kindness. Jesus showed this superbly in his story of the two debtors. The master had compassion on the servant with his astronomical debt and freely forgave him (Matt. 12: 27ff). 'I forgave you all that debt!' And that is what God does to us. But see what it cost him. The master suffered the loss of all that money when he forgave the man freely. It is a most costly thing to do. What happens when you forgive anyone? Precisely the same as the master in Jesus' story of the debtor. It means *you pay!*

I remember Bishop Stephen Neill, a Christian deeply versed in other faiths, describing the uniqueness of Christian forgiveness with moving simplicity. He explained how in Hinduism the principle of *karma* prevails everywhere: the Hindu doctrine of retribution. Your actions incur indebtedness in a multitude of ways. These debts have to be worked off in a further reincarnation. If you do well, your next life will be on a higher level. If not, it will be on a lower level. But always *karma* drives you on. There is no possibility of forgiveness. Indeed it would be immoral, for you must pay your debts. The iron hand of *karma* rules all. The ethical structure of the world is parallel to the physical. The law of *karma* is as omnipresent as the law of gravity. And it says to the Hindu 'You sin . . . and you pay.'

What a contrast Christianity presents! Grace instead of retribution. Forgiveness instead of endless working-off of debts. Eternal life instead of countless reincarnations culminating in a sea of non-being. Because of what Christ did on Calvary the message of God to the believer is totally different from the Hindu concept. It says 'You sin . . . and I pay.'

That makes no sense in commerce: it makes excellent sense in personal relationships. It happens every time we forgive.

How do I know that God is like this? Calvary is the answer. It shows what God has been like from the beginning. It is the effective symbol in time of what God eternally is. The cross shows the cost of forgiveness to God. It cost him no less than crucifixion to forgive us and to have us back in his family.

Forgiveness is costly to give. It is humbling to receive. So the wronged party who offers forgiveness often needs to stand alongside the one who has done the wrong, and help him to a fresh start. He will take the one who has offended him as a friend. It is in this context that the word *hetairos* is signficant in the Gospels. It means 'friend' – almost 'old fellow'. Three times Jesus speaks of someone thus. In each case the words come from the injured party to the one who has done the wrong. Once it is said by the owner of the vineyard, reproached by one of the men who had worked for the whole day when he gave a full day's wage to those who had only worked the last hour. 'Friend,' said the owner, 'I am doing you no wrong. Did you not agree with me for a denarius? Do you begrudge my generosity?' (Matt. 20: 13, 15). Once it is said by the king to the man who had barged into the wedding feast in his own clothes and had refused the proffered wedding garment. 'Friend, how did you get in here without a wedding garment?' (Matt. 22: 12). And the man was speechless, because he had rejected free grace, and had regarded his own garments as good enough. And the third occasion is full of pathos. Jesus says to Judas,

Judas who has come to betray him, 'Friend, why are you here?' (Matt. 26: 50). Grace, forgiveness, are making their final bid for the heart of Judas, but in vain.

If God forgives, he must be a suffering God. Christians have often got confused at this point with the impassibility of God. *Paschō*, to suffer, can be used in two senses. One is simply 'to suffer'. That God has always been doing, bound up as he is with suffering humanity. And he reached the nadir of suffering on the cross. The other sense of *paschō* means 'to have something done to you without your consent'. In this sense God is impassible. But suffer he does, and he must. For love makes you vulnerable. And this is what makes the cross of Jesus credible.[1]

To be sure, then, the category of law is not broad enough to embrace the cross of Christ, but it is an essential aspect of that cross. Forgiveness, however, operates in a different world from law, the world of personal relationships.

*For Christ to die in our place would be unjust*
Even if we agree that our sins merit death, both physical and eternal, how can it be urged in the name of justice that Christ suffered in our place? What magistrate on earth would allow such a miscarriage of justice?

There is much force in this objection. It does not apply to the biblical teaching on the subject, but it does apply to much common preaching about the cross, where it is suggested that God the Father (one party) punishes Jesus (another and innocent party) for the sins of a third party (guilty mankind). The teaching of the New Testament is far more profound and not liable to the same critique. There, the doctrine of an objective atonement rests on a full and real incarnation. 'God was in Christ, reconciling the world to himself' (2 Cor. 5: 18), while at the same time 'God made Christ to be sin for us, Christ

---

[1] I should like to acknowledge my indebtedness to Bishop Stephen Neill for his great help and illumination over the nature of forgiveness.

who knew no sin, so that we might become the righteousness of God in him' (5: 21). Here we see as forceful an expression of objective atonement as could be imagined, but note how it is qualified.

In the first place, God is not here, or anywhere else in the New Testament, said to be reconciled to us by the death of Christ. He is the source of the reconciliation. It is indeed something God does, rather than something God has done to him, and to that extent the liberal objection to objective atonement is fully justified. But notice, second, that Christ who does the sinbearing is in solidarity with both parties. In no sense is a holy God punishing an innocent Jesus for guilty men. The word 'punish' is significantly not used of the death of Christ in the New Testament. Thirdly, Jesus is one with God and one with us. It is only 'in him' that we can become the very righteousness of God. So what looks like the most external of understandings of the cross is really far from it. Linked to God Jesus accepted the place of total identification with human sin. But he did so while at the same time being the man Christ Jesus. In a profound sense it was no third party who was suffering on that cross, but the Proper Man, the head of the human race, the one who represented us all. We were involved in what was done: in some mysterious sense we were caught up 'in him'. God the Father, too, was involved in what was done: he was in Christ, reconciling the world to himself. How did this happen? He was able not to count their trespasses against them, simply and solely because he, in Christ, was burdening himself with that appalling weight of human sin.

So a full recognition of the deity as well as the humanity of Jesus prevents us from making the error of supposing that a wrathful God was punishing an innocent Jesus for sinful men. In the whole drama of Calvary we see God himself taking responsibility, in the human flesh of Jesus, for the guilt of a whole world awry.

A clear understanding of this enables us to avoid the most common objection raised by thoughtful people to an objective atonement made vicariously for us on the cross by Christ. They say that it separates the Father from the Son in our redemption. It drives a wedge into the Godhead. Of course, it does nothing of the sort. Jesus made it abundantly plain that his death was his Father's will, as we saw in chapter 3: it had been the heartbeat of God from all eternity. Jesus always did his Father's will. There was no shadow of divergence in their attitude to Calvary. God was in Christ, reconciling the world to himself. To be sure, Jesus shrank from it in the Garden of Gethsemane: did not his Father shrink also? It was only during that time of sinbearing on the cross that the Father's face was hidden from the Son in whom he delighted: even that does not suggest any divergence in attitude between them. It simply follows from the terrible nature of sin: sin does cause separation from the presence of God. How could Jesus possibly enter into our sins and draw their sting without the inevitable entail of sin taking its effect? Truly, he experienced the horrors of Godforsakenness on the cross. But such was the will both of Jesus and his Father, in order that a whole world of sinners could be reconciled. Is there anything unjust in this most perfect meeting place of mercy and judgment? Who but God could have devised a remedy for human sin at once so loving and so utterly just?

*For Christ to die in our place would be incredible*
This objection takes a number of forms. A common one is to ask how the death of Christ 1,900 years ago could avail for all men everywhere down the ages. The answer lies partly in the relativity of time: 'a thousand years with the Lord are as one day, and one day as a thousand years' (Ps. 90: 4; 2 Pet. 3: 8), for the death of Christ was 'foreordained before the foundation of the world' (1 Pet. 1: 20). The Lord who is above and outside time entered time for us. 'In the beginning was the Word, and the Word was with God and the Word was God ... the Word became flesh and dwelt among us' (John 1: 1, 14). Isaiah's instinct had been right when he said of the Suffering Servant: 'The Lord has laid (or, caused to meet) on him the iniquity of us all' (Isa. 53: 6). It was as if Christ died at the mid-point of time,

and his death availed retrospectively as well as prospectively. Abraham and the saints of the Old Testament were justified because of what Christ *would* one day do at Calvary: men in generations since by what he *has* done. God had been forgiving penitent sinners from time immemorial: only the ground of that forgiveness had not been made plain. Since Calvary it has been made abundantly plain.

Another query connected with time has a similar answer. How, it may be asked, could a few hours' suffering of Christ on the cross avail to rescue the whole world from eternal loss? In so far as that question is open for mortal men to discuss, it would seem that the key to it is the person of the sufferer. Christ is *qualitatively* distinct from the whole mass of mankind. There is no question of quantitative equivalence in what Christ suffered and what men alienated from God might suffer. The one who hangs there brings totally different considerations to bear. We should be more distressed by the pain of a child for an hour than by the death of hundreds and thousands of mice, because we know there is something qualitatively different. So it is when the Son of God tastes death for every man.

It has sometimes been a problem to the tidy-minded that they have thought of the death of Christ in quantitative terms, precisely equated with the number of the elect. It would be important, on such a view, to ensure that there be no waste in the saving work of Christ. Thus some of the more stringent of the Calvinist theologians have argued the theory of limited atonement. Christ, on this view, did not die for the world but only for the elect. Thus there is no waste, so to speak, incurred by people refusing to respond to his sacrifice. Such a theory verges on the blasphemous, and it totally contradicts 1 John 2: 2 where the writer assures us that 'he is the expiation for our sins, and not for ours only, but for the sins of the whole world'. There is a glorious prodigality of grace in God. There is no parsimonious precision and precise equating of the work of Christ with those who will in due course respond. Think of such parables as the Great Supper, overflowing with generosity and grace.

Some are not able to respond – small children, those who die young, the infirm in mind. Did Christ not die for them, too? Did he not die for the masses of heathen who have never heard his name? Of course he did, and there may well be in heaven many of all races who knew nothing of Christ but somehow trusted in God to accept them though they knew themselves to be unacceptable. That is how David and Abraham, Isaac and Jacob were accepted. They had no idea how it could be. But they entrusted themselves to God, and he accepted them, knowing the atonement that was to be made. There is generosity enough and to spare in the Father's house. All who call on his name, however ignorantly and tentatively, will not be disappointed. On that matter he has given his solemn pledge (Rom. 10: 11–13).

To some the doctrine of an objective atonement seems incredible because it seems inconceivable that guilt should be transferable. How could my guilt possibly pass to Christ, and his righteousness to me?

It depends on how you construe guilt. If I steal twenty pounds from you I have contracted a liability to the criminal law, and I can be judged for that: I have defrauded you and wronged you; and I have done something evil in the sight of God, something which builds yet higher the wall of alienation between him and me. Clearly the cross of Christ cannot affect my guilt before the law. I may well be prosecuted, and if convicted I shall have to shoulder my punishment. Neither can the cross of Christ affect the fact that I have wronged you. I need to make reparation for that. But there is a third area which can be and gloriously is transformed by the cross of Christ. That is the 'being-in-the-wrong-with-God' which is ultimately the most serious aspect of guilt.

Guilt has little to do with guilt feelings. These, as modern psychiatry has shown, are often prompted by a variety of sources unconnected with the supposed offence. Christianity is not about guilt feelings. But Christianity has a lot to do with objective guilt. It has a message of complete and free acceptance for the man who knows he is most unacceptable.

And that makes a new man of him. It is in this sense that Christ took our guilt. He stood in for us at the point of our total inability to face God. As man, he went to that bitter cross, that place of guilt and shame. As God the sacrifice he made there is eternally valid. As the head of the new humanity he shouldered our responsibility towards God. The weight of it spelt a cross. In that sense he did indeed bear our guilt (though the New Testament writers prefer to speak of him bearing our sins). In the simplest of language, we sinned and he accepted the responsibility.

There are still two objections to this doctrine of an objective salvation achieved for mankind on Calvary. One is that the whole thing is rather like a transaction, external to us. It is finished, it is painted into the past. Nothing could be further from the truth. The date of Calvary may be in the past, but the effects remain. Not only did Christ 'sit down' having 'offered for all time a single sacrifice for sins' (Heb. 10: 12) but he is the living one; he rose from the grave and is alive for ever (7: 25). And he confronts us, challenges us to decision, calls us to discipleship, and to enter by baptism and faith the dying and rising life of which he is the forerunner and supreme example. As we shall see in a later chapter, the heart of discipleship is dying and rising with Christ. The cross and resurrection are far from external to us. They become internalised within our very being once we open our lives up to the Christ who died and rose.

Finally there remains the nagging doubt in many minds whether the offering of Christ in our place could be fair. The answer is an unequivocal No. For the cross of Christ far transcends any conception of justice we could ever entertain. If we are looking for justice we can have it. 'The wages of sin is death'. However, as Romans 6: 23 goes on to say 'but the gracious gift (*charisma*) of God is eternal life through Jesus Christ our Lord.' With undreamed-of generosity God has met us at our point of deepest need. He has acted with perfect justice. The curse of the broken law need never haunt us, for he has taken it upon himself (Gal. 3: 10, 13) and with open arms he welcomes us to his heart of love.

Actually, I do find the cross and resurrection incredible. But incredible because I am astounded that God should bother like that for sinners. It is unbelievably good news, the best mankind has ever heard.

Here was no overlooking of guilt or trifling with forgiveness; no external treatment of sin, but a radical, a drastic, a passionate and absolutely final acceptance of the terrible situation, and an absorption by the very God himself of the fatal disease so as to neutralise it effectively.

So wrote C.F.D. Moule in *The Sacrifice of Christ*, p. 28, admirably summarising what Christ did for us on Calvary. Thank God for it. Thank God too that such is only half the story. Jesus is no dead Saviour, but alive for evermore. 'If while we were enemies we were reconciled to God by the death of his Son, much more, now that we are reconciled, we shall be kept safe by his life' (Rom. 5: 10). We are not dependent in the Christian life on a Christ who lived and died; but on a Christ who lived, died and rose again, so as to share with us the power of his endless life. Thus even forgiveness is not an end in itself. It clears the barriers out of the way so that we may live with him.

# Part B

## The Resurrection

# Chapter
# 7

Empty Cross, Empty Tomb?

Jesus of Nazareth was executed at Passovertime in the year 30, 31 or 33 – the experts continue to debate the matter. It was while Pontius Pilate was prefect (his proper title, as an inscription found at Caesarea makes clear) of Judea. Shortly after his death a new and very dynamic religious movement arose, maintaining that death had been unable to silence Jesus: he was alive, and he was Lord.

This seemed so improbable as to be laughable. But it was the sole belief which differentiated the new movement from Judaism. They were ordinary Jews in every other respect except this: they believed that God's Messiah had actually come, been unrecognised by the people, been done to death on the cross, and had been gloriously raised by God to the power of an endless life. Such was the conviction. And it spread so fast that within thirty years large numbers of the Jewish priesthood had become believers; Rome had been heavily affected, so had Alexandria, Ephesus, Antioch and the other main cities of the Empire. More, it had spread into the country parts, in North Africa, inland Turkey and to the Russian border. Clearly something had happened – but what?

Christianity is not, as Bertrand Russell once claimed, based on the belief that fairy tales are pleasant. Its central claim concerns the supposed resurrection of someone who was a contemporary of those who first proclaimed it; indeed a close personal friend. To be sure, there had been myths in Greek poetry of Orpheus and others coming back from the underworld, but the Christian claim is quite different. It maintains that in the case of one whose life and teaching, whose miracles and impact were unparalleled, even death proved unable to hold him. Such a claim has never been made with any shred of credibility for any other person on this earth. If true it is unique, and any description of it in the sources must necessarily hover on the borderlands of experience and even of language. What evidence is there upon which to assess such a claim?

*The evidence of the cross*
First, there is the cross itself. It might be said, and has been said, that since Jesus apparently expired in such a short time, about six hours, he might not have been really dead, and could subsequently have emerged from the tomb. This is substantially the position maintained in H. Schonfield's *The Passover Plot*, but quite apart from its psychological improbabilities such a view is hard put to explain away the plain facts of the case. They were very plain, and very public. A squad of four executioners put him to death in full view of a large crowd. They were experienced at this grisly task, since crucifixions were not uncommon in Palestine. They knew a dead man when they saw one. They could see that the other two men were not yet dead: that is why they broke their legs so that they could gain no relief from the 'saddle' on the cross, and would rapidly expire, Jesus they saw was already dead. Their commanding officer had heard Jesus' death cry, and certified the death to Pilate (Mark 15: 39, 44). But just to make doubly sure, the soldiers pierced his heart through with a spear. So we are told on the authority of one who claims to have been an eyewitness, and this testimony is included in St. John's Gospel (19: 34, 35). It is clear that the eyewitness attached great importance to what he saw: it is no less clear that he did not understand it. Hardly surprising. Nobody did until the rise of modern medicine. The witness maintains that when the side of Jesus was pierced, out came 'blood and water'. Had Jesus been

alive, strong spurts of bright arterial blood would have emerged. Instead, the observer saw semi-solid clots seeping out, distinct and separate from the accompanying watery serum. This is evidence of massive clotting of blood in the main arteries, and is exceptionally strong medical proof of death. Dr. E. Symes Thompson researched this matter with care many years ago in his book *On the Physical Cause of the Death of Christ*. His conviction is that the death of Jesus was brought about by rupture of the heart through excessive agony of mind, and he is able to quote a number of other cases where this has been established as the cause of death. Within a short time of death the blood of Jesus, released into the pericardium, would have coagulated, and when the spear wound took place, would have come out as separated clot and serum. The 'blood and water' is proof positive that Jesus was dead.

In any case, quite apart from this remarkable observation of an eyewitness, crucifixion was not something from which escape was common. I know of only one instance in ancient literature which is remotely comparable. Josephus (*Vita*, 75) tells of a time when he saw a number of captives being crucified; and, noticing three of his friends among them, he asked Titus, the Roman commander, for a reprieve. This was granted, and the men were taken down at once. It seems that they had only just been crucified, but despite being given every care by the most expert physicians available, two of the three died. It is incredible that Jesus, who had not eaten or slept before his execution, who was weakened by loss of blood through the most brutal flogging, who was pierced in both hands and feet, could have survived unaided had he been alive when taken down from the cross. It is even more incredible that he should have been able to emerge from the tomb, and persuade his followers that he was conqueror of death. There can be no doubt that Jesus was dead. That must have been evident not only to the executioners but to the hostile crowd round the cross and the friends who hastily embalmed his body. Moreover, had the centurion, had the governor made a mistake over the execution of a messianic pretender, their jobs and probably their lives would have been on the line. Jesus was dead. If the resurrection took place, it reversed the process of nothing less than death.

## The evidence of the church

The second relevant evidence concerns the Christian Church. It is indisputable that shortly after the execution of Jesus an entirely new religious movement of great vitality sprang into being. It was normal when charismatic leaders arose in the troubled province of Judaea for the followers to return, disillusioned, to their homes once the leader had been disposed of. Josephus records a number of such events: the Acts of the Apostles alludes to one of them, the abortive rising of Theudas (Acts 5: 36, cf. Josephus *Ant.*, 20.97-9). But in this case the disciples did not melt away. They grew and spread rapidly over the known world. Tacitus records with distaste, that 'a most mischievous superstition, thus checked for the moment (i.e. by the crucifixion of Jesus) *again broke out*' (*Annals*, 15.44). Their own account of their origins was plain. They were brought into being as the community of the resurrection. Nobody could deny that such was their claim.

Associated with the rise of the church are several subordinate but significant things. The Christians had two sacraments. One was baptism, the sacrament of Christian initiation. The other was the eucharist, the sacrament of Christian growth. Both were rooted in the resurrection. Baptism was seen as a personal re-enactment and appropriation of the death and resurrection of Jesus: as the candidate goes down into the water he dies to the old self-centred life and rises to new life in and with Christ (Romans 6: 3f). And the Holy Communion was no memorial feast in honour of a dead founder. They broke bread with *agalliasis*, exultation (Acts 2: 46) because they believed the risen Lord was in their midst as they took the tokens of his death for them. Both sacraments would have been a complete travesty had the earliest Christians not believed that Jesus rose from the dead.

In addition to the sacraments, there was the preaching of the good news of salvation. The core of this was that the Messiah Jesus had risen from the shameful death inflicted upon him, and was even now Lord of the universe, in power at the right hand of God his Father. Moreover, modern critical study of the New Testament has made it abundantly plain that the new literary genre which the Christians brought into being, the Gospel, is permeated through and through by the resurrection. The whole thing is written from the perspective of the risen and living Lord. It is neither biography nor history, *tout simple*. It is governed by the conviction that the Jesus who walked the streets of Judaea and Galilee is alive and reigning, and present with believers.

There is another remarkable aspect of the church's life, which would be hard indeed to explain if the resurrection did not loom at the very forefront of their thinking. They succeeded in changing the day of rest from its time-honoured Saturday to Sunday. It is impossible to exaggerate the importance of the sabbath in Judaism. It was inaugurated by express divine command to celebrate God's rest after creation. But these men managed to change it to Sunday, because Sunday was the day when Jesus rose from the dead, and they reckoned that the new creation which that signified was even more important than the creation remembered by the sabbath. It is not very easy to change the day of rest, especially among Jews! Something very significant must have happened. The earliest church was sure that something very significant had happened: something unprecedented.

*The evidence of the appearances of Jesus*
The third strand of evidence which needs to be weighed is the resurrection appearances. D. E. Nineham, although himself a very radical critic of the New Testament, has drawn attention to the heavy stress on eyewitness when the resurrection appearances are mentioned (*Journal of Theological Studies*, 1960, p. 253). Paul, in writing to the Corinthians in c. A.D. 53 is remind-

ing them of the cardinal nature of the resurrection for the truth of the whole Christian faith. He names the apostles, and in particular their acknowledged leader, Peter, and the head of the Jerusalem Church, James. He adds a third key name, his own, the apostle to the Gentiles. He caps it by saying that 500 brethren at once saw the risen Christ, 'most of whom are still alive, though some have fallen asleep' (1 Cor. 15:6). The implication is plain: 'If you aren't convinced, go and talk to them.' The appearances are attested by a formidable array of eyewitnesses.

This passage of Paul's in 1 Corinthians 15 is of inordinate importance. Such a statement in a genuine letter written by someone in close touch with the other eyewitnesses less than twenty-five years after an event is as strong evidence as one could hope to get for something that happened nearly 2,000 years ago. Very few ancient events are supported by such early and good evidence. But we can go a good deal further.

In the first place this passage is written by a convinced enemy of the Christian heresy, as he thought it, who was himself brought round full circle by the resurrection appearance of Jesus to him. He then became Christianity's greatest protagonist.

Second, the message of the resurrection which he is writing about is no optional extra to the Christian case. It is 'of the first importance' (15: 3). On its truth or falsity the whole Christian case rests – or so Paul believes (15: 14ff).

Third, in talking about the resurrection message Paul uses two words which have a long history. They are 'I delivered ... I received'. Those Greek words, and their Hebrew originals, were used of receiving and passing on *authorised tradition*. Paul is claiming that what he is telling the Corinthians had become traditional by the time he received it after his conversion. That is to say, it had originated and had become almost sacrosanct among Christians within five years or less of the event itself, because it would be hard to date Paul's conversion later than A.D. 35. Moreover, he seems to be quoting some list, probably written, because he uses a fourfold *hoti* ('that'). The traditional material of which he speaks maintained *that* Christ died for our sins according to the scriptures; *that* he was buried; *that* he was raised again the third day according to the scriptures; *that* he appeared to various close friends and to 500 believers. Those *hoti*s are almost quotation marks. They delve back into that traditional material of which Paul reminds his Corinthian readers and which is attested by three of the most famous names in early Christianity, each of them won to faith because of the resurrection of Jesus.

It is impossible to exaggerate the importance of 1 Corinthians 15. This scrap of half a dozen verses embodies the oldest document in the Christian church. It derives from the key people concerned, and within a very few years of the event. It is not surprising that it became 'tradition' very early on in the Church.

The main thrust of this remarkable passage is the sequence of appearances by the risen Jesus which convinced his followers that he was alive. The Gospels record many more such appearances: the two on the way to Emmaus, the women at the tomb, Mary Magdalene, the disciples on the Lake, Thomas, and so forth. The appearances of Jesus are as well authenticated as anything in antiquity. The precise status of these appearances we shall consider in the next chapter. But there can be no rational doubt that they occurred, and that the main reason why Christians became sure of the resurrection in the earliest days was just this. They could say with assurance, 'We have seen the Lord'. They *knew* it was he.

### The evidence of the tomb

The fourth strand of evidence is the empty tomb. Though it will not bear the apologetic weight sometimes placed upon it – there could be many reasons why the tomb was empty – it will not do to dismiss it out of hand as a late fabrication with anti-docetic tendencies, as is often done. That is to play fast and loose with the evidence. For the empty tomb is a powerful supporting factor in the case for the resurrection. Indeed, it is impossible to imagine how the preaching of the resurrection could ever have got off the ground if the body of Jesus had remained in the tomb of Joseph of Arimathea. As C.H. Dodd put it 'When they said "He rose from the dead", they took it for granted that his body was no longer in the tomb; if the tomb had been visited it would have been found empty. The Gospels supplement this by saying, "it *was* visited and it *was* empty"' (*The Founder of Christianity*, p. 166).

Matthew, Mark, Luke and John all are totally explicit on the point, and John adds some remarkable eyewitness material about the graveclothes. In the most graphic of narrations he tells how Peter and 'another disciple' (probably John himself) ran to the tomb when the first tidings of its emptiness were brought them by the women who had gone to complete the embalming of their friend on the first Easter morning. 'Peter went into the tomb; he saw the linen cloths lying, and the napkin, which had been on his head, not lying with the linen cloths but rolled up in a place by itself . . . and he (i.e. the other disciple) saw and believed' (John 20: 6-8). Why should this have made such an impression upon the two disciples? Because the wrappings seemed to them like a chrysalis case when the pupa has emerged. The graveclothes had encircled Jesus, and were interlaced with a great weight of embalming spices. The head covering was a small distance away, retaining its original shape surrounding the head of Jesus. *But his body was simply gone!* No wonder they were convinced and awed. No grave-robber would have been able to enact so remarkable a thing. Nor would it have entered his head. He would simply have taken the body, graveclothes and all. Had Jesus merely been resuscitated, he would presumably either have used the clothes or laid them aside. But as it was, all the signs pointed to Jesus' having risen to a new order of life, a new sphere of existence. He left the graveclothes behind as the butterfly emerging to a new dimension of life leaves the cocoon behind it. That sight convinced Peter and John.

*Naturalistic explanations*
Naturally nobody would resort to the hypothesis of a divine

raising of Jesus if a naturalistic explanation of the empty tomb could be found to hold water. But none has been found. It would be ludicrous to suppose that the Jews moved the body of Jesus. They had at last got him where they had long wanted him, dead and buried. They would never have given colour to the resurrection preaching which soon began to shake Jerusalem by so crass a folly as removing the body. And if, by some egregious blunder, they had done just that, they would easily have been able to produce the mouldering corpse as soon as the Christians began to claim that he was alive. And that happened very soon. *The third day* is strongly embedded in the earliest references to the resurrection. That is embarrassingly early. It is an indication of how threadbare rationalistic arguments were becoming by the end of the second century that such unlikely people as the Jewish gardener were being suggested as agents of grave-robbery. 'This is he... whom the gardener removed', wrote Tertullian with biting irony, 'lest his lettuces should be injured by the crowds of visitors' (*de Spectaculis* 30).

It has been suggested, of course, that the disciples of Jesus removed his body and then claimed that he had risen from the dead. That is what Matthew says the Jews feared would happen (Matt. 27: 63-6) and what the late and malicious treatise *Toledoth Yeshu* says did happen. It is at first sight a plausible explanation, but it will not survive careful scrutiny. There are two good reasons why it is false. The disciples could not have done it if they had wanted to, and they would not have done it if they had been able.

The disciples could not have removed the body because there was a guard on the tomb. It is fashionable to disregard the story of the guard, because it is only recorded in St. Matthew's Gospel, and looks like a bit of Christian propaganda. However it is attested by two of the apocryphal Gospels of the second century, *The Gospel of the Hebrews* and *The Gospel of Peter*. The former, probably the oldest of the apocryphal gospels, says of Pilate 'he delivered unto them armed men, that they might sit over against the cave and keep it day and night'. *The*

*Gospel of Peter* was certainly circulating by A.D. 150 and is both docetic and anti-Semitic. But it records that Pilate set Petronius, a centurion, with soldiers to watch over the tomb of Jesus. Early on the sabbath, crowds from Jerusalem come to see the sealed tomb. Early Sunday morning two angels approach the tomb. The soldiers rouse Petronius. They see three beings emerge, two supporting a third, and a cross following them. The guard reports this to Pilate, who tells them to keep silence.

The account is manifestly legendary: in the authentic Gospels nobody ever claims to have been present at the resurrection, and Jesus never appears to other than believers. But the story of the guard has a firm place in the tradition; it is found also in Justin and Tertullian in the second century. Furthermore it is just the sort of thing one might expect, given that mixture of law and intrigue which went to make up the administration of Judaea at that time. The body of a condemned criminal remained Roman property. That is why Joseph had to go and ask no less a personage than Pilate himself for it if he wanted to give a burial. Normally such bodies were thrown into a common grave, but recently the discovery of the bones of a young man, crucified, in an ossuary in a rock-cut tomb to the north of Jerusalem, dating from about A.D. 50, has shown that the Romans could be compassionate in allowing the bodies of crucified people to be given a decent burial.

As soon as Pilate made this concession to Joseph, the whole situation changed. The body was now back in Jewish custody. Responsibility for any riots that might ensue would fall on Jewish shoulders. The ball was now uncomfortably back in their court. That is what made the Jewish leaders pluck up courage to beard the governor once again, although they knew he was in a black mood, in order to try and persuade *him* to place a guard. Pilate refused to be drawn. That, if not quite certain, is highly probable. Matthew 27: 65, *echete koustōdian* could just be translated as an imperative, 'Right, have your guard.' But much more naturally the words would be construed as indicative: 'You already have a guard.' That interpretation is confirmed by the fact that the guard subsequently reported not to the Roman but to the Jewish authorities (28: 11) – quite apart from the fact that for a Roman soldier to sleep on duty was a capital offence, so it is unthinkable that he could confess to it. The apocryphal gospels are wrong, then, in saying that it was the Romans who set the guard. It consisted of the Jewish temple soldiery. This guard was set over the tomb by Jewish authorities who recalled the allusions made to a possible resurrection even as recently as at the trial (Mark 14: 56, 57). But neither the guard nor the stone succeeded in preventing the tomb from being empty on the third day. So afterwards the priests had to produce the lame story of soldiers sleeping on duty while the disciples made off with the corpse. Embarrassing in the extreme, but better than admitting the reality of the resurrection.

The presence of the guard would have prevented anybody from rifling the grave. They had been mounted for that express purpose, and the first thing they would do on taking up their position would be to inspect the tomb and ensure that all was in order. Probably in the early hours of Sunday morning some disturbance in the tomb associated with the resurrection caused them to roll aside the stone and investigate. They found the grave empty, and at once went to report to the chief priest.

But could this whole story of the guard not be a piece of Christian apologetic? Doubtless it served apologetic purposes in arguing with Jews, but it could not have arisen in that way. Two words make that certain. No Christian could have made up those two words *hēmōn koimēmenōn* ('while we slept') and put them in the mouth of the guards (28: 13). The story would only have been any use for Christian propaganda if the guards *had stayed awake!*

The only possible reason, therefore, the story of the guard circulated is that it was true. There had been a guard. It had not prevented the resurrection. And it is eminently credible that the Jewish authorities bribed the soldiers to say that the disciples came and stole the body while they slept. The authorities were simply making the best of a bad situation. All in all, the guard on the tomb, together with the millstone on the door make it very difficult to suppose that the friends of Jesus could possibly have removed the corpse.

In any case, is it psychologically credible? The disciples were shattered by the events of the passion. They were utterly disheartened. So far as we can tell, thoughts of resurrection never entered their heads. They had backed a failure, and all they wanted to do was to go away and hide and forget all about the fiasco. Moreover, we must take into account the astonishing sequel. These disciples, once so dispirited, became new men. Their lives and outlook were transformed, and the man who had quailed before a servant's taunts at the trial of Jesus now dared to take on the whole sanhedrin with his gospel of the resurrection (Acts 4: 8-12). You could command these Christians to be silent, but it did no good. You could imprison them, but their followers were just as confident and just as fearless. Goguel disposed of the theory of imposture on the part of the disciples with great brevity. 'On peut se laisser persécuter pour une illusion' he wrote, 'mais non pour une fraude.' And Joseph Klausner, himself a Jew, will hear nothing of it. 'That is impossible,' he wrote. '*Deliberate imposture* is not the substance out of which the religion of millions of mankind is created ... The nineteen hundred years' faith of millions is not founded on deception' (*Jesus of Nazareth*, pp. 357, 359).

If neither the friends nor the enemies of Jesus removed his body, one possibility remains. God raised him up. Take together the empty tomb, the resurrection appearances, the launching of the church, the meaning of its sacraments, the conversions of those most opposed to the new faith, the passionate centrality of the resurrection in the church's preaching and writings, the changed day of rest, and it is very difficult to resist the conclusion to which the New Testament writers came. 'If Christ has not been raised your faith is futile ... But in fact Christ has been raised from the dead.' Such was the conclusion of a distinguished Jewish rabbi nineteen hundred years ago. Pinchas Lapide, an orthodox Jewish rabbi of our own day, has just published a book, *The Resurrection of Jesus.* Its conclusion? 'I accept the resurrection of Jesus not as an invention of the community of disciples, but as a historical event.' No other conclusion is warranted by the evidence.

# Chapter
# 8

Objections Considered

The claim that Jesus arose from the dead is so shatteringly
unique that it has understandably aroused a host of objections.
So it ought. Credulity is not a Christian virtue, and if the case
for the resurrection is not good enough it ought to be ruthlessly
and courageously scrapped. Let us therefore in this chapter
examine and assess some of the difficulties that have been felt
about the full-blooded Christian claim that Jesus left the tomb
on the first Easter day and is still alive.

*'The resurrection is impossible'*
The most basic objection of all is very simply expressed. Dead
men don't rise, so it is inconceivable that Jesus rose. This
objection is often heard in circles influenced by the natural
sciences: it is scientifically impossible for the effects of death to
be reversed. Put like this, the claim looks rather unscientific.
Such dogmatism is not the normal way in which reputable
scientists examine a problem. True, there is an impatience with
miracle in many scientific circles, but it is matched by an
increasing recognition of the limitations of our knowledge and
of the mystery of the universe. Many things which would
unhesitatingly have been declared impossible by scientists a
century ago are a normal part of our existence: television,
space travel, antibiotics.

If, then, it is asserted on scientific grounds that the
resurrection *did* not happen because it *could* not happen, there
are two main points to make. The first concerns scientific

method. This is unashamedly inductive. That is to say, it begins with phenomena and then seeks to arrive at the generalisations or natural laws which account for them. It does not begin by ruling out of court facts which are inconvenient. Instead, it patiently examines them. And many of the advances in scientific knowledge have taken place when scientists have wrestled with the one inconvenient fact which did not fit in with the prevailing theory of the day. In principle there is no scientific reason why Jesus could not have risen from the tomb.

But secondly, we are not claiming that there is a certain class of people who are in the habit of emerging from their graves. The first-century writers were not claiming that either. What Christians do maintain is that Jesus was no ordinary man. They believe that there are good reasons for supposing he shared God's nature as well as ours. How, then, can we be so certain that he could not have overcome death, just because nobody else has been observed to rise from the dead? He lived an unsullied life, one that not even his detractors could credibly slander, one that even his judge could not fault. How can we be certain that a perfect life which had given no foothold to sin might not also master death, which scripture asserts is in some mysterious way connected with sin? We have no other example of the 'sinless' category to compare Jesus with. There are no parallels by which to measure the possibility of his unique rising from death. It ill befits the competent scientist or the open minded enquirer to say 'It could not have happened'. The proper course is to apply stringent criteria in examining whether in fact it does seem to have taken place. That is good scientific procedure. Prejudice is not appropriate in serious investigation of truth.

### 'The resurrection is not a historical event'
The very uniqueness of Christian claims about the resurrection have led to another form of dogmatic scepticism. We can know nothing about what, if anything, happened at Easter. Thus Bornkamm, in his influential book *Jesus of Nazareth* (p. 180) claims that 'the last historical fact (available to scholars) is the

Easter faith of the disciples'. The resurrection, whatever it may have been, was not an event accessible to the historian. It was trans-historical. Many sophisticated people think like this. The most celebrated was Rudolf Bultmann who believed that the cross and resurrection are so identified in the apostolic preaching as 'saving events' that it is impossible to think of them apart. They 'bring judgment on the world and open up for men the possibility of authentic life' (*Kerygma and Myth*, p. 39). 'The resurrection narratives', he maintains, 'and every other mention of the resurrection is nothing more than an attempt to convey the meaning of the cross.' Again 'the resurrection is not itself an event in past history. All that historical criticism can establish is the fact that the first disciples came to believe in the resurrection'. In other words, Bultmann believed that it is improper to seek to examine the Easter event. We are not able to pierce back behind the Easter faith. Bultmann even argues that 'the historical problem is not of interest to Christian belief in the resurrection'. What matters is 'the historical event of the rise of the Easter faith' (*loc. cit.*). Bultmann rightly holds that the death and resurrection of Jesus belong together in Christian proclamation. He rightly sees that the empty tomb is totally unimportant compared with the presence of Christ in the kerygma and in the believer. So he abandons faith in the physical resurrection of Jesus, locates his Christian confidence in the kerygma of the early Church, and construes the Easter faith as meaning that the cross, which he regards as the end of the Jesus story, has saving significance.

Bultmann speaks out of a particular historical situation. He is heir to the radical scepticism of Wrede. He is a disciple of the existentialist Heidegger. Like Lessing he is unwilling to allow faith to be propped up by history lest it cease to be authentic faith. Having said that, he is in a vulnerable position on many counts, and one of his most stringent critics has been Karl Barth, who rightly insisted on the powerful evidence for the objectivity of the resurrection. There are three important questions that clamour to be asked of Bultmann's position, and others like it which affect disdain for history.

First, granted the importance of the Easter faith, what Easter *fact* gave rise to it? Something assuredly did, and it cannot be irrelevant to the question of whether or not that faith is valid.

Second, if Jesus did not rise from the dead, what sort of sense does it make to profess faith in him as the living Lord, to be met in the kerygma? Bultmann, in some ways heir to Luther, believed that the kerygma should not be argued with: it should evoke our faith in response to the preaching of the word. True enough, provided the message of that word is true! But only if so.

Third, if history is inimical to Christianity, then Christianity is false, and it is much better and more honest to say so. A number of Bultmann's close disciples have in fact taken that step. The fact of the matter is that there is very strong, very varied and very widespread evidence for the historicity of the Easter event, and no attempt to dissolve it into mythology can be said to have succeeded. Christianity is not a mystery religion which succeeded. It is not a form of acquiring authentic existence. It concerns the God who raised Jesus from the dead. If the evidence can be shown to discredit that position we should give up the Christian faith. We should not seek to make Christianity the handmaid of existentialism or whatever the contemporary intellectual fashion happens to be.

### 'St. Paul knew nothing of the empty tomb'

Those who find the resurrection of Jesus incredible stumble most at the concept of an empty tomb. Often they are happy with some idea of spiritual survival, but maintain that the tomb of Jesus of Nazareth remains full: his bones are mouldering somewhere in Jerusalem. In support of this position they commonly adduce the oldest mention of the resurrection in the New Testament, the passage in 1 Corinthians 15 to which we have already given some attention. They argue that Paul did not know of the empty tomb, or he would have mentioned it here. The Gospel accounts of the empty tomb are likely, therefore, to be later and anti-docetic pieces of embroidery.

I find it hard to regard this argument as other than special pleading. A close examination of the text of 1 Corinthians 15 makes it almost impossible to credit that St. Paul was not aware of, and did not believe in the empty tomb.

In the first place, Paul normally says very little about the ministry and teaching of Jesus. In this passage in 1 Corinthians 15 he says a good deal: Jesus was crucified, Jesus was buried, Jesus was raised, and Jesus was seen by a large number of people. Paul is certainly much more interested in the Christ of faith than the Jesus of history. That is obvious. But in this passage he is careful to link the two together. The contemporary Christ springs from the historical Jesus through his emergence from the tomb in which he was laid.

Second, he quotes as of prime importance the fact that Jesus was raised *on the third day*. What does this tradition imply? It must mean here, as in Acts (e.g. 10: 40) that on the third day the tomb of Jesus was found to be empty, and Jesus was encountered, alive. The mention of that third day is decisive. It shows Paul knew about the empty tomb.

Third, when Jews spoke about the resurrection, they meant only one thing. They did not mean the survival of the soul, for the Hebrews regarded human personality as a unity. They meant bodily resurrection, the reintegration of the whole person, when they spoke of resurrection. They would not know what to make of the 'spiritual' survival which is what some modern writers wish to attribute to Paul's understanding of Christ's resurrection. To a Jew, if Jesus' bones were still in a Palestinian tomb, there could be no argument about it. He was not, in that case, risen. Throughout 1 Corinthians 15, Paul asserts the reality of the resurrection in the most robust terms. There would have been nothing exciting or new about the view of mere spiritual survival: such a view was common in Greek culture, and it did nothing to cause a stir. Paul was a Jew, and could not exclude the physical from his understanding of the resurrection. You have to search the rabbinic writings for a long time before finding any mention of any purely spiritual resurrection – and on the rare occasion that you do it is late and heavily influenced by Hellenistic thought.[1] But here we are talking about a movement which arose in the heart of conservative Judaism, in Jerusalem itself. The earliest believers were all Jews. We are told that 'a great number of priests became obedient to the faith' (Acts 6: 7). It is simply naive to suppose that a 'spiritual' understanding of the resurrection will cover the facts and account for the rise of Christianity. When Paul said 'risen' he meant that the tomb was empty. To speak of Jesus as having died, been buried and then raised cannot do other than imply that the tomb was empty. Paul nowhere says that Jesus survived death. He was always raised by the action of God – *ēgerthē* or *egēgertai*.

The fourth piece of evidence that Paul took the empty tomb for granted and simply assumed it without argument, is this. He goes to some lengths in explaining, during the second part of this long chapter, that our destiny is to be made like Christ. We shall have a resurrection body like his. 'Just as we have borne the image of the man of dust, we must also bear the image of the man of heaven ... this perishable nature must put on the imperishable, and this mortal nature must put on immortality' (1 Cor. 15: 49, 53). Just as the physical body of Jesus was transformed at the resurrection, so will it be with the Christian.

Curiously enough, it is with this point that Dr. Lampe, in *The Resurrection*, finds greatest difficulty. He believes the resurrection of Jesus is the pledge of our own. He observes that we do not rise physically after death and concludes that therefore Jesus did not rise physically either. But that is to mistake the whole force of what Paul is saying. The apostle does not for one moment imagine that when Christians die they immediately rise from the tomb like their master. He sees Jesus as the firstfruits in time of the eschatological hope for redeemed mankind (v. 20). That final destiny of believers is

---

[1] See further the discussion of the resurrection body in chapter 15.

always reserved in the teaching of the New Testament for 'the last day'. The staggering thing about the resurrection of Jesus is that in his case, and his alone, the destiny of all the people of God at the last day has been anticipated. No Jew would have been surprised at the message of resurrection at the last day (see John 11: 24). What amazed him was the message of *resurrection now*, in the person of Jesus. So although Paul does not expect Christians to rise as Jesus did immediately, he does at the end, when the stuff of this world is taken up and transformed, as it was with the body of Jesus. Gerald O'Collins rightly says in *The Easter Jesus* (p. 43f),

> What Paul says about the risen body [1 Cor. 15: 35ff] is far from contradicting the tradition of the empty grave. His account of the risen body would be ruled out if Jesus' corpse had still been in the grave. He maintains a reversal of death and entombment, a *transformation* of our mortal bodies, not the (creation and) substitution of brand-new risen bodies. For Paul to assert that God had raised Jesus from the dead necessarily implies a passage from the tomb – however difficult it may be to imagine such.

Finally on this point, it is important to remember that Paul is not informing the Corinthians of something they did not know, nor is he trying to counteract scepticism about life after death: nearly all Greeks believed in that. Nor is he trying to persuade them of the truth of Jesus' resurrection. If he had been, his treatment would have been very different. He is simply reminding them in headline fashion of what they did already believe and what he had preached more fully to them when he evangelised Corinth. Luke gives us a good example of the place of the empty tomb in Paul's evangelistic preaching by his report in Acts 13: 29f. 'They took him down from the tree and laid him in a tomb. But God raised him from the dead, and for many days he appeared to those who came up with him from Galilee to Jerusalem.' Paul certainly believed in the empty tomb. And when writing 1 Corinthians 15 one of his main aims was to show the necessity of the bodily resurrection of Jesus for the whole Christian gospel. Not survival of the soul as an inherent quality of man: but resurrection of the body as a sheer gift of God. And it was anticipated and pledged by the resurrection of Jesus Christ from the tomb.

### 'There is no external attestation'

Well, there is some. We have the *Annals* of Tacitus (15.44) describing the Great Fire in Rome in A.D. 64 for which Christians were made scapegoats by the Emperor Nero. He writes:

> The name Christian comes to them from Christ, who was executed in the reign of Tiberius by the procurator Pontius Pilate; and the pernicious superstition, suppressed for a while, broke out afresh and spread, not only through Judaea, the source of the malady, but even throughout Rome itself, where everything vile is fêted.

Pliny, one of the other main classical sources for the end of the first and beginning of the second century A.D., was governor of Bithynia in Turkey. He wrote, about A.D. 112, to ask the Emperor Trajan what he should do about the rapid spread of the Christians in his area. Their monotheism was threatening the sale of pagan sacrificial animals, the survival of pagan temples and the prestige of the Emperor. Pliny says the Christians lived exemplary lives, but would not worship the gods, and met on a fixed day (i.e. Sunday, the day of resurrection) and sang before dawn in alternate verses a hymn to Christ as God (*Epistles* 10.96).

But the most interesting external testimony comes from Josephus, the Jewish general turned historian, who wrote shortly before the turn of the century. His work contains information about many of the people we meet in the New Testament, but there is a particularly remarkable passage concerning Jesus and his reputed resurrection, which is worth quoting in full:

And there arose about this time Jesus, a wise man, if indeed we should call him a man; for he was a doer of marvellous deeds, a teacher of men who receive the truth with pleasure. He won over many Jews, and also many Greeks. This man was the Messiah. And when Pilate had condemned him to the cross at the instigation of our own leaders, those who had loved him did not at once fall away. For he appeared to them the third day alive again, as the holy prophets had predicted, and they said many other wonderful things about him. And the race of Christians, so called after him, has not yet died out (*Antiquities*, 18.3.3).

Josephus was far from being a Christian. He was out to whitewash Judaism before the Roman reading public after the disastrous Jewish War of A.D. 66–70. So this testimony in his writings is very surprising and very suspicious. It has attracted a lot of attention. Many scholars cannot believe it was written by Josephus, because of the sentiments expressed. But the manuscript tradition is uniform. Our manuscripts give this passage as it stands; so they did in Eusebius' day, though there is a fourth-century A.D. Arabic text which gives a shortened version. There may be some Christian interpolation here, though it is hard to imagine Christian interpolators being so restrained. But a totally impartial writer like R. Marcus, editing the Loeb Classical Library edition of Josephus, gives a sober and powerful secular defence of the text as it stands. Some of the passage is doubtless sarcastic. 'If indeed we should call him a man' may be a snide allusion to his divine claims. 'This man was the Messiah' may well refer to the charge affixed in three languages to his cross, while the passage about the resurrection may simply refer to popular hearsay and Christian preaching. It must be remembered that many Jewish leaders and members of the priesthood had become Christians early on (Acts 6: 7) and the facts on which Christianity stood were well known among the Jews. All in all, we have here a remarkable independent testimony to the person, death, resurrection and continuing influence of Jesus among Jewish circles at the end of the first century.

There is even some archaeological evidence which may bear on the resurrection. A remarkable inscription, belonging to the principate of either Tiberius (A.D. 14–38) or Claudius (A.D. 41–54) has turned up. In it the emperor expresses his stern displeasure at reports he has heard of the removal of dead bodies from the grave, and he warns that he will punish, by the unusually harsh expedient of the death penalty, any further tampering with tombs. This inscription was found in Nazareth, the home town of Jesus. Pilate must have reported about Jesus to the emperor in Rome. Tertullian, a Christian lawyer in Rome at the end of the second century even claimed (with what truth we know not) that Pilate's report was still extant in the imperial archives. Presumably Pilate would have taken the line, alluded to in Matthew 28: 11ff, that the disciples came and stole the body of Jesus. This would be quite enough to account for the sharp imperial rejoinder.

*'The resurrection appearances were hallucinations'*
This position has often been urged in a variety of different forms against the resurrection appearances. The assault is shrewd. For the disciples did not rely on an empty tomb: it formed only a very small part of their proclamation. They believed that they had met Jesus after his death. The New Testament accounts of the resurrection appearances 'are trying to justify, even to rationalise, what was for the original witnesses an immediate, intuitive certainty needing no justification. They were *dead sure* they had met with Jesus, and there was no more to be said about it'. So wrote C.H. Dodd (*The Founder of Christianity*, p. 170). If that assurance of the earliest disciples can be reduced to mere subjective visions, hallucinations, wish fulfilment or delusions (all have been suggested) then it is not one doctrine of Christianity which collapses, but the whole structure. For the Christian faith rests fairly and squarely upon the resurrection of Jesus from the dead and his appearance to

his disciples for a limited period of forty days before he ceased to manifest himself in that way but continued to abide with his followers world wide through the Spirit.

Is Renan right when he says, beautifully, 'It was love which resurrected Jesus'? Is Guignebert right (*The Life of Jesus*, p. 503) when he imagines Peter back home in Capernaum lovingly remembering Jesus while hope dawns in his breast which demands that the Crucified appear? As Strauss cryptically assumes, did the disciples pass from the position 'He must live' to the position 'He does live! He has appeared'? (*Life of Jesus*, 2, p. 643ff).

No explanation of the resurrection appearances is without difficulty but any delusion or hallucination theory fails to convince for a number of reasons, and there are few serious theologians – or psychologists – who would commit themselves to it.

Let us glance, first, at the evidence put before us in the New Testament accounts. The Gospels profess to give us only a selection of events in the Jesus story (John 21: 25) but even so there is an impressive list. Jesus appeared to Mary Magdalene (Mark 16: 9; John 20: 1–18), to the two Marys (Matthew 28: 1–10), to Simon Peter (Luke 24: 34; 1 Cor. 15: 5), to the disciples on the road to Emmaus (Luke 24: 13–31), to the eleven and other disciples (Matthew 28: 16–20; Luke 24: 36–49; John 20: 19–23; 21: 1–14; Acts 1: 3–9; 1 Cor. 15: 5–6) to Thomas (John 20: 24–9) to James (1 Cor. 15:7) to Joseph and Matthias (Acts 1: 22ff), to 500 people at once (1 Cor. 15:6) to Peter and John together (John 21: 15–24), to Nathanael and some other disciples on the lake (John 21: 1–14) and to Paul (Acts 9: 4ff; 1 Cor. 9: 1; 15: 8).

Taken together, these appearances to individuals and to groups, to men and to women, in country and in town, in the upper room and by the open lake, on the road and on the hillside, constitute testimony to the resurrection that needs to be taken very seriously indeed. But there are some very strange things in this list.

One is the omission of the appearance of Jesus to the women

in Paul's account in 1 Corinthians 15 which we have already examined. Why is this? Surely because Paul is summarising the Jerusalem gospel tradition which he had passed on at Corinth. And the Jerusalem gospel, proclaimed by Jews, would not have made use of female testimony. One of the oldest commentaries on the Law of Moses rejects testimony from a woman (*Siphre* on Deuteronomy, 190). In the light of this, is it not charmingly in character for Jesus to reveal himself alive first of all to despised *women*? And is it not totally incredible that if anybody had been fabricating the resurrection appearances they would have made the first witnesses of the resurrection women, unqualified to give evidence?

A second peculiarity is the inclusion of Paul in the list. The appearances ceased with the ascension of Jesus. It was as if Jesus spent six weeks showing them that he was indeed risen from the dead, and training them for mission; then he made a decisive break. Thereafter he would be known by his Spirit in the hearts of believers, not by appearances to a limited number of people on spasmodic occasions. But Paul was sure that the Lord had made an exception in his case. He knew a vision when he saw one: he had had considerable experience of visions, as 2 Corinthians 12: 1ff makes plain. He was quite clear that the Damascus Road experience was no vision. It left him physically blinded for a few days. This appearance was extremely important to Luke: he seems to recognise that it was quite exceptional. He tells the story three times in Acts (chs, 9, 22, 26). Luke believed, and Paul believed, that this appearance of the resurrected Christ was in some sense objective and not simply a vision. He placed it as in the same genre as the appearances to the original disciples over the forty days. Despite the ascension, despite the cessation of these appearances, Paul was confident that an exception had been made in his case, summoning the apostle to the Gentiles to the service of Christ. 'Last of all, he appeared to me, as to one untimely born (or "afterbirth", v. 8).' This untidiness, attested also by St. Luke, is perhaps a salutary reminder that it is impossible to tie God down.

A third peculiarity about these appearances concerns the mode of appearance. Throughout, we are given a picture not of wish-fulfilment on the part of the disciples, as if they had been waiting for this; on the contrary, we read of doubt, disbelief, and initial failure to recognise Jesus. Had these appearances been visions, this would not have been the case. They would have envisaged Jesus just as they knew him. As it was, they were dubious if not sceptical (Matt. 28: 17; Luke 24: 11, 16, 31, 37; John 20: 14, 25f; 21: 4) but, once convinced, they were radiantly certain (John 21: 12; 20: 16, 28; Luke 24: 31–5). There is something to be said for Theodor Keim's belief that in the resurrection appearances we have 'a telegram from heaven'. They were divinely sent objective visions. Something rather like this view has been reverently and competently revived by M.C. Perry in *The Easter Enigma*, where he argues that a telepathic hypothesis best fits the material of the Gospels. But not only does this accord ill with the empty tomb, and the conviction of Paul that although he knew visions this was not a vision: it also comes up against the strangely physical streak in the appearances. In 1 Corinthians 15 this is not apparent, because Paul is tabulating the appearances very briefly. But the repeated *ōphthē* ('he was seen' rather than 'he appeared') is emphatic. In Mark's original short ending there are no appearances, so the physical aspect does not arise. But in Matthew 28: 9 we read that 'they took hold of his feet and worshipped him': subsequently he came and met them on a mountain in Galilee. All very physical. In Luke the physical side is even stronger: Jesus walks, talks and eats with the two disciples on the Emmaus road, and then we find him eating with the whole group of his followers. ' "Why are you troubled, and why do questionings arise in your hearts? See my hands and my feet, that it is I myself. Handle me and see; for a spirit has not flesh and bones as you see that I have." They gave him a piece of boiled fish, and he took it and ate before them' (Luke 24: 13–35, 38–43). In St. John, Mary tries to hold on to his feet, Thomas is presented with his wounded hands, feet and side, and the disciples have breakfast with him by the lake (Chs. 20, 21).

It is perfectly possible to discount all this testimony if you try hard enough and are sufficiently ruthless. Many scholars maintain that there is an increasing objectifying of the body of Jesus the later the tradition is, doubtless in an anti-docetic direction. But that is hardly an honest way to treat three quite independent accounts. It is possible to disprove anything if you destroy enough of the evidence! And the evidence as it stands suggests that the disciples were at their wits' end to know how to describe the indescribable. They had no means of communicating what relationship with a resurrected (as opposed to a resuscitated) body meant. It was beyond the scope of language, and it is not surprising that now they speak as if Jesus were pure spirit, and now as if he had a physical presence. They were simply shattered, and their accounts were as impressionistic as they could make them. We should not look for precision in all the details. But we have a right to look for an honest attempt on the one hand to show that the risen Jesus was no resuscitated corpse: he was risen to a new order of life. And on the other hand he was no vision or ghost: he was a resurrected 'body' or entity, and was capable both of sharing our human conditions by eating and walking; and of transcending them, by passing through closed doors and vanishing.

We could only fault the earliest witnesses if we were experts in resurrection bodies. Instead, we might be wise with St. Paul to wait for the day when 'this perishable frame shall put on the imperishable, when this mortal nature shall put on immortality, when death is swallowed up in victory'. It is sensible to remember that 'all flesh is not the same flesh... There are celestial bodies and there are terrestrial bodies... So it is with the resurrection of the dead' (1 Cor. 15: 53ff, 39ff). Indeed, Paul said it all with his analogy of the corn of wheat, perhaps derived from the teaching of Jesus on the subject (1 Cor. 15: 37, John 12: 24). The complete ear springs from the 'death' of the single grain in the ground. It has a manifest similarity, yet an equally manifest difference. The ear is far more beautiful and glorious than the single grain: its properties are marvellously multiplied. Yet throughout the whole process there is an identity of life, though in the ear God has given the grain a 'far more glorious body'. So it seems to have been with the resurrected body of Jesus, the firstfruits of the ultimate crop.

In the light of these considerations, let us return to the hypothesis that the appearances were, after all, hallucinations, subjective visions, or the like, and see if it bears critical examination.

Normally, only certain types of people are subject to hallucinations. Someone like Mary Magdalene might fill the bill, but scarcely men of such diverse temperaments as Peter, Thomas, James and Paul.

Hallucinations are normally individual things. It is noticeable how weak is the evidence that Michael Perry is able to adduce for group hallucination. But in the case of Jesus the same 'hallucination' is observed by fishermen, tax collectors, rabbis, close relations, a determined foe, and 500 people at once.

Hallucinations generally come to people who have been hankering after something for a long time. The wish becomes father to the thought. But here we find no wish-fulfilment. As we have seen, the disciples were not expecting anything of the sort, and they proved most reluctant to accept even the evidence of their own eyes.

Hallucinations tend to recur over long periods. Someone who suffers from obsessional appearances continues to suffer from them. But here they ceased as dramatically as they began. It all took place within six weeks.

Hallucinations are generally restricted to a particular person, a particular time and a particular place. In this case, the diversity could not have been wider. The appearances took place at early morning, at noon, at night. Seashore, roadside, upper room, garden – the locality made no difference. And those who experienced these 'seeings' were a very varied crowd.

The appearances did not become increasingly bizarre, as is often the case with visions. Rather, they remained very restrained in character. The contrast with the apocryphal gospels is dramatic in this respect. Moreover, far from mounting in frequency and pitch, as hallucinations often do, these meetings ceased entirely after forty days, never to return.

Hallucinations, of course, do not have the physical element which we have seen to be such an ineluctible strand of the resurrection stories. They are not in any sense objective. Nor do they tend to produce in those who have them a remarkable change of character from dishonesty to truth, from fear to confidence, from sorrow to joy – in short, hallucinations are incapable of accounting for the rise, the maintenance and the growth world wide of the Christian church. The Easter faith did not manufacture the facts. On the contrary, the events of Easter gave rise to this astonishing and world-changing faith.

Taken as a whole, these appearances seem to have an order and a logic about them. They start in the garden by the tomb itself. They progress in Jerusalem and its environs. They move into Galilee on mountain and lake, and they direct the disciples towards world mission after their Lord is taken from their sight. These meetings, in short, assure the disciples of the reality of the resurrection, make plain Jesus' determination to leave them (yet pledge his presence with them always), and prepare them for evangelism to the needs of the world. When these functions of the resurrection appearances had been achieved, the need for them ceased. From now on Jesus who had walked the streets of Palestine, Jesus who had died and risen, was with them by the Spirit until the end of history. That was the meaning of Pentecost. And Pentecost was the birthday of world mission.

### 'The accounts are full of contradictions'

Many scholars regard the Gospel accounts of the resurrection as so diverse as to be irreconcilable: this, they believe, casts doubt on the whole claim that Jesus rose.

Even if there were major contradictions two things would

need to be remembered. In the first place, the writers are struggling to express something never previously seen or experienced in human history, something on the borderland of this world and the next. And secondly, even if there were major discrepancies, that would not necessitate the conclusion that Jesus did not rise. As William Barclay has observed,

> it is a notorious fact of ancient history that Polybius, the Greek historian, and Livy, the Latin historian, represent Hannibal in his invasion of Italy crossing the Alps by completely different routes, routes which can by no stretch of the imagination be harmonised, yet no one doubts that Hannibal most certainly arrived in Italy (*Crucified and Crowned*, p. 157).

But are there such major diversions in the accounts? The one most commonly adduced seems to me the weakest of all. It is the claim that in Matthew (and by prediction in Mark 16: 7) you get appearances of Jesus in Galilee; whereas in Luke and John you get appearances in Jerusalem. But this objection is totally jejune. Matthew does indeed give a Galilee appearance, but he gives a Jerusalem one as well, by the tomb itself (28: 9f). Luke certainly gives Jerusalem appearances, but then in his Gospel he offers us a continuous narrative from the resurrection to the ascension in highly compressed style, and he has a clear theological emphasis on Jerusalem as the centre from which world mission spreads out until it takes over Rome itself. Though he selects Jerusalem resurrection material, that does not mean he is unaware or sceptical of Galilean appearances. He tells us that Jesus 'presented himself alive after his passion by many proofs, appearing to them during forty days' (Acts 1: 3), so he affords plenty of opportunity for appearances to have taken place in both locations. John has both Jerusalem and Galilee appearances (ch. 20, 21), and both are implied by Paul's list which includes appearances to Peter and James (manifestly in Jerusalem), to 500 (manifestly in Galilee) and to himself (in Syria). Why on earth not?

In point of fact one can make a tentative but harmonious reconstruction of the probable course of events, which makes room for almost all the material contributed by our six accounts. John Wenham has a brilliant book on this topic, *Easter Enigma*, going through the press. I have not been able to consult it in detail but it may well prove to have solved with great probability the apparent contradictions in the accounts. In the following analysis I am largely indebted to M.C. Perry's treatment in his book entitled *The Easter Enigma*.

1    On the Saturday, as it began to move into Sunday (*tē epiphōskousē*, i.e. just before 6.00 pm in Jewish timing), Mary Magdalene and Mary the mother of James visit the tomb, not to embalm, but to explore the situation (Matt. 27: 66–28: 1). To be sure, they were resting on the sabbath (Luke 23: 56) but this was within a sabbath day's walk.

2    Towards dawn on Easter day the stone is dislodged, and the guard scatter in panic (Matt. 28: 2–4).

3    A little later the women arrive at the tomb and find it empty. They included Mary Magdalene, Mary the mother of James, Joanna, and Salome (Mark 16: 1–4; Luke 24: 1–3, 10; John 20: 1). Mary Magdalene alone is mentioned in St. John's account, for it was she who ran to give Peter the news: others were with her, as the 'we' in John 20: 2 shows.

4    While Mary Magdalene runs off (John 20: 2) the other women enter the tomb and see an angel (two in Luke) who speaks to them (Mark 16: 5–7; Matt. 28: 5–7; Luke 24: 4–7).

5    The women leave the tomb, and follow Mary to tell the disciples about the angel's message (Mark 16: 7, 8; Matt. 28: 8; Luke 24: 8–11). Mark cannot mean by his enigmatic 'they said nothing to anyone, for they were afraid' that their awe-induced silence was long-lived: the previous verse had said 'go, tell'.

6    Peter and 'the beloved disciple' run to the tomb, and depart puzzled but with dawning faith induced by the graveclothes (John 20: 3–10). Luke 24: 12, which suggests Peter alone ran to the tomb, is omitted in the best texts of Luke.

7    Mary Magdalene returns to the tomb; when she arrives it is deserted. She sees the two angels inside the tomb, and

turning away meets the risen Christ. She returns to tell the disciples, but they do not believe her (John 20: 11–18; Mark 16: 9–11).

8  Some time early in the day Peter meets the Lord (Luke 24: 34; 1 Cor. 15: 5). This is prior to Jesus' appearing to any other of his male disciples.

9  In the afternoon, Jesus appears to the two disciples walking to Emmaus. They rush back to town to tell the eleven (Luke 24: 13–35; Mark 16: 12f).

10  On the first Easter evening, Jesus appears to the disciples in the upper room. Cleopas and his companion are there, but Thomas is away (Mark 16: 14–18; John 20: 19–23; 1 Cor. 15: 5). Jesus speaks of the Spirit he is about to send on them.

11  A week later, still in Jerusalem, there is another appearance to the disciples, including Thomas (John 20: 26–9; Luke 24: 49).

12  The disciples go back to Galilee where seven of them see Jesus after a night's unproductive fishing on the lake (John 21: 1–22).

13  Further appearances follow in Galilee throughout several weeks (Acts 1: 3, cf. John 20: 30), including an appearance to a crowd of 500 at once on a mountain where world mission is broached (1 Cor. 15: 7; Matt. 28: 16–20). The identification of these two events is not certain but plausible. The 500 must have been in Galilee: there were only 120 disciples in Jerusalem by Pentecost (Acts 1: 15).

14  Jesus returns to Jerusalem just before Pentecost. He appears to James, his brother (1 Cor. 15: 7). But this might have taken place in Galilee after the 500 (which it immediately follows in Paul's list). The *Gospel of the Hebrews* says that James saw Jesus in Jerusalem on the day of resurrection. We do not know exactly when and where. But it is clear that some such encounter took place. James, an erstwhile sceptic, becomes leader of the Jerusalem Church (Mark 3:21; John 7: 7; Acts 15: 13–21).

15  The final appearance takes place outside the city, on

Olivet. Jesus leaves them and is taken into heaven (Mark 16: 19; Luke 24: 50–2; Acts 1: 6–11; 1 Cor. 15: 7).

16    The ending of Jesus' time with the disciples gives way to the beginning of the age of the Spirit. At Pentecost (Acts 2: 1ff) there is a mighty visitation of the Spirit on the infant church, and he has not been withdrawn. With the exception made to transform Saul of Tarsus into Paul the apostle to the Gentiles, there were no more appearances.

That reconstruction may not be precisely correct in every detail. But it does show that it is perfectly possible to work out a credible course of events from the resurrection to the ascension, and that the various accounts are far from a bundle of contradictions.

# Chapter
# 9

The Implications of Easter

The resurrection of Jesus was never intended to be a matter for academic discussion. It has very practical implications, and they touch the most profound areas of human life and enquiry. In this chapter we shall restrict ourselves to three of the most important questions it is possible to ask.

When Paul discusses the resurrection in 1 Corinthians 15, he shows a ruthless integrity in drawing the inferences. If Jesus did not rise from the grave, then Paul's preaching has been a waste of time, their faith is futile, and they remain unforgiven. What is more, all Christians misrepresent God, dead Christians are finished, and live Christians are deluded. That is how he summarises the importance of the issue in verses 12–19 of that chapter.

On the other hand, if Christ did rise from that grave, then he is alive to be encountered (15: 4ff). He has cleared our accusing past (15: 3). He has broken the fear of death (15: 54). His resurrection is the pledge of our own (15: 22). He can change human nature (15: 57). And he has a plan for our lives (15: 58). In other words, it is very difficult to exaggerate the importance of the resurrection of Jesus from the dead. Its implications are immense.

Modern man, however, remains unimpressed. He does not think it matters very much whether or not Jesus rose from the dead. When it comes to religion the man in the street is not asking 'Did Jesus Christ rise from the grave on the first Easter Day?' but much broader questions like the following: 'Is there a

God?', 'Aren't all religions much the same?' and 'What happens after death?'.

These are indeed questions of vital importance for everyone, but there is not much evidence that we are getting nearer to agreed answers to them. Could it be that we are looking in the wrong direction? Is it possible that in the resurrection of Jesus of Nazareth we have the clue to these queries which are so much aired these days? If so, there will be no further disinterest in the resurrection. It will come into its own as the master key to unlock those three intractable locks. It could be that the resurrection is the proper starting point if we are to find our way through the maze of muddled thinking on these questions. Let us look at them in turn.

*Is there a God?*

I am constantly surprised to see arguments continuing to pass to and fro, even in learned journals like *Mind*, seeking to prove or disprove the existence of God. The whole procedure is quite inappropriate, because, although there are good reasons for believing in a Supreme Being, personal existence can neither be proved or disproved. It must be encountered. And the only God known to the Bible is not the First Cause or the Unmoved Mover discussed in philosophical argument, but the living God who made man, who cares for him, and who comes to meet him in Jesus Christ. It is beside the point to argue for or against the traditional 'proofs' for God's existence. The Bible never uses them. It never argues about God's existence at all, but always assumes him as the basis for all else. It points, instead, to Jesus Christ, who claimed that he was revealing God to us. 'No one knows the Son but the Father, and no one knows the Father but the Son and any one to whom the Son chooses to reveal him. Come to me, all who labour and are heavy laden, and I will give you rest' (Matt. 11: 27ff). Claims like this make the imagination boggle. They mean – if they can be relied on – that behind this world there is a loving, personal God who has created all there is. This God cares for us men so much, despite our waywardness and rebellion, that he chose to come and share our world, and to make known to us his nature and his will in the only terms we intimately understand, the terms of human life.

And what a life! A life that has influenced art, music, culture and literature more than any other before or since. A life which has inspired most of the ideals of modern education, hospitals, social services, freedom, the trade unions and the welfare state. A life which embodied every virtue known to man, and was free from all human vices. However you look at it, the character of Jesus was unparalleled. He set the highest standards for human conduct that any teacher has ever set, and unlike any other teacher, he kept to those standards.

Not only is the life of Jesus admired far beyond Christian circles. So is his teaching. It is widely recognised as the best and noblest that has ever been offered to mankind. And yet we cannot stop there. For in the course of his teaching Jesus made the most staggering claims, such as the one quoted above. There is no close parallel to them anywhere in the religions of the world. They are far too plentiful to be discounted as textual insertions; they are far too important to be ignored, as is commonly done by those who regard Jesus as just a great teacher. Yet if we are compelled to accept them as part of the authentic record that has come down to us about Jesus, attested in every strand of the material that has gone to make up the New Testament, then at once the cosy picture of Jesus as merely a good man and a great teacher disintegrates. As C.S. Lewis so crisply expressed it in *Miracles*, 'The discrepancy between the depth and sanity, and (let me add) *shrewdness* of his moral teaching, and the rampant megalomania which must lie behind his theological teaching unless he is indeed God, have never been satisfactorily got over.' For Jesus claimed to be authorised by God to forgive sins, to give life, to raise men from the dead at the last day, and to be the final judge of all mankind (Mark 2: 5; John 6: 35; 11: 25; 5: 27ff; Matt. 7: 21–7; John 5: 22). Imagine any other teacher saying that the eternal destiny of his hearers depended upon their obedience to him! He would not long escape the attentions of the psychiatrists.

Moreover, Jesus accepted as his due the worship thought proper to God alone. Peter fell at his feet and said 'You are the Christ, the Son of the living God' (Matt. 16: 16). Thomas, in the upper room, cried out 'My Lord and my God' (John 20: 28). In both cases Jesus accepted this tribute quite naturally. Contrast that with the horror of Paul and Peter when engaged on their missionary work in Acts (Acts 10: 25; 14: 14). They were appalled at the blasphemy. Not so Jesus. He took it as his right.

Claims such as these are breathtaking. They would sound like the ravings of a lunatic, were it not for the character and moral teaching of the man who uttered them. But how did he propose to authenticate his claims? Not by miracles. He refused to work these to order. In any case, miracles could never compel belief: men would always find some alternative explanation. So Jesus made the whole of his credibility rest upon the resurrection. There is a somewhat sardonic account in Matthew 12 of Jesus healing a blind and dumb demoniac, and the scribes and pharisees cynically coming to him and saying 'Teacher, we wish to see a sign from you.' What more did they want? What more could they need in order to believe? So Jesus says 'An evil and adulterous generation seeks for a sign. But no sign shall be given to it except the sign of the prophet Jonah. For as Jonah was three days and three nights in the belly of the whale, so will the Son of man be three days and three nights in the heart of the earth' (12: 39, 40). As everyone knew, Jonah was the man who spent three days in the great fish: so Jesus would, he said, spend three days buried in the earth. That would be the authentication of his claim. And that is precisely what happened at the resurrection. Jesus was as good as his word.

A Ugandan friend of mine sees the implication clearly. 'For me, he is not a mere hero of history, like those who fought and died in two World Wars. He is my God, in full power of deity.' That is what Paul meant when, apparently drawing on an even earlier formulation, he says this about Jesus. 'He was descended from David according to the flesh, and designated Son of God in power according to the Spirit of holiness by his resurrection from the dead, Jesus Christ our Lord' (Rom. 1: 3f). The most compelling argument for the existence of God, and the sort of God described in scripture, is Jesus Christ. By his incarnation, his teaching, his death, and supremely by his resurrection, he has shown us what God is like. He has shown us that God is personal. He has shown us that God is holy. He has shown us that God is love. He has shown us that God forgives – at infinite personal cost. He has shown us, by the resurrection, that evil will not have the last word in God's universe. In the risen Christ we have the answer to our doubts about God.

## Which religion?

Comparative religion has come of age in the global village. It is partly because of the multiracial nature of much of the world. It is partly due to the current decline in absolutes in any area of life. But undeniably the common assumption in many minds is that there are countless roads up the mountain to God, and that it does not matter very much which one you take. This is represented at a more sophisticated level by the replacement of departments of theology in universities by departments of religion, or of the phenomenology of religion. It is represented in some Missionary Societies by the replacement of evangelism by 'dialogue'. It is very deeply rooted, and confusing to many genuine enquirers after truth.

Very often, of course, people take refuge from personal involvement in any religion by pointing out that there are so many. Often such people have no knowledge whatever of other religions. If they had, they might think again. What religion in the world apart from the Judaeo-Christian faith, is intellectually coherent, morally dynamic, and big enough to embrace culture and science, creation and redemption, life and death, the individual (whatever his colour or class) and the community as well, the present generation and the future of mankind? But for those seriously troubled by the diversity of world religions, the resurrection might prove to be the most useful and secure starting point.

There is all the world of difference between the resuscitation of a corpse and the resurrection of Jesus. Christians are most certainly not asserting that a certain man died 2,000 years ago, was brought back to life for a while, and then was overtaken by death. On the contrary, they are claiming that almighty God took our human nature on him; that in that human nature he died, that he rose victorious over death, and will never die again. 'We know that Christ, being raised from the dead, will never die again; death no longer has dominion over him' (Rom. 6: 9). His resurrection affirms his claim to be the Way, the Truth and the Life. It was not just any old person who rose. It was *this man*. And the resurrection vindicated his claim to share the nature of God.

The resurrection therefore is the place for the honest enquirer to begin. He need not examine every religion under the sun from animism to Islam. Let him wrestle with the evidence for the resurrection of Jesus.

Once he is persuaded, he need look no further.

There is of course much to admire, much to learn in other religions, as well as much that is cruel and disgusting. God Almighty has not left himself without witness in the hearts of men throughout his world. But world religions do not contain anything which is good and true which cannot be found in Christianity. And none of them but Christianity will tell you about a God who loves you enough to die for you, to rise from the grave as a pledge of your future, and to be willing here and now to come and share your life with you. You will find nothing of that elsewhere. Islam has ninety-nine names for God, but none of them is Father. Hinduism can offer you no power of forgiveness to break the iron grip of *karma*. The Maharishi cannot come and indwell his disciples.

If Jesus did rise from the dead, then he is indeed the way to God. God has vindicated him and set him on high. In that case the exclusiveness of the Christian claim makes sense. It does not amalgamate with other faiths, because it is so very different. The risen Jesus is not just one of the many, he is unique. It is not that Christians are narrow-minded or uncharitable about other faiths. But if Jesus is indeed, as the resurrection asserts, God himself who has come to our rescue, then to reject him, or even to neglect him, is sheer folly. That is why Jesus is not, never has been, and never can be, just one among the religious leaders of mankind. He is not even the best. He is the only. Among various examples of the relative he stands out as the absolute. In the risen Jesus God Almighty confronts us with shattering directness. He offers us total succour; but he demands of us total allegiance. It is important to have an interest in other faiths. The early Christians lived in a world far more syncretistic in beliefs than even our own. But they were clear that Jesus was unique. The more you know of other faiths, the more clearly is this seen to be the case. And the key to Christianity is the resurrection.

Christianity is a historical religion. It claims that God has taken the risk of involving himself in human history. The evidence lies open before us. It will stand, as it has stood over the centuries, any amount of critical investigation. But if we conclude that Jesus Christ did indeed rise from the dead, then that settles the questions of other religions. Christ can no longer appear to us as the finest of men and the best of teachers. Although completely human he shares the nature of God. And as such he claims our ultimate loyalty and obedience.

The point is well made by the celebrated meeting of Auguste Comte, the French philosopher, and Thomas Carlyle. Comte said he intended to found a new religion, which would sweep away Christianity and everything else in its wake. Carlyle's devastating reply ran something like this. 'Splendid! All you need do is to speak as never man spoke, to live as never man lived, to be crucified, rise again the third day, and get the world to believe you are still alive. Then your religion will have some chance of success.'

*What happens after death?*
A few years ago the British *Sunday Times* ran a series of articles in which distinguished men and women gave their ideas about what would happen after death. They included

Christmas Humphreys the Buddhist, Lord Dowding the spiritualist, Basil Henriques the Jew, Bertrand Russell the atheist, and so on. The articles aroused a lot of interest, and were subsequently published as a book, *The Great Mystery of Life Hereafter*. The motley collection of views brought together in this way showed a number of things: that man is fascinated by this problem; that there is general belief (even among rationalists) in some sort of survival; and that there is a most bewildering difference of opinion on the matter. One view seems as good as another: nobody knows for sure, for none of the writers had experienced life after death. It would seem that mortal man is reduced to guesswork; we can, by definition, get no certain knowledge.

It seemed like that in the Middle Ages over the possibility of a sea route to India. There was a great deal of speculation about this in the political and economic circles of European capitals. Was there a way to the rich land of spices and perfumes around the southern tip of Africa? Nobody knew for sure, though many believed there was. All attempts at rounding the Cape had failed. So much so that this treacherous headland was known as the Cape of Storms and it was the scene of many a wreck. However, one determined sailor determined to try again. He succeeded in rounding the Cape and reaching the East. Indeed, there is still a monument to this famous mariner, Vasco da Gama, in China today. Ever since he sailed back to Lisbon in triumph it has been impossible to doubt that a way to the Orient exists round the bottom of Africa. The very name of that perilous Cape was changed to its present title, the Cape of Good Hope.

The enigma of life after death is rather like that. Until the time when Jesus died and rose again death was like that Cape of Storms, littered with wrecks. Until his successful rounding of that Cape and return, men had nothing but speculation to go on about any after life. Now we know. His resurrection has turned it into the Cape of Good Hope. He has opened up for men the way to a new and rich land which he has shown exists. And because he has safely circumnavigated that dangerous

Cape he is well equipped to act as pilot to others. Christian optimism about the future life is not (as Bertrand Russell complained in his article in the *Sunday Times*) 'built on the ground that fairy tales are pleasant', but founded on the solid basis of the resurrection of Jesus Christ from the dead (which Russell appears not to have investigated). And this same Jesus promised his followers that he would go to prepare a place for them, so that where he is, they might be also (John 14: 2, 3).

'He has' wrote C.S. Lewis in his book *Miracles*, 'forced open a door that had been locked since the death of the first man. He has met, fought and beaten the King of Death. Everything is different because he has done so. This is the beginning of the New Creation. A new chapter in cosmic history has opened.'

If we want an answer, supported by solid evidence, to three of the most fundamental and baffling questions a man can ask (and does ask very frequently), then it is the resurrection of Jesus Christ which provides the clue. We are constantly reminded of the importance of asking the right questions. The trouble is that in religious matters we do not know what the right questions are. So we pose these disconnected queries about the existence of God, the different religions, and life after death. However, the Bible does not encourage us to ask these questions at all. To do so is to court inconclusive and unsatisfactory answers. The New Testament writers urge us to make up our minds about Jesus of Nazareth and his resurrection. For the resurrection shows us clearly that there is a God, that Jesus Christ is the way to God, and that death for the Christian leads into the nearer presence of God. Those are implications of Easter of the utmost importance. There are many others. We shall meet them in the chapters which follow.

# Chapter
## 10

The Heart of the Good News

Christians did not proclaim a new way of life, a new discipline or philosophy. They did not preach an ideal, or a guru. Good news was their business: the good news that God had come and brought about the messianic salvation promised long before.

*The heart of the good news ... not example*
A great many religions stress the character of their founder. His life, his character, his personality are held up to the faithful as an example. While there is a sense in which the example Jesus was unparalleled, in that he not only taught the most exacting standards but kept them, it is noteworthy how little the example of Jesus figures in the evangelistic preaching of the early church. Naturally, enquirers and new believers would be asking the original missionaries 'What was Jesus like, and what was his teaching?' and the Gospels sprang, partly at least, out of the need to answer that legitimate enquiry. But that is not what the apostles preached. They gave only enough material about the historical Jesus, it would seem, to ground him very firmly in recent local history. That done they proceeded to speak of his death on the cross and his resurrection. There lay the heart of the matter. The longest account of the actual ministry of Jesus to be found in any of the Acts sermons comes in 10: 38f. 'God anointed Jesus of Nazareth with the Holy Spirit and with power; he went about doing good and healing all that were oppressed by the devil, for God was with him. And we are witnesses to all that he did both in the country of the Jews and

in Jerusalem.' That is all about Jesus' ministry. Immediately Peter proceeds to the cross and resurrection. 'They put him to death by hanging him on a tree; but God raised him up the third day and made him manifest, not to all the people but to us who were chosen by God as witnesses, who ate and drank with him after he rose from the dead'. Peter does not leave it there. As constantly in the apostolic kerygma, he challenges his hearers to repent of their sins and receive the forgiveness God wants to offer them through Jesus.

*... not mythology*
This particular passage illustrates admirably another important factor in the early preaching. The apostles did not present a mythical hero of the past, but a highly contemporary Jew, known to many of their hearers, and intimately to themselves. Here was something quite different in kind from the ravaging of Hades by an Orpheus or a Heracles, fabled mythological figures of the distant past. Indeed, it is astonishing, on reflection, that the myth theory of Christian origins, discredited so long in Germany, should have reappeared afresh in recent years. Walter Künneth is devastating in his critique of this sort of approach to the resurrection. 'Whenever revelation is cut off from its moorings in history,' he insists, 'we find a tendency to reduce it to general truths of reason...' 'Myth is the expression of anthropocentric religion. To combine myth and the resurrection of Jesus therefore represents a fundamental misunderstanding. The word of the resurrection... is the proclamation of a reality which is not at the disposal of man in himself, of which he cannot be even mythologically aware, and which must first be told him.' (*The Theology of Resurrection*, pp. 47, 54f). He goes further. 'It is superficial and unfounded to say that the history of religions has shown the dependence of the resurrection of Jesus on mythology. On the contrary, it is precisely the comparison with the history of religion that gives rise to the strongest objections to any kind of mythifying of the resurrection of Jesus', 'The special character of the spiritual atmosphere of Israel is distinct from the syncretistic world

around... Its whole outlook stands in contrast to mythological assumptions' (*op. cit.* pp. 58ff). He rightly points out
that when the Christian gospel began to be preached it was not
treated as a new but basically similar myth. On the contrary, it
was recognised (and rejected, very often) in all its starkness and
offensive otherness. This witness to the one Lord Jesus, 'in
contrast to the tolerance of the whole mythical world, comes
with an intolerant claim to absoluteness which calls in question
the validity and truth of all mythology' (*op. cit.*, p. 62). It is
impossible to exaggerate the absoluteness of the Christian
claim. Peter before the Sanhedrin was typical: 'And there is
salvation in no other. For there is no other name under heaven
given among men by which we must be saved' (Acts 4: 12).

### ...not even the incarnation

The cross of Jesus remains offensive as it always has been, even
in the household of the church. Therefore it is no surprise to
find the emphasis in some modern theological writing which
locates the centre of the Christian faith not so much in the
example of Jesus or his teaching, not in some timeless myth
about the dying and rising life which he represents, but in the
supreme fact of his incarnation. It would, of course, be
ludicrous to play the atonement against the incarnation.
Without the incarnation there would have been no atonement.
Nevertheless when theologians like Karl Rahner see the
incarnation as the climax of the history of the human race, it is
not surprising that the cross and resurrection are almost
regarded as appendages: 'In virtue of the inmost essence of the
incarnation, seen as a formally salvific act, the one event,
composed of death and resurrection, is implied' (*Theological
Investigations*, 4, p. 185). That is very far removed from the
preaching of the apostles. In the Acts sermons his pre-existence
is not mentioned. In Paul it is (Rom. 8: 3; Gal. 4: 4). But it is not
given anything like the prominence of the cross and
resurrection. Both the Pauline references go on from
mentioning the incarnation to its purpose and culmination in
the atonement. The heart of the matter, for the apostles, was

not Christmas, wonderful and indispensable as that was: it was Good Friday and Easter. 'I delivered to you as of first importance what I also received, that Christ died for our sins according to the scriptures, that he was buried, and that he was raised on the third day in accordance with the scriptures' (1 Cor. 15: 3). *That* was the heart of the apostolic proclamation.

### ... but the cross and resurrection

In other words, it was the action of God in Christ for sinful men that the earliest missionaries stressed. He had done something of supreme significance. He had dealt with the barrier of human sin; he had broken the prison bars of death. In virtue of those achievements he could offer both forgiveness of sins and the gift of the Holy Spirit, the pledge of the age to come which was available now to believers. Jesus was the supreme revealer of God: he was also the unique redeemer of men. Hence the confidence and joy with which they made this good news known.

'This Jesus,' says Peter on the Day of Pentecost, 'you crucified and killed by the hands of lawless men. But God raised him up, having loosed the pangs of death because it was not possible for him to be held by it ... This Jesus God raised up, and of that we are all witnesses ... And having received from the Father the promise of the Holy Spirit, he has poured out this which you see and hear' (Acts 2: 24ff). They must repent, and be baptised, and then they will receive the double gift: forgiveness of sins and the indwelling of the Holy Spirit. That is how Luke records the first Christian preaching. It accords well with Paul's fundamentals of the faith in 1 Corinthians 15: 33ff.

The other sermons in Acts have much the same thrust. 'You denied the Holy and Righteous One ... and killed the Author of life, whom God raised from the dead. To this we are witnesses.' What must they do, in the light of this? 'Repent, and turn again, that your sins may be blotted out, that times of refreshing from the presence of the Lord may come' (3: 14f, 19). In 4. 10ff Peter says 'Be it known to you all, that by the name of

Jesus Christ of Nazareth, whom you crucified, whom God raised from the dead, by him this man is standing before you well'. Again comes the implicit challenge to repentance and new life in the powerful claim to uniqueness which follows: 'And there is salvation in no one else, for there is no other name under heaven given among men by which we must be saved.' Summarising the characteristics of the infant church, Luke observes, 'With great power the apostles gave their testimony to the resurrection of the Lord Jesus' (4: 33), and in 5: 30f we find them at it again. 'The God of our fathers raised Jesus whom you killed by hanging him on a tree. God exalted him at his right hand as Leader and Saviour, to give repentance to Israel and forgiveness of sins. And we are witnesses to these things, and so is the Holy Spirit whom God has given to those who obey him.' It was the same message to Cornelius: 'They put Jesus to death by hanging him on a tree; but God raised him on the third day and made him manifest.' Why? 'That everyone who believes in him should receive forgiveness of sins through his name'. And 'while Peter was still saying this, the Holy Spirit fell on all who heard the word' (Acts 10: 39f, 43f).

It was the same message during the missionary journeys: man's sin in crucifying Jesus, God's power in raising him, and the offer of forgiveness and new life through commitment to him in repentance, faith and baptism (Acts 13: 29-39). This message was, as always in the economy of God, to the Jew first; but when so many of the Jews would not receive it, the apostles began to fulfil the Old Testament prophecies about the Gentiles which had lain unheeded or uncomprehended hitherto. Paul and Barnabas said in the synagogue at Pisidian Antioch 'It was necessary that the word of God should be spoken first to you [Jews]. Since you thrust it from you, and judge yourselves unworthy of eternal life, behold, we turn to the Gentiles. For so the Lord commanded us, saying, "I have set you to be a light for the Gentiles, that you may bring salvation to the uttermost parts of the earth." And when the Gentiles heard this, they were glad ... And the word of the Lord spread throughout all the region' (Acts 13: 46ff).

It would be otiose to pursue this theme throughout the New Testament. If we turn to Paul we find him saying that God will acquit those who believe 'in him who raised from the dead Jesus our Lord, who was put to death for our sins, and raised for our justification' (Rom. 4: 25). That was the divine action through which men can be reconciled with God. How then should Christians live? 'No longer for themselves, but for him who for their sake died and was raised' (2 Cor. 5: 15). It is the same with Peter. In his greeting at the outset of his letter he prays peace on those who are sprinkled with the blood of Jesus and sanctified by his Spirit; and soon we find him luxuriating in the cross and resurrection by which he had been made a new man. 'By his great mercy we have been born anew to a living hope through the resurrection of Jesus Christ from the dead ... You know that you were ransomed from your futile ways ... with the precious blood of Christ ... Through him you have confidence in God, who raised him from the dead and gave him glory, so that your faith and hope are in God' (1 Pet. 1: 3, 18, 20f). It is perfectly plain that the heart of the good news by which men and women from Jewish and Gentile backgrounds alike were 'born again' (1: 23, 25) 'ransomed' (1: 18) and 'saved' (1: 9) was the death and resurrection of Jesus Christ.

The death of Jesus alone could lead to a very static view of salvation, a very backward-looking faith. The resurrection alone could lead to an exhilaration with the powers of the age to come which failed to make room for suffering and discipleship here and now. During the history of the church both imbalances have occurred, and as a result the church has gone seriously off course. It is the death and resurrection of Jesus, the empty cross, which lies at the heart of the apostolic Christianity and is God's good news for the world.

*How would the pagan world understand the gospel?*
But would the world have understood this message? Would it have appeared double Dutch to the first hearers? Martin Hengel of Tübingen has brought a superbly documented answer to that question in his book, *The Atonement*. He has

unearthed and put together a mass of classical material which shows beyond all possible doubt that the first hearers of the gospel, Jews and Greeks alike, had more than enough pointers within their own background to understand the heart of the good news about a saviour who suffers for our rescue.

Let us begin with the Greek world in which Christianity was soon to make such tremendous strides. How comprehensible was the message of vicarious suffering there?

Hengel shows that the ancients were well aware of death's being the necessary precondition for the exaltation of a hero, like Achilles or Heracles. They knew of many instances of voluntary death 'for mankind'. The Greeks greatly valued those who died for the city, or for their friends, for the law or for the truth, and this was enthusiastically taken up by the Maccabean martyrs in the days of Antiochus. All this Hengel carefully documents. But his most interesting material concerns the familiarity of the idea of atoning sacrifice to Greek minds. It was a common theme in Greek tragedy. Agamemnon sacrificed his daughter Iphigenia to avert the wrath of Artemis and secure the success of the Trojan War; and that story was disseminated to all strata of Greek society through its celebration in the *Iliad* of Homer, the *Agamemnon* of Aeschylus, the *Electra* of Sophocles and the *Iphigenia* of Euripides. But Euripides went further. He took up the theme of atoning sacrifice and saw it as the voluntary surrender of one's life for a higher end. This theme plays a prominent role in no less than five of his extant plays (*Alcestis, Hecuba, Heraclidae, Phoenissae,* and *Supplices*).

Furthermore, the phrase *apothnēskein huper*, 'to die for', passed into common Greek usage. We meet the scapegoat in many places (significantly the scruffiest, most broken-down animal in your flock!). The averting of divine wrath was a commonly accepted idea, and it was done through the death of an innocent animal or, sometimes, person. This atoning sacrifice was often called *pharmakos* or 'medicine'. And when the *pharmakos* was cast into the sea as a sacrifice for Poseidon, the people cried 'Be our means of atonement, that is, salvation and redemption' (*soteria kai apolutrōsis*). Perhaps the most celebrated and moving example of the *pharmakos* in all antiquity was Oedipus, who, in order to rid the land of the curse he has unwittingly brought on it, blinds himself and allows himself to be driven from home, as a criminal. He believes 'that one soul can intercede for thousands, and expiate this' and so he voluntarily embraces his fate. Finally he finds grace (*charis*) in the shrine of the Eumenides who had been affronted by his sin but propitiated by his sufferings, and he finds a peaceful passage over the threshold of death. Everyone in antiquity knew that story: indeed, most educated people still do today. And Hengel points out that, despite all the differences, the figure of Oedipus is the closest thing in all Greek drama to the passion and resurrection of Jesus in the Gospels.

In Abdera, a scholiast tells us, 'a man was sacrificed each year for the sins of the citizens, but people proscribed him seven days earlier, so that in this way he alone would take upon himself the sins of all'. But the most amazing parallel to the sacrifice of Jesus is found in Lucan's *Pharsalia*, 2.304-9. The younger Cato offers himself to die for the bloodguilt of the civil war, and so atone for it.

So may it be. May the strict gods of the Romans receive complete expiation, and may we not cheat war of any of its victims. If only the gods of heaven and the underworld would allow this head to expose itself to all punishment as one condemned!

The hordes of the enemy cast down Decius, the consecrated one: may the two armies [involved in the civil war] pierce me through. May the barbarians from the Rhine make me the target of their shots, and exposed to every spear, may I receive all the wounds of the whole war. This my blood will ransom all the people; this my death will achieve atonement for all that the Romans have deserved through their moral decline.

It is well to remember that the writer of this passage was a contemporary of St. Paul. He died in A.D. 65 on Nero's orders. It is not difficult to see why the Christian message was so readily understood in Rome and the other great cities of the Empire.

Hengel concludes this part of his study thus:

> The message of the death of Jesus of Nazareth, the Son of God, on the cross for all men was not incomprehensible even to the educated audience of the Greek world. Its linguistic and religious categories were largely familiar to this audience. Nevertheless the primitive Christian preaching of the crucified Messiah must have seemed aesthetically and ethically repulsive to them and to be in conflict with the philosophically purified nature of the gods . . . It appeared to contemporaries as a dark or even mad superstition. For this was not the death of a hero from ancient times, suffused in the glow of religion, but that of a Jewish craftsman of the most recent past, executed as a criminal, with whom the whole present and future salvation of all men was linked (*op. cit.*, p. 31).

But however comprehensible the message was, it totally overflowed the banks of previous thinking in this area. Here was no hero dying for his city, no philosopher dying for his friend, but God in human form dying for the sins of a whole world. Here was no averting of impersonal wrath by human sacrifice: here was God himself providing the means of atonement for his enemies who could now become his friends. Here was no occasional intervention to atone for a particular crime, but the eschatological salvation, the judgment and the salvation of the whole world. The pagan in the ancient world was, therefore, provided with the categories of sin and suffering, atonement and ransom which enabled him to understand the message of the gospel: but the message utterly transcended any concept of atonement that could have crossed his mind. Such was God's *praeparatio evangelica* in the pagan world.

*How would the Jewish world understand the gospel?*
But what of the Jewish world? Would they have understood the apostolic proclamation of a personal atoning sacrifice? To some extent we have already answered that question in chapters 3 and 4. The whole New Testament *kerygma* is rooted in the Old Testament revelation, which lay at the heart of Judaism. The sacrificial system, the Passover lamb, the expiation of sin, the sprinkling of blood, the creation of covenants, the sin offering, all this and more is taken up from the Old Testament and applied to the atonement achieved by Christ. It is seen as the shadow of the real thing, the trailer for God's main film. So from one point of view, the Jew was ideally prepared for what was to come to him in the proclamation of Jesus.

From another point of view one can only marvel at the newness of it all. There was no suggestion in first century Judaism of a suffering and dying Messiah. It was totally scandalous: for it meant that God's chosen one had failed, had ended in disgrace, and had even died under the curse of God (Deut. 21: 23). It was not until well into the second century that you find the figure emerging of a suffering Messiah of the tribe of Ephraim: the idea sprang from the terrible catastrophes of the Jewish War (A.D. 66–70) and the Bar-Cochba rising (A.D. 132–5).

Moreover, though Israel had many martyrs, she did not, until the late first-century A.D. *Similitudes of Enoch* (71), regard any of them as fulfilling the role of the Son of Man, exalted by God to his throne (Dan. 7: 14). So the Christian claim of Jesus' exaltation, based on the event of Easter and prefigured in the messianic Psalm 110: 1, was strikingly new.

So, curiously enough, was the phrase *apothnēskein huper*, to die for. This phrase was common in classical Greek, as we have seen. But it occurs nowhere in the LXX of the Old Testament.

Yet it quickly became a major way of describing the achievement of Jesus' death.

Nor does there seem to be much anticipation that a crucified man might be of religious value. There is only one example of a crucified martyr in rabbinic Judaism, Jose ben Joezer, a celebrated teacher in Maccabaean times. Little wonder that the message of a crucified Messiah was such an offence to the Jews. How could any man be a great religious leader, let alone God's promised Messiah, if he died in the place of the curse?

Finally, there does not seem to be any rush of candidates in pre-Christian Judaism to fulfil Isaiah 53. Indeed, there is no clear evidence in Judaism before the time of Jesus that this mysterious prophecy was ever applied to the idea of a suffering Messiah. However, we know little of the pre-Christian exegesis of Isaiah 53. It is *possible* that it was seen messianically. There is a hint of this in the *Manual of Discipline*, viii, among the Covenanters at Qumran. Certainly by the time of Justin's *Dialogue with Trypho* in the middle of the second century A.D. Trypho the Jew concedes 'It is quite clear that the scriptures announce Christ had to suffer... We know that he should suffer and be led as a sheep. But prove to us whether he must be crucified and die so disgracefully and so dishonourably the death accursed in the Law. For we cannot bring ourselves even to consider this' (*Dial.*, 90). It was not so much a suffering Messiah that stuck in the throat of the Jew. After all, they had known suffering all through their history, and none more than the prophets and righteous men. But it was the scandal of a crucified Messiah whom God raised from the dead – that was the real sticking point for orthodox Jewry. And the Christians did not attempt to evade it. They accepted the teaching about the curse; and, we have seen, they boldly maintained that the curse Christ bore on that cross was not his own but ours – the sinless taking the place of the guilty.

*The empty cross: its wide appeal*

There were, then, many pointers to the gospel's already

existing in the Jewish as well as in the pagan world of the first century. But in both it broke in as something wonderfully new, comprehensive and breathtaking in its breadth and scope. Here was the unheard-of offering of the Son of God for guilty sinners. Here was the astounding scandal of the Messiah crucified by the most shameful of deaths. Yet here was what the ancient world most needed to hear, the universality of atonement for Jew and Greek, for virtuous and obviously sinful alike. Here in the midst of time was God's ultimate act of deliverance. In the cross, judgment and salvation were anticipated; so even was the eschatological verdict of acquittal. Through the resurrection, the powers of the age to come broke in, defeating death, attesting God's acceptance of the Messiah, and enabling the gift of the Spirit to be poured out in the hearts of believers. The centre of the good news was the empty cross, and it more than transcended every partial anticipation of it in the Greek and Jewish worlds.

The ultimate deliverance has broken in. The final day of God has dawned. The Lord has come and died, and is risen and alive. His Spirit is with us. Those were the convictions on which the infant church was launched. What had they to differentiate themselves from other Jews? Nothing, except the assurance that the Messiah had come, had died, had been raised by God to his right hand, and was even now leading them out into mission and pouring his Spirit into their hearts. That alone explains the rise of the early Christians. That is why they were so brave in persecution, so joyful in hardship, so confident in prayer. That is why they outlived and outloved the pagans and the Jews alike: God's own love, Calvary love, had been shed abroad in their hearts by the Holy Spirit who had been given to them. That is why the early church soon became involved in education, medicine and the liberation of the oppressed. Had not the Messiah done these things? And was not his risen presence with them through the Spirit?

The ancient world was hungry for salvation, exhausted by a century of civil war which had devastated the known world before the emergence of Augustus to undisputed pre-eminence in 28 B.C.. Grateful subjects called him *Sōtēr tēs oikoumenēs*, 'saviour of the world', and hailed his principate as the start of 'the eternal age': I have documented this fully in my book *The Meaning of Salvation*. There was a lot of truth in all this: the roads and seas were safe, the pirates and brigands quelled, the frontiers of empire secured, and much more. And yet the hunger of the human heart remained unmet. Men and women were oppressed by guilt, by powerlessness, and by total uncertainty about the world to come. The gospel of the crucified and risen Jesus met those needs.

Because Jesus had made full atonement for all the sins of the world upon the cross, men were offered, if only they would be humble enough to accept it, complete forgiveness from all their sins and guilt. Another had dealt with them. Guilt is not commonly recognised except in monotheistic circles. It is only when you realise there is a unified centre of life and morals, and that you have utterly failed to live up to your standards, that you become aware of real guilt. The Jews realised it: the Law and the sacrificial system were both deeply concerned with the question of human responsibility, standards, and guilt. But the Gentiles, too, were by the first century becoming increasingly monotheistic. Behind the popular animism and polytheism of the Empire, there was a growing consensus that one supreme source of deity existed. Even as long ago as Homer there had been a dim recognition that Zeus was the 'Father of gods and men'. This had grown under the influence of the philosophers and indeed of the Jews. Their monotheism was immensely attractive to the Gentile world: hence the number of 'Godfearers' who thronged the synagogues but balked at the final step of 'mutilation' by circumcision. Increasingly, then, real guilt was seen to be a problem to Gentile and Jew alike. Imagine, therefore the relief, the wonder, when joyful, liberated men and women began to show how 'through this man forgiveness of sins is proclaimed to you, and by him every one who believes is freed from everything from which you could not be freed by the law of Moses' (Acts 13: 38f).

It was not only pardon, but power that was such an

attractive feature of the early preaching of the empty cross. Here was the one who had broken the power of death. He was risen and alive, and very much to be reckoned with. The powers of the age to come were clearly being dispensed by the risen Christ to the disciples. The spiritual gifts of tongues and prophecy, of healing and exorcism were displayed in their assemblies. The grip of greed and lust, of sectarianism and materialism was broken among these people of Jesus. Their lives made their talk about the new age credible to many. If you had to put it in three words, they could be the ones thrown at Paul in Athens: he was always going on about *Iēsous kai anastasis*, 'Jesus and the Resurrection'. Although the preaching of the resurrection at Athens caused much mirth, a church was born there, and before long produced one of the great intellectuals of the second century A.D., Athenagoras. He wrote two books. One of them, *Resurrection from the Dead*, is a stout defence of that resurrection faith which had brought a new power to Athens and to his life. Tatian, his contemporary, discovered the power of the risen Jesus breaking the grip of demonic forces in his life. He bursts out in praise to God who has snapped the power of 10,000 tyrants within him (*Orat.*, 29). The empty cross spelt moral power such as Jewish and Stoic ethics had never been able to inculcate.

What is more, the empty cross meant that death was vanquished by Christ, and what was true for the master would be true for the servant too. The fear of death was as common in ancient society as in our own, and more readily admitted. At some palatial banquet a remembrancer would stand near the head of the table and say to him during the feast, *'Memento mori'*, 'remember, you must die!' Skull and cross-bones are common wall decor in Herculaneum and Pompeii, as is the phoenix, the mythical bird which was said by the poets to die and be reborn from its own ashes. That shows the prevalent hunger for life after death. One mid-first-century picture of the phoenix in Pompeii has this envious inscription, 'O phoenix, you lucky thing'. And Clement of Rome, writing in the nineties of the first century, after arguing for reasonableness of the resurrection from the fact that seeds die and come to life again in new flowers, makes the phoenix the climax of his argument. He really believed it existed! Naturally, in this he was a child of his age. Nevertheless it is not the phoenix he was interested in. It served merely as an emblem of the risen Christ. Jesus by his resurrection had brought life and immortality to life, and had solved the problem of life after death. Here was something far more tangible than could ever be offered in the Eleusinian Mysteries. Nobody but Jesus had died and risen again.

Finally, this holding together of the crucifixion and resurrection in the Christian good news made sense of the worldly and the other worldly in people's lives. In the midst of sorrow and agony, life was shot through with the resurrection. In the most exalted moments of ecstasy and joy, the marks of the cross could not be eradicated. Here in the empty cross was the symbol that made sense of the whole of life, its incarnation and transformation, its joys and sorrows, its materialism and values, its 'already' and its 'not yet'. It spoke – and speaks still – to the hunger of the human heart as no symbol in the world has ever spoken. The empty cross takes us to the heart of human need and to the heart of God's provision.

# Part C

## The Empty Cross

# Chapter
# 11

The Empty Cross and the Theologian

Theologians are among God's important gifts to his church. They are charged with the responsibility of examining the Christian revelation in depth, and relating it to the contemporary needs and thought forms of the society in which they serve. Theirs is the privilege of being paid to spend their time working on the content of the faith, wrestling with its problems, relating it to secular thought and other world views. Theirs is the responsibility of feeding the Church with their studies in such a way that leaders on the ground, the clergy and teachers, can be helped to a more balanced, well-considered and relevant presentation of the gospel to which both theologian and preacher are committed. The theologian is not in bondage to the church, as if he might never be allowed fresh opinions and discoveries; nor is he independent of the church, as if what he has to say has no relation to its life and faith. He is part of the church, and he is called to love within its fellowship and witness. He has a position of great trust, responsibility and privilege.

But he also occupies a most difficult and dangerous position. Pressures come on him from all sides. Often the churchman regards him as a threat, and his academic colleagues as a sort of appendix, left over from some previous age of man. Gone is the day when theology was seen as the queen of the sciences, concerned as it was with God, the ultimate source of both man and matter. She has become the Cinderella instead, and is often only acceptable at the ball of university disciplines if she dresses up as student of ancient Near Eastern literature or of the phenomenology of religion. In many a university today the theologian is a very lonely person: his colleagues think of him as a quaint oddity who retains belief in God, and the Christian often regards him as a sceptic – or a quisling.

### Pressures on theologians

The pressures on the modern theologian in academic life are very powerful. Here are five of the more obvious.

The astonishing advance of the natural sciences and the technology deriving from them have in recent decades upstaged many arts subjects and none more than theology. There are at least four attitudes in the successful world of science and technology which blow a chill wind towards the theologian. There is an optimism about man in scientific circles, induced by the amazing success of the discipline. It stands in sharp contrast to the pessimism about man in many arts circles, and the Christian doctrine of man both as creature and as fallen. Second, there is, at best, agnosticism about God. He is no longer needed to plug the gaps in scientific knowledge. 'Sire' as Laplace said to Napoleon on the subject of God, 'I have no need of that hypothesis'. Third, there is impatience with miracle: ours is a world of observed and reliable uniformities where direct divine intervention cannot be detected. And fourth, in the wake of Bishop Wilberforce's disastrous debate with Darwin in the last century over Genesis and evolution, it is commonly held in scientific circles that the Bible is discredited and is a farrago of myths which we have outgrown. All of this, often uncritically assumed, rather than explicitly stated, makes life hard for the theologian today.

The second pressure on the theologian derives from history. It is a composite pressure, composed of at least three strands. First, there are the parallels of history. Greater knowledge of the past shows many parallels for elements in Christianity which had been hitherto thought unique. There are parallels of sorts for the creation narratives, the virgin birth, the miracles of Jesus, the descent to hell and the resurrection. Wherein lies the uniqueness, wherein the superiority of the Judaeo-

Christian tradition? Second, there is the precariousness of history. If you really take history seriously, faith seems at once too insecure and too improper. Insecure because it lies at the mercy of historical research; and improper because faith buttressed by history is in danger of being no longer faith. These factors explain the 'flight from history' in much modern theology. And third, there has been increasing stress since Lessing on the irrelevance of history. How can accidental facts of history ever become necessary proofs for faith? Thus Bultmann claimed, 'The historical Jesus is no more part of the kerygma than my book on Jesus is.' Both existential theology and redaction criticism are influenced by this disjunction between history and faith which goes back in Germany through Weiss and Wrede to Lessing and Schleiermacher.

A third area of pressure on the theologian is philosophy. Here again there are at least three interlocking strands. First, there is the breakdown of a unified world view. So long as you believe that both man and his unified environment, mind and matter, spring from a personal creator God, a unified world view is possible. Once remove that concept of a personal creator God, and things begin to fall apart. The world of aesthetics and values is divorced from the world of physics and biology. Matter evolved from chaos, and values are merely man made. A holistic approach to knowledge is ruled out. Hence the decline in philosophy, now largely concerned with what the ancients would have seen as the prolegomena to true philosophy, linguistic analysis. It is impossible to overestimate this *volte-face* in philosophy. Absolutes are ruled out. So is contradiction. Words no longer mean what they say: there is a widespread use of connotation language when the entity itself is discredited. There is plenty of God talk left among theologians who scarcely believe in God any longer.

The rise of existentialism has had an enormous influence on philosophy and theology in the middle of this century. This is a very anthropocentric outlook on life, an intellectual, social and moral reaction against the chill hand of authority in philosophy, history and theology. Arising as it did in occupied

Europe during the war, it has exercised, through writers like Sartre and film directors like Bergman, an enormous influence on ordinary people. Indeed, it is one of the major influences behind the so-called 'Me generation.' I become myself in encounter, in choice, in decision, in love, in dread. History and philosophy–and bourgeois ethics for that matter–are dead, part of the old 'I-it' world of classical categories. What is important is 'I-Thou' encounter, untrammelled by the past or the conventional. Hence a good deal of the subjectivism in modern theology, influenced as it has been by Bultmann and his followers in the existentialist school.

Curiously enough, in a hard-headed and materialistic age, there is a new resort to mysticism. This is very noticeable in secular writers, but is no less prevalent among theologians. Redaction criticism allows scholars to go on studying the 'meaning' of a Gospel story when they do not believe it ever happened. Words like 'pantheism' give a pseudo-theistic respectability to a concept which would otherwise have little to commend it; 'everythingism' is not an edifying world view! The connotation language of the resurrection is used by writers who do not believe that anything remotely like the resurrection of Jesus in the Gospels ever happened: Geering's 'idiom of resurrection' helps to fudge the edges while retaining some of the value of the word resurrection. 'Christ-event' can be used by the most sceptical instead of the proper name, in order to gain a spurious currency for agnostic or heretical Christ-ologies. 'Faith' is a notable example of the resort to mysticism. It used to be the correlative of grace: the faculty by which man grasped the divine initiative. Now, since the divine is discounted, there is precious little grace to grasp; so faith has moved upstairs. It is our refuge when the downstairs of life is too intolerable. With these mystical and often pantheistic emphases that have been pressing on theologians, it is hardly surprising that the language and thought of Hinduism and Buddhism is increasingly to be seen in the writings of theologians like Don Cupitt, H.A. Williams and John Hick.

Finally, the modern theologian is not exempt from the

pressures of ordinary modern society. There is a great tendency towards universalism in a world that makes God in its own tolerant image. There is a tendency towards syncretism in a world that has shrunk to a global multi-faith village. There is a tendency towards secularism: with both the historic faith and the future hope soft-pedalled in so much modern theology, Christianity is frequently presented in terms of love alone. And finally, there is an ever growing tendency towards indifferentism. Alongside a shrinking world, a shrinking hold on biblical revelation, a growing ecumenism, goes a declining interest in doctrine. It derives, as we have seen, from the philosophical question of the absolute and contradiction. Truth is relative. The black I see and the white you see are no longer contradictory: they are complementary. Heaven and hell are all one, for truth is no longer objective. Doctrine is arrived at, both in politics and religion, largely by head counts: norms have degenerated into what most people of good sense and good will approve.

*Weaknesses among theologians*
It is not hard to see how these and other pressures have affected a great deal of theological writing. A shrewd critique was mounted some time ago by C.S. Lewis in his article 'Fern Seed and Elephants' in *Christian Reflections*. With humour and skill he raises a number of problems which he, as a non-professional theologian, has with much of the work of the professionals.

First, he is unimpressed by theologians as literary critics. He hears great tracts of the Gospels being dismissed as romances and legends by distinguished theologians, and he wonders how versed they are in legends and romances.

> I have been reading poems, romances, vision-literature, legends, myths, all my life. I know what they are like. I know that not one of them is like this...
> ... These men ask me to believe they can read between the lines of the old texts; the evidence is their obvious inability to read (in any sense worth discussing) the texts themselves.

They claim to see fern-seed and can't see an elephant ten yards away in broad daylight. (pp. 194,197).

His second complaint is that many theologians suppose that the real purpose and teaching of Jesus was speedily misunderstood and altered by his followers, and has only been recently recovered by modern scholars. 'There is', he says, in this sort of arrogance, 'an *a priori* improbability which almost no argument and no evidence could counterbalance' (*op. cit.*, p. 198).

Third, he finds that many theologians believe that the miraculous does not occur. They do not believe in the possibility of prophecy, and so anything in the words of Jesus which looks like a prophecy must, on their view, be considered a *vaticinium post eventum*. 'That is very sensible,' he remarks sardonically, 'if we start by knowing that inspired prediction and the miraculous never occur'. He points out that the presupposition 'if miraculous, then unhistorical' is not one on which scholars can speak with any more authority than anyone else. This scepticism about miracles is something they bring to their studies, not one they have learned from them. They have surrendered to the secular spirit of the age (*op. cit.*, p. 198).

Fourth, he amusingly reflects on the motives, the subtleties, the mistakes ascribed to him by reviewers, and shows how totally beside the point they are. He is, accordingly, unimpressed by the suggestion that modern scholars 2,000 years after the event can rewrite the story of Jesus and the New Testament. 'Dr. Bultmann never wrote a Gospel. Has the experience of his learned, specialised, and no doubt meritorious life given him any power of seeing into the minds of those long dead men who were caught up into what, on any view, must be regarded as the central religious experience of the whole human race?' (*op. cit.*, p. 202).

These are formidable points. He could have added many more, which will immediately be evident to any who have spent half a lifetime, as I have, studying the literature of the subject.

I see an unwarranted scepticism in many quarters, a

surprising preference for tendentious sources, like Josephus, or late sources like the Mandaeans in preference to the clear testimony of New Testament writers. It is significant that this scepticism is not shared by secular ancient historians, who almost to a man have high regard for the New Testament material.

I see a bondage to the historical-critical method, which very properly seeks to get back to the original text, the original setting and the original meaning. All too often when this is done, the possibility of inspiration is totally discounted. The biblical writers are treated as if they made no claim to inspiration, and displayed no marks of it.

I see a bondage to presuppositions. These can, all unconsciously, vitiate the scholarly approach. Theologians sometimes display reluctance to accept biblical evidence because of *a priori* assumptions which go in another direction. This is particularly noticeable in the case of the resurrection: it *didn't* happen because it *couldn't* happen. No amount of evidence will convince wilful blindness or remove blinkers. There are many fundamentalisms, as Bishop Cyril Bowles pointed out years ago in his article of that name: many liberals are a great deal more fundamentalist about their assumptions than the biblical fundamentalists are about the Bible.

I see among some theologians a misplaced assurance, often mixed with contempt for others, on matters which are, to say the least, patient of another interpretation.

I see an almost universal antipathy to the 'deadly sin' of harmonising. If there are the smallest discrepancies in the biblical account these are exploited to the utmost, attibuted to diverse if not contradictory sources, and often both accounts are rejected. To suppose, as John Wenham and Michael Perry, for example, have done, that it is possible to make a convincing reconciliation of all the five accounts of the resurrection appearances is almost equated with intellectual suicide.

Perhaps the greatest occupational danger of the theologian is the same that beset the scribes and Pharisees in the time of Jesus: justification not by faith but by footnotes. There is a tendency towards logic-chopping, and arguing about the constitution of bread while multitudes perish from hunger.[1] Sometimes there seems to be a lack of social involvement, and even of deep commitment to the life of the church. Sometimes familiarity with holy things inoculates against holy living, adventurous faith and bold proclamation. Jesus arraigned the Pharisees in his day for their love of top places in processions and honorific titles. He warned of the danger of making the word of God ineffective through the weight of their tradition. He blamed them for compassing heaven and earth to make one proselyte, and then making him twice as much a child of hell as themselves. It is not infrequently the case that after studying theology a man loses his faith, which was once radiant. And it is all too possible for the modern professor, like the scribes, to take away the key of knowledge of God in the course of theological education: 'you did not enter yourselves, and you hindered those who were entering' (Luke 11:52). I know that is easily done as a theological teacher. To my shame, I have done it myself.

*Theological imbalance and the empty cross*
Turning to the cross and resurrection, it is all too obvious that these pressures have been at work among theologians. But they have worked in a curiously chiastic way. Always in the Bible,

---

[1] A classic, and alas, not unrepresentative example has just come to my attention as I write this chapter. It is a review of *From Chaos to Covenant: Prophecy in the book of Jeremiah*, by Robert P. Carroll. His basic contention is that 'the Jeremiah tradition was constructed out of the poetry of Jeremiah, worked on by many redactional circles including a major deuteronomistic redaction, and produced over a lengthy period of time'. This view, as the reviewer observes, precludes any assured information about the historical Jeremiah. 'The book of Jeremiah is a metaphor of the redactional and community activity which produced it.' Carroll does maintain, amazingly, that a primary tradition attributed to Jeremiah, does exist, in Jeremiah 4: 23-6! The methods which produce such conclusions are, the reviewer laconically informs us, those of higher criticism with particular emphasis on redaction and especially function. (Review by David L. Petersen, *Religious Studies Review*, October 1982, p. 375). Is it any wonder that theologians are often laughed at by their secular colleagues and distrusted by Christian churchmen?

from the Flood and the Exodus onward, event and interpretation are carefully held together. The God who speaks is the God who acts. But with the cross, theologians accept the event, but often reject the interpretation given by the first Christians. With the resurrection, they accept the interpretation but often reject the event. In the first instance, a Liberal abhorrence of categories such as redemption is at work: in the second, plain disbelief in the possibility of miracle.

The empty cross of Jesus is one of the prime focal points for unearthing the prejudices and presuppositions of those who write about it. This is well brought out in extended examinations of various theological approaches, to be found in books such as G. O'Collins, *The Easter Jesus* (chs. 9,10), J.N.D.Anderson's *A Lawyer Among the Theologians* (chs. 1,3, 4) and Hans-Georg Geyer's 'Survey of the Debate' in *The Significance of the Message of the Resurrection for Faith in Jesus* (ed. C.F.D. Moule). We have already seen how variously theologians have interpreted the death of Jesus. It is much the same with those who have written about the resurrection.

For instance, it is fatally easy in the pursuit of a particular position to denigrate what one is opposing. In his article in *Kerygma and Myth* Bultmann argues his 'mythical' reinterpretation of the cross and resurrection, and says 'The difficulty is not simply the incredibility of an event like the resuscitation of a corpse...' Who in his right mind ever claimed that this is what happened at Easter? Bultmann makes a man of straw and then burns him.

Again, dogmatism easily creeps in, in lieu of evidence. Thus Christopher Evans, in *Resurrection and the New Testament*, dismisses the Matthaean account of the resurrection as 'a tissue of improbabilities'. Its additions to the Marcan account 'are either legendary and apologetic... or interpret the events by a crudely literal version of the supernatural' (pp. 82, 57). Dogmatism is very common among German theologians, and one of the most sceptical writers on the resurrection, the New Zealander Lloyd Geering, is an outstanding example of unsupported assertion. Thus 'Jesus truly died. He remains dead for all time' or 'the literary form of Mark's tomb pericope shows definite signs of having been developed in three stages' (*Resurrection: A Symbol of Hope*, pp. 220, 52). It is a case of 'argument weak–shout loud!'

The hatred of harmonising comes through in many writers on the resurrection. Schmiedel's article in *Encyclopaedia Biblica* claims that the Gospels exhibit 'contradictions of the most glaring kind'. 'Nothing', says Gardner Smith (*The Narratives of the Resurrection*, p. 60) 'can be made of a jumble of contradictory statements'; and Christopher Evans asserts 'It is not simply difficult to harmonise these traditions, but quite impossible' (*op. cit.*, p. 128). In point of fact, such harmonisation is perfectly possible, as we have already seen. But I am concerned here not so much with whether or not it can be done, but with the *partis pris* by the writers quoted. How different the modest, unprejudiced words of Michael Ramsey in the Preface to his book, *The Resurrection of Christ*.

> So far from disregarding historical criticism, I believe that it leads us to the radical conclusion that we cannot with certainty reconstruct an ordered plan of the Easter traditions in the Gospel narratives. But I also believe... that our inability to do so is not surprising and does not destroy the historical value of the traditions as congruous with the apostolic preaching that Christ was raised on the third day.

Another way in which writers are influenced by the *Zeitgeist* is shown in some shrewd words of Alan Richardson, in his *Introduction to the Theology of the New Testament* (p. 196). He was referring to the view, increasingly canvassed, that it was possible for Jesus to live on in some spiritual sense while his bones mouldered in a Palestinian tomb.

> The notion that the resurrection of Christ was a purely 'spiritual' affair, while his corpse remained in the tomb, is a very modern one, which rests on theories of the impossibility of miracle drawn from nineteenth-century physics.

Bultmann is, of course, one who is deeply influenced by nineteenth-century physics, but his scepticism about the historical resurrection and his emphasis on the cross as saving event have other causes. 'Faith in the resurrection' he thinks, 'is really the same thing as faith in the saving efficacy of the cross.' He rightly maintains that the early preaching always held the cross and resurrection together. 'And the Easter faith is just this–faith in the word of preaching.' We must not question the preaching. 'The word of preaching confronts us as the word of God. It is not for us to question its credentials' (*Kerygma and Myth.*, p. 46). Those brief citations show the variety of assumptions which lie behind this complicated giant in New Testament studies. We see the scepticism of Wrede and of Lessing. We see the existentialism of Heidegger. We see the stress on the cross as saving event, characteristic of a chaplain who has sought to evangelise in the trenches. We see Luther's emphasis on the preached word which confronts us, and on faith alone which justifies.

So we could go on. Barth is strong on the historical resurrection because he sees it as the ground on which faith can rest. Pannenberg, equally correctly, sees the physical resurrection of Jesus as the validation of his divinity. Geering, who does not appear to believe in life after death at all, is constrained to see the resurrection as merely a symbol of hope. Enough has been said to show how often the conclusions people come to on these matters are less related to the evidence than to *a priori* assumptions.

The theologians in the New Testament were clear that the cross and resurrection were central in the purposes of God for mankind. It might be helpful to conclude this section with a glance at the way in which various theologians have removed the cross and resurrection from the centre of the stage.

*Theological flight from the empty cross*
O'Collins is particularly acute on these tendencies. He points out first how Christendom has given far more place to Good Friday than to Easter Day. This has a number of causes and

consequences. The soul, its supposed immortality, and the 'inner life' came soon to bulk larger in religious imagination than the resurrection of the body. Manichean and Gnostic distaste for physical being plays its part in the downgrading of the resurrection. Western individualism led to a decline in interest in the corporate life implied by the resurrection. Western Pelagianism shied off it: resurrection is a very God-centred, not man-induced, affair! The link between the cross and the eucharist, developed so strongly in the Middle Ages, leaves out both the resurrection and the Holy Spirit. New Testament theologians like Paul, John and Luke, all related the Holy Spirit to the risen Christ: it is not surprising therefore that in the Western Church the decline of interest in the Holy Spirit and in the resurrection went hand in hand. O'Collins has a splendid passage where he observes:

> Generally speaking, both Catholic and Protestant theologians have proved loyal successors to St. Anselm (A.D. 1033-1109) who managed to discuss the redemption in his *Cur Deus Homo?* while completely ignoring Christ's resurrection. So long as full credit for our redemption is ascribed to Christ's death, his resurrection becomes at best a highly useful (if not strictly necessary) proof of Christian claims.
>
> Looking back on such Western theology, we might parody Paul and cry out: 'Resurrection is swallowed up in crucifixion. O Resurrection, where is thy victory? O Resurrection, where is thy sting?' (*The Easter Jesus*, p. 118).

This separation by theologians between cross and resurrection has facilitated the tendency to subsume them under some other aspect of the Christian faith. We have seen how to men like Rahner, standing in the tradition of much Alexandrian Christianity, the supreme miracle was the incarnation. Christ's death and resurrection can appear, to such an outlook, as logically inevitable but not theologically necessary.

To men like Ebeling and Fuchs it is the ministry of Jesus, not his cross and resurrection, that are at the heart of the gospel. We are meant to believe like the historical Jesus, to 'let him give us the freedom to believe'. The same could be said not only of existentialists like themselves but of many of the older Liberals.

Others erode the meaning of the cross or resurrection into personal experience. Bultmann, as we have seen, has no place for the resurrection as such: 'the Easter message tells me the significance of the cross as saving event for me'. Evely maintains 'It matters little whether Christ rose from the dead ... It is of no importance whether we ourselves will rise on the last day ... The most important resurrection of all is the one that we experience' (*The Gospels Without Myth,* pp. 154, 157).

Throughout history, apocalyptic sects in Christianity have played down both cross and resurrection in favour of heightened eschatological expectation. They have developed millennial descriptions, timetables of the Rapture, and geographies of heaven and hell. No doubt they believe in the cross and resurrection as events in the past, but they have little significance in the here and now: their gaze is unambiguously on the future. They have sacrificed an inaugurated eschatology for a future one.

Others, like Marxsen, have such an emasculated idea of the resurrection that it becomes another way of saying that 'the cause of Jesus goes on'. New life can happen for me now, if I accept the message of Jesus. In a word, the resurrection is to be found only in the kerygma.

All such minimising interpretations either attempt to run away from the cross and resurrection, or else display a significant shift in emphasis from that of the New Testament. We have, in preceding chapters, seen both the centrality of the cross and resurrection in the writing and preaching of the first Christians, and also the variety of implications in these saving events. Most of the views we have been surveying here have been minimising views: in one way or another they have sought to evade that centrality, that historicity and those implications. The words of James Denney long ago are an apt comment on this tendency among certain theologians:

To say that the faith produced the message–that Jesus rose again in the souls of his disciples, in their resurgent faith and love, and that this, and this alone, gave birth to all the stories of the empty tomb and the appearances of the Lord to his own–is to pronounce a purely dogmatic judgment. What underlies it is not historical evidence as the documents enable us to reach it, but an estimate of the situation dictated by a philosophical theory which has discounted the evidence beforehand (*Jesus and the Gospel*, p. 110).

*Factors for theologians to recall*
Theologians are indispensable for the Christian Church. But if the theologian is to fulfil his commission, there are several factors he would do well to remember.

First, he is a sinner, just like everyone else. He occupies no privileged position from which to observe the follies of the world. Therefore he needs to come in repentance and faith to the Christ who died for him and rose again. He needs to come under the spell of that empty cross. He needs to know he is forgiven and accepted in the Beloved. He needs to draw on the power of the risen Christ in his writing and research, in his speech and behaviour. These things are by no means self-evident among many theologians.

Second, he is a member of the Body of Christ, just like everyone else. His position is no more and no less important than that of other Christians. But he is bound up in the corporate life of the church with them. He is not to write in the seclusion of an ivory tower, but in the context of God's believing people whom he has the privilege of helping by means of the gifts God has entrusted to him. His work is not independent of the life of Christianity in his university and country. It is bound to affect it, if he is heard. It is therefore imperative for him to recognise his responsibilities to the body as a whole.

Third, he is a slave. The New Testament writers revelled in that most opprobrious title. They saw themselves as bond-slaves of Jesus Christ. Whatever they did, they did in the name of the Lord Jesus and in order to honour and exalt him and make him known. It is salutary to reflect that they did not do their theology in the comfortable confines of a divinity faculty library, but in prison, on the road, by hastily dictated letters in the middle of the night and in response to pastoral crises. The theology of the New Testament was hammered out in the heat of conflict and persecution, of vital Christian ministry and prayer. The best theologians were the spiritual leaders, the confessors, the evangelists; men who hazarded their lives for the Lord Jesus. It is not so today. Nor should it necessarily be. We cannot court persecution and martyrdom. But we can all be engaged in active Christian ministry. We can be immersed in prayer. We can and should seek to bring others to a faith however good theologians we may be: indeed, the better the theologian, the more sensitive and effective should be his approach to colleagues who are without Christ. But do most modern theologians give the impression that they are bondslaves of Jesus Christ, consumed with the passion to understand him better and make him known? Or are they more anxious to make themselves known by lecturing and writing, whether or not it subserves the glorifying of their Lord?

Fourth, he is a child of his age. His age will speedily go out of date, and so will his own theological positions. It is humbling but necessary to reflect that no theologian has any finality. His novelty today will be old hat tomorrow, and maybe heresy as well. This does not invalidate the theological enterprise. Far from it. It is altogether necessary to interpret the faith afresh to each generation and to various strands within it, cultural, educational and ethnic. But our theology is very ephemeral. And this should make for humility. It certainly does nothing to support the brash and arrogant claims often made by theological writers. The bookshops are cemeteries of un-saleable second-hand theological tomes, which were once the last word from the presses...

Fifth, he is a frontiersman. He is situated on the very horizon of conventional understandings of the faith, and is always seeking deeper understanding, ways ahead which do not negate the past, and the integration of Christian truth with the ever-expanding corpus of human knowledge. He must seek truth wherever it leads him. He must have intellectual freedom. But he is, *ennomos Christou*, under the law to Christ, as Paul put it: he is not a freelance. He must beware the insidious pressures of the *Zeitgeist* to which he is exposed as much as any Christian, and more than most. 'I beseech you' said Oliver Cromwell, 'in the bowels of Jesus Christ, think it possible that you may be mistaken.' The theologian needs to eschew the syncretistic, secularist presuppositions of his non-Christian colleagues. He needs to press on in search for deeper levels of truth in the Christian revelation; sure that it *is* a revelation, rooted in the kerygma, abiding in the living Christ, living under the shadow and the blessing of the cross. Then his theology will be marked by the lineaments of Christ, not by the scepticism of those who are strangers to the Lord. Unfortunately, it is often the case that those who do not claim to be Christians, like Lord Eccles in his book *Half Way to Faith*, are actually nearer to the theology of Christ and the apostles than those who are supposed to be Christian theologians.

Sixth, he must seek simplicity. This is rarely to be found among theologians. They are as difficult to understand as any other technical expert who has not taken the trouble to translate his jargon for the benefit of those who are laymen in his discipline. When one considers that the greatest theologian of all, Jesus himself, clothed his unfathomable truth in the simplest and most memorable of language, often stories, and when one considers that Paul and Peter and John wrote to a constituency which had no biblical encyclopedias or dictionaries and consisted largely of ill-schooled members of the ancient world, it is tragic that so much theological writing these days is practically incomprehensible to the lay ear. If the theologian is to serve the church he must learn to put profound thought into language which is not only easily understood but is graphic and memorable in this television age when competition runs high.

Finally, the theologian is a person, too. He cannot live

cocooned in his theological teaching and writing. He must in most cases be husband and father. He must be teacher. He must be pastor. He must live. And he must die. And unless he lives in the light of the cross and in the power of the resurrection he will make a mess of these responsibilities, however unexceptionable his theology. Theologians are people too. They will all have to face the person who died for them and rose again. Unless their studies and teachings prepare them for this supreme encounter, all will have been in vain. But if they live in the shadow of the empty cross their effect on the Church will be immensely beneficial.

# Chapter
## 12

The Empty Cross and the Preacher

The cross of Christ is a many-splendoured thing. Like a diamond, it has many shining facets. And the preacher is charged with the responsibility of holding those facets up to the gaze of the congregation he serves. He is failing in his responsibility if he always speaks about the same aspect of the cross. It is the wisdom of God and the power of God, and he needs to dig deep into its mystery.

This is all the more necessary because of the great spread of moods and needs in mankind. In any one church there will be represented a whole host of needs, of prejudices, of approaches and of personality types. No preacher can reach them all at any one time with any one presentation of the empty cross. But he ought, in the course of a balanced ministry, to expose them to a variety of interpretations of the empty cross of Christ, for it is indeed the broad-spectrum antidote to the maladies of the human spirit.

In what follows, therefore, I shall attempt to take seven aspects of the passion and show how they complement one another and how they speak to differing needs within the heart of man. They are far from exhaustive, but they may perhaps indicate that our presentation of the cross need never be monochrome.

*Jesus the sufferer*
At some time or other in life, everybody has to suffer. It is universal. Physical suffering, mental suffering, spiritual

suffering affect every household, and embrace every nation and colour and creed. The problem of suffering is the greatest stumbling-block for many to believing in a good and loving God. What has Christianity to say to this most pressing cry of the human heart in anguish 'Why should this happen to me'? God has given us the cross of Christ *non ut dicamus sed ne sileamus*. It is not the final and complete explication of the problem of pain, but it does shed a blazing patch of light upon it. A chapter like Matthew 27, depicting Jesus on his cross, enables us to see a number of positive factors even in the midst of outrageous suffering and injustices.

This chapter displays Jesus supremely as the sufferer. Betrayed by his friend, denied by his right-hand man, deserted by his followers, Jesus was subjected to a mockery of justice. He endured several trials, a corrupt judiciary, the hatred of the priests, the vacillation of the crowds, the weakness of Pilate. Jesus is brought before us as the sufferer par excellence: the agony of the cat-o'-nine-tails, the indignity of stripping and exposure, the unspeakable anguish of crucifixion, the shame of dying naked and exposed to public derision. The St. Matthew Passion indeed! Nor does the evangelist conceal the utter innocence of Jesus (Matt. 27: 4, 12-14, 19, 23, 24). He was not only innocent, he was perfect. Never does the obscenity of innocent suffering affront us so sharply as in the crucifixion of Jesus of Nazareth.

We see suffering these days as an unmitigated evil without redeeming quality. We go to great lengths to avoid it for ourselves and others. But Jesus had dared to call the sufferers blessed (Matt. 5: 11). And he showed it by the manner of his death.

First, the crucifixion of Jesus shows that there can be a fellowship in suffering. God does not torment us and leave us on our own. He may not have given full explanation of pain, but he has come to share it. God is a suffering God. He does not stay immune from the anguish of his creatures. It breaks his heart. The cross of Christ means we can never say to God 'You don't care' or 'You don't understand'. He is in there with us.

There is no suffering we can bear which he does not know from the inside. There is no injustice we can suffer which he does not comprehend from personal experience. And in times of greatest suffering it is not explanation we need so much as companionship. That God has provided for us in the sufferings of Jesus, and in his risen presence.

Second, we see from Calvary that there is a value in suffering. It is not fruitless and in vain. For much of our suffering Hebrews 12: 11 holds true: 'For the moment all suffering seems painful rather than pleasant; later it yields the peaceful fruit of righteousness to those who have been trained by it.' Certainly the cross of Jesus has been incalculably fruitful. He has seen the fruit of the travail of his soul–and been satisfied (Isa. 53: 11). There is always value to be found somewhere in suffering, though it is usually only afterwards that this becomes apparent.

Third, peace is possible in suffering. Even in the paroxysm of death Jesus maintained a peace which enabled him to hand over his spirit to his Father (Matt. 27: 50). His example was not lost on Peter. 'Therefore let those who suffer according to God's will do right and entrust their souls to a faithful Creator' (1 Pet. 4: 19). In the midst of anguish and desolation, there is a rock beneath. God knows what we can bear, and will temper our trials to enable us to endure them in peace, the peace to which Christ showed the way.

Fourth, there may be healing in suffering. In a strange passage in Matthew 8: 17 the evangelist makes a secondary application of the Suffering Servant motif of Isaiah 53 to the healings of Jesus. He maintains that 'He took our infirmities and bore our diseases'. Many who have suffered the horror of being neglected from the earliest days of their life, many who have been seared by the most terrible inner hurts, have found healing at the cross of Jesus when they understood what he endured for them of desolation and rejection.

Fifth, there is a royalty in suffering. Many a watcher at a bedside has realised that. And it was supremely displayed in the way Jesus met his suffering. Matthew goes to considerable lengths in this chapter to underline the royalty of Jesus. He is very much the King of the Jews, even here, at his most vulnerable (27: 11, 17, 22, 29, 37, 40, 42, 43, 54). He wears his pains as a hero wears his medals. So much depends on our attitude. If we resent suffering, struggle against it, we show our worldliness. But if the Messiah of Israel, the Son of Man, could learn obedience through the things that he suffered, why should his followers be exempt? Royalty *in* suffering (not merely after suffering) is a badge of the suffering Father's sons and daughters.

Sixth, there is an outcome to suffering. For the Christian the cross can never be separated from the resurrection. And the resurrection speaks of God's triumph over suffering. Jesus drained the cup of suffering to the dregs, and it failed to poison him, or embitter him, or make him distrust his Father. Accordingly, Good Friday was followed by Easter Day. Suffering, if this world were all, would be inexplicable and unjustifiable. But this world is not all there is. What is sown in tears will be reaped in joy. It was so for Jesus. It will be so for his suffering followers.

The cross empty of Jesus, therefore, has much to say to the sufferer. We should not be surprised when suffering strikes, nor expect to be exempt from it. We should allow it to draw us closer to the crucified Jesus. If we suffer with him we shall also reign with him. No tears fall unnoticed on the ground of Calvary.

*Jesus the substitute*
Many men besides Jesus have suffered unimaginable torment, and yet they have been forgotten. What makes the cross unique? The answer takes us to the heart both of God and of the human predicament.

There is in the Gospels an astonishing concentration on the death of Jesus. Very nearly half the Gospels concern the last few days of his life. Moreover, there is a strange note of compulsion about it: 'the Son of Man must suffer...', 'the Son of Man must go as it has been determined...' St. Luke, for example, when giving his account of the crucifixion of Jesus in chapter 23 of his Gospel makes it very plain that the death of Jesus is no mere miscarriage of justice, no appalling accident, but the fulfilment of biblical prophecy. Verse 33 takes us back to Isaiah 53: 12 'he was numbered with the transgressors'. The next verse is equally rooted in Isaiah 53: 12 'he made intercession for the transgressors'. Psalm 22 is prominent also. 'They divided his garments, casting lots' and the psalmist's cry 'My God, why has thou forsaken me' find obvious fulfilment in the account of the passion. The mockery of verse 35 recalls the psalmist's complaint 'All who see me mock at me, they make mouths at me, they wag their heads: "He committed his cause to the Lord; let him deliver him, let him rescue him, for he delights in him".' Verse 36, on the proffered vinegar, goes back to Ps. 69: 21.

All the evangelists make this same point. Calvary was no accident. The whole of God's progressive revelation pointed that way. Jesus was indeed 'delivered up by the definite plan and foreknowledge of God' (Acts 2: 23).

But why was the death of Jesus so important? Basically because ours is a broken and sinful world. And sin matters to God. He cannot overlook it. His wrath, that is to say his personal though not vindictive reaction against sin, is active. In the end, it is a blessing that this is so. It would be no comfort to us if God pretended that evil did not matter. For then good would not matter either. God would not be a loving Creator but an indifferent fiend. God's holiness and our sin can no more mix than can light and dark, oil and water. Separation between the parties is inevitable (1 John 1: 5). Indeed it is already at work (Eph. 2:1; Rom. 1: 24, 26, 28 with its triple 'But God gave them up'). If it is not dealt with, this separation will be final (John 7: 34; 2 Thess. 1: 9). And physical death will put the final seal on that separation which already exists (John 8: 24; Rom. 6: 23). That, incidentally, is why man feels God to be so far away: our sins separate him from us (Isa. 59: 1, 2). And that is what brought Jesus to Calvary. He came to share, and so to remove our alienation. He came to take man's place as sinner though he was Son of God, in order that we, though sinners, might share his place as sons of God.

But why was it necessary that Christ should die on a cross, that very unJewish means of execution? Here again the answer lies in the long shadow cast by the Old Testament. Deuteronomy 21: 21f makes it plain that anyone exposed to die upon a tree was to be seen as resting under the curse of God. It is, then, of the utmost significance that the New Testament writers do not shrink from repeatedly calling the cross a 'tree' (*xulon*). Luke himself calls it by this evocative name in Acts 5: 30, 10: 39, 13: 29. He is clear that both Peter and Paul understand the cross in this light, and significantly both apostles use it in their writings (1 Pet. 2: 24; Gal. 3: 13). Paul's usage is particularly bold and explicit. He has just said in Galatians 3: 10 that all of us lie under the curse of God for having broken his law: and three verses later he explains with triumphant joy, 'Christ redeemed us from the curse of the law, having become a curse for us–for it is written "Cursed is everyone who hangs upon a tree"'. It is impossible to express this idea of substitution more clearly. Christ bore for us the judgment of his holy Father against sinners. We broke the law of God. He took the place of the lawbreakers.

All through the Bible there had been trailers of this epic event. The Passover Lamb. The Sin Offering. The Suffering Servant. And on Calvary all this was fulfilled. 'Christ died for sins, once and for all, the righteous for the unrighteous, that he might bring us to God' (1 Pet. 3: 18).

No wonder the Fathers of the Church wax lyrical on this subject. 'Who ever paid for the death of another by his own except the Son of God?' mused Tertullian. 'He came for this purpose, that he himself, free from all sin, and altogether holy, should die for sinners' (*de Pudicitia, 22*). 'The Son of God did not disdain to take the flesh of man, and although he was not a sinner, himself to carry the sins of others' exclaimed Cyprian (*On the Goodness of Patience, 6*). Augustine was succinctly to the point when he declared 'If man had not sinned, the Son of Man would not have come.' And what did his death achieve? 'He underwent death to give satisfaction for those who were under judgment' (*Sermon*, 174. 2, *Concerning Flight from the World*, 7. 4).

The Fathers merely expressed what touches ordinary sinners so greatly. Once I see that Christ cared enough for me to die in my place, to bear the alienation that my selfishness had chosen, to endure the curse that rightly fell on me–why, that brings freedom to the enslaved, self-respect to the downtrodden, cleansing to the guilty and the blessing of a conscience free at last. Christ my substitute means that I can look at my sin in all its filth and say, 'Thank God! He has dealt with it. I could not. He did it for my good. He did it in my stead. I can neither contribute to it nor deserve such undreamed of mercy. Because he died, I live. Because he took evil at its flood and endured its full onslaught he has exhausted its powers and can with utter justice offer me forgiveness and reinstatement'. What a message!

Substitution is not the only side of the cross. It is not even the main thrust of New Testament teaching about the cross. But it does speak to troubled consciences as nothing else does. It is a truth, as we have seen in earlier chapters, which is all too easy to abuse. Analogies from lawcourts or the punishment of third parties are particularly to be eschewed. But despite the dangers of misunderstanding and misinterpretation, this mode of understanding Calvary is quite essential. It enables us to see how God could be both just and the justifier to him who believes in Jesus. Stripped of all its legal imagery, it makes one central point which lies at the heart of the atonement. He did for me on Calvary all that was necessary to put me in a right relationship with God. And that is something I could never, never have done without him. It goes further. It makes the even more fundamental point that but for the cross of Christ, God would not be to me what he is. Calvary did not merely show something: the love of God. It achieved something: the reinstatement of sinners. And it cost the Son of God his life, no less.

There is nothing automatic about this reinstatement. We for

our part need to stretch out our hand to the bloodstained hand of the Saviour. Only then is contact made. St. Luke was clear about this in his account of the passion. One dying robber was saved on that terrible Good Friday, so that nobody need despair. But only one was saved, so that nobody could presume. And when a man follows that penitent thief and entrusts himself to the Substitute, then like Bunyan's Pilgrim he can (and frequently does) give three jumps for joy as he sees the burden on his back fall off and disappear into the bottomless pit opened up at the foot of Calvary's cross.

### Jesus the representative

There used to be a good deal of acrimony between theologians who adopted the representative and the substitutionary approaches to the atonement. Ordinary mortals were left puzzled, because it seemed to them that there was little or no difference between a representative and a substitute. However, there clearly is a difference. In a football match a player gets injured. He is not replaced by a representative, but by a substitute. On the other hand, if the shop floor in some industrial firm believes it is being unfairly treated, it will send a representative, not a substitute, to discuss matters with the management. To put it epigrammatically: a substitute is provided outside of me by others, while a representative is provided by me to represent my views.

When we talk about the atonement, the same difference remains. Christ my substitute did in my place what I could never do for myself. But Christ my representative does in me and as my head what I too must do as a Christian. In a word, he heads my destiny, and he enables my discipleship.

Christ is seen as our representative in many places in the New Testament. His death is representative: it is intended to enable us to 'die to sin and to live to righteousness' (1 Pet. 2: 24). His resurrection is representative: he is 'the firstfruits of those who have fallen asleep' (1 Cor. 15: 20). He is the head of the new humanity of which his followers are all members. This theme of the representative of course goes back to his own teaching about the cross. In Mark 8 Jesus astounds his followers first by telling them that he is to go to the cross, and then by assuring them that they too must deny themselves, take up their cross and follow him. Where the head goes, the body must follow.

This accounts for much of the teaching of the New Testament on the solidarity between Jesus and his people. In Jewish thought the Messiah was inconceivable without his *qahal*, his people. They share his sufferings, the Messianic birth-pangs, and also his triumph. We find that unity brought out in a number of ways. Hebrews sees Jesus as the ultimate high priest who represents his people when he goes into the Holy Place, and as the elder brother who is not ashamed to call us 'brothers' (Heb. chs. 7–10 and 2: 11). Paul sees Jesus as the head of the body which comprises the church (Eph. 1:22f; 4: 13–16; 1 Cor. 12; Rom. 12; Col. 1: 17ff). He sees him as the architect of human destiny: we are baptised into his death and resurrection, and that is what constitutes us as Christians (Rom 6: 1ff). He sees Jesus, significantly, as the last Adam, and this is a highly representative term. Both are inclusive personalities: they hold all men within them. The one is the cause of the fall for everyman, the other of rescue for all who will unite with him. For we are, of course, 'in Adam' by nature, whereas we become 'in Christ' only by faith. The comparison and contrast between the first and the last Adam and our solidarity in both, is worked out in several places by Paul (1 Cor. 15: 22f; Phil. 2: 5ff), but nowhere in greater detail than in Romans 5 at the end of the great chapter on justification. It reminds us forcibly that the doctrine of *Christ for me* in the first part of that chapter needs to be held firmly together with *I in Christ* in its latter half.

All these images are designed to stress the indissoluble link between vine and branches, between Christ and disciple. It shines through even in tiny pointers like prepositions. Whereas the New Testament does teach that Christ died in our place (*anti hēmōn*) it asserts much more frequently that he died *huper hēmōn*, that is to say on our behalf and as our representative. But, as we shall see in Chapter 14, the main concern of the biblical writers is to make clear to us that the dying and rising of Jesus must have a counterpart in our own lives. That is the point of 2 Corinthians 4: 7-12; Colossians 3: 1-17; Philippians 3: 10, 11; Galatians 2: 20; 1 Peter 2: 24; 4: 1ff. The old preconversion nature needs to be crucified daily by the followers of the crucified: and it can only be done in the power of his resurrection. The self-centred 'I' needs to be mortified so that the Spirit of Christ can possess my mortal body. The *imago dei*, marred by the Fall, needs gradually to be restored in me by him who is at once both the image of the invisible God and also the ideal man.

It is vital to hold the doctrine of Christ our representative along with that of Christ our substitute. They are totally complementary. The atonement is no cold legal transaction done outside of me by someone totally alien. No, Christ as my kinsman, my brother, sharer of my humanity did for me and without my aid what I could never have done for myself. But also, praise God, he works out his purpose in me as limb of his body and branch of his vine. Christ for me: that is the logic of the substitute. I in Christ: that is the logic of the representative. And both are needed in any balanced doctrine of the atonement.

Has this teaching of Christ our representative, our head, the proper man in whom God himself delights, not got a great deal to say to our contemporary situation? Modern man is agonisingly in quest of destiny. He is aware of lordship over creation, aware, too, of bestiality lurking within. No longer a series of islands off the continent, with each individual self-sufficient, we are all too well aware that the world belongs together, and that we sink or swim together. Human solidarity has become very crucial in a nuclear age, when the act of one man could play Adam and destroy the whole of mankind. To modern, fearful, atomised man this doctrine of Christ the representative, Christ the head of renewed humanity, makes sense and gives hope. We neglect it at our peril.

*Jesus the trail-blazer*
The New Testament writers assert by a variety of images that

Jesus, through his death and resurrection, has blazed a trail into the very presence of God for us to follow. And this is an important and relevant aspect of the atonement which is much neglected by contemporary preachers. Modern men feel lonely and cut off. They frequently feel shut off from the places of decision making and power. 'There is no way out, or round, or through' concluded H.G. Wells in his last book, *Mind at the End of its Tether*. In every trade dispute people are looking for a 'breakthrough'. In the Theatre of the Absurd a major theme was 'No Exit'. And that is how a great many people feel. They cannot get through.

The cross of Jesus shows us that this need not remain the situation. There is a way through.

Paul himself takes up this theme with his marvellous word *prosagōgē*. In Romans 5: 2 he imagines God as an Eastern potentate, and Jesus as heir to the throne. In our own name we should never have a chance of access. But he takes us by the hand, leads us past the guards, through the anterooms, and into the very presence of his Father. Access! What a superb understanding of the empty cross.

But the most startling teaching on this subject comes in Mark's account of the passion. The climax of his story is in 15: 37, as Jesus dies. Then he takes us away from Golgotha back to the city and informs us that the curtain of the temple was ripped in half from top to bottom. Then immediately back to the site of execution, and the centurion's confession 'Truly this man was the Son of God'. And all in three verses! Is this literary incompetence? Or had Mark a deep purpose?

The curtain in the temple was no ordinary one. It was sixty feet high, and very thick. It was designed to keep people out of the Holy of Holies, the place which God inhabited. That curtain spelt the message 'Keep out'.

Only one man ever went inside: the high priest.

Only once a year did this happen: on the Day of Atonement.

Only after making sacrifice for his own sins and the sins of the people could he enter.

Clearly it was a 'No Go' area, a quarantine, to remind one

and all of the holiness of God.

So what is Mark trying to teach us? Surely, that the death of Jesus made a permanent way through to the presence of God. It blazed a trail through the barriers. The quarantine was ended. The 'No Entry' signs were removed. If man had split the curtain, it would have been from the bottom to the top. Mark tells us that it was rent from top to bottom: God's work, no less. And that spells access. There is a way through.

Mark's artistry is not done. He moves to the man in charge of Jesus' execution, and records a strange comment he made. 'Truly this man was the Son of God'. On Roman lips this would express admiration of Jesus as a superb man. But of course Mark means us to see more in the comment than that. It is as if the first Gentile is availing himself of the access provided within the curtain, into God's very presence. For the Christian baptismal confession was precisely this: 'Jesus Christ, Son of God, Saviour'. In that centurion we are meant to see the first Gentile entering into the Holy of Holies, saved by the death of a Jew. The first access into the presence of God is offered to the man who had slain his Son! Abundant access, indeed.

But that is what God is like. That is the astonishing love he shows to those who reject him. That is grace indeed.

And Hebrews 10: 19 picks up this incident and meditates on it. It sees the curtain, keeping us out. And then, as in a twin projector, one picture fades into another. That curtain is replaced by Jesus Christ on the cross. His wounds replace the split in the curtain. This is a new thing in the history of the world. The blood sacrifice had to be offered afresh each year when the high priest had gone in. But the blood of Jesus is described as 'ever fresh', its validity eternal. The high priest of Israel went in with the names of the tribes of Israel on his garments, although they could never follow him. This high priest had blazed a trail within that curtain which his disciples were entitled to follow. They could enter behind their high priest, for the curtain had been torn asunder and the blood was ever fresh.

The implications of this for modern man are immensely

suggestive. It is not true that there is no exit. It is not true that there is no way out or round or through. It is not true that we are imprisoned within inexorable circumstances, or that breakthrough is impossible. Jesus has broken through! I need not remain shut in and cut off. The heavens are not brass, nor the universe silent. In Christ my trail-blazer I can get through. And is not that precisely what modern man needs to hear?

## Jesus the reconciler

This is not a very common category of interpretation in the New Testament, but it is very useful today with the breakdown of relationships in homes, at work, and between classes, colours and nations.

It is important to observe that the Greek word for 'reconcile', *katallassō*, has a very different usage in the New Testament from that in our own day. With us to reconcile means to find a *modus vivendi* between different positions, to discover a compromise solution. Not so with Christ's atonement.

The reconciliation of which the New Testament speaks is entirely God-given. It is something for which we do not bargain: we either receive it or reject it. We do not have some right on our side, some claim to consideration: we were enemies! Such is the stirring emphasis of Romans 5: 10f. 'Enemies... reconciled by his death... saved through his life'. Once again the cross and resurrection are held firmly together as saving events.

This objective aspect to reconciliation in New Testament usage makes the word hard to translate. Perhaps 'remove the barriers to fellowship' might be a more accurate, though cumbersome, rendering. 2 Corinthians 5 bears this out. Sin has produced not one but two barriers between us and God. Each time I sin I build up my wall against God and stand behind it. It is the wall of my rebellion. Each time I sin God sadly has to build up his wall against me. It is the wall of his righteous judgment. The good news of the gospel is that God in his amazing generosity has pulled down his wall, by allowing it to fall on himself! 'All this is from God who *has reconciled* us to himself... In Christ, God was reconciling the world to himself, not counting their trespasses against them' (2 Cor. 5: 18, 19). It was exceedingly costly. 'For our sake God made Jesus to be sin, who knew no sin, so that in him we might become the righteousness of God.' That is one side of the truth. The other, without which it would be neither possible or moral, was this: 'God was in Christ, reconciling the world to himself'. This, then, is what God has done. He offers a completed *katallagē*: 'Christ reconciled us to himself'. In our usage we could not use the word 'reconciled' until the parties were actually at one. When Paul says that 'Christ reconciled us' he is saying that God has, so to speak, pulled down his barrier to fellowship. His judgment against human sin has been exhausted—by bearing it himself. So there is a complete *katallagē* to offer to mankind.

But this does not mean that everybody is automatically reconciled. Far from it. Christians are entrusted by God with the message of this wonderful *katallagē*, and are sent as loyal ambassadors to his rebel subjects, bidding them pull down their barriers to fellowship, just as God has pulled down his. 'We beseech you on behalf of Christ, be reconciled to God' (5: 20). There is no compromise on either side in this reconciliation. Both sides make a clean and decisive act of will, God wills to pay our debts. Man wills to surrender to grace. That is the reconciliation, so costly to him, so free to us, which the empty cross of Jesus proffers to us. In any reconciliation the mediator has to be in complete harmony with both sides. That happened on the cross. There we see God in Christ, reconciling us to himself. There we see God, identifying the sinless Christ with the sins of humanity. On those terms, not of shallow compromise but of profound and double identification, guilty sinners can be reconciled with God.

This is therefore a category of interpreting the achievement of Jesus which is highly relevant to modern man. Reconciliation and arbitration procedures are the order of the day. ACAS, the statutory arbitration agency for industrial disputes, has a permanent and much needed place in British life. People readily understand about the barriers which disputes and intransigence create, and do not find it difficult, on reflection, to realise that God must have a dispute with them. If the preacher, having shown the similarity between the breakdown of relations in the modern and the biblical situation, then produces the unprecedented and utterly astounding generosity of God (the wronged party) to his people on strike, by personally bearing all the pain and responsibility for the breakdown–why, then, the gospel will be seen to be clothed in overalls, totally relevant to the lives and working conditions of ordinary people, and yet soaring in its generosity above anything we are aware of in human conciliation procedures.

But people will not believe this unless the Christian church shares the character of the reconciler. Perhaps that is why Paul uses this word-root for the new bond between Jew and Greek forged at the cross, as the middle wall of partition, separating each from the other and both from God in strict apartheid, comes crashing down (Eph. 2: 13–16). Not all Jews, not all Gentiles could bring themselves to accept this costly reconciliation. But the Church did, and the Church still does. Our community must have no class barriers, no colour barriers, no sex, no economic barriers between those who have been reconciled to God. Unless we demonstrate reconciliation we can never proclaim it credibly. Reconciliation and brotherly love between Christians is both the demonstration to a critical world of the truth of the atonement, and also a powerful agent by which that atonement spreads, for God has committed to us the ministry of reconciliation. That is, if I may be personal for a moment, why I am in the habit of taking 100 or so from the congregation of our church on an annual fortnight's mission to some city which invites us. It is not so much the preaching of reconciliation which wins new converts to the Lord: certainly not that alone. But what touches people is the quality of life and love among the team. They demonstrate, artlessly and unconsciously in their mutual relationships, that reconciliation which is being proclaimed day by day in the pulpit, in the schoolrooms, in the prisons, in the homes and in the streets. And when people see that this doctrine of reconciliation with

God really makes a large and qualitative difference to the lives of those who profess it, then, and not until then, do they begin to want it for themselves.

### Jesus the conqueror

The supreme paradox of Calvary is this: it looks like defeat, but it is victory. The throne of the universe belongs to self-sacrificial love. The cross is the supreme glory of the Servant Messiah. There is no lifting up higher than the gibbet of Calvary. It is there, as St. John insists, that we see the glory and the exaltation of the Saviour.

St. John's account of the passion is full of profound irony. As Jesus is put on trial for his life, who is the real victor? A terrified governor? Roman justice? A squad of soldiers? Religious intransigence? No. Jesus is clearly portrayed as the victor. Pilate could have no power over him had not God given it to him (19: 11). It is God and God's Servant who hold ultimate power. Power is only delegated temporarily to earthly rulers. And so throughout John's account Jesus is portrayed as the victor (19: 14, 15, 19, 21, 22). He even 'dismisses' his spirit (19: 30). Christ is the conqueror on that dark day. The victim is in charge of events.

This aspect of the passion receives much attention in the New Testament, and nowhere more than in the Book of Revelation. Written against a background of anti-religious totalitarianism as strong as anything in Eastern Europe today, it concentrates the reader's gaze on the throne of God. The Lord is reigning. The Lamb with the marks of slaughter on him is in the midst of the throne. No wonder the redeemed break out 'worthy are thou...' (5: 13). For there is no power in the universe greater than self-sacrificing love. Nothing can obliterate it. Nothing has obliterated it.

Therefore, when preaching about the cross and resurrection, the preacher must not lose his dimensions. It is the pledge of final victory. It is the doorway to the last Easter.

Jesus is conqueror over suffering. He shared our pains. He drained the cup of suffering to the dregs. And he rose again. He will finally wipe away every tear from every eye. 'Neither shall there be mourning nor crying nor pain any more, for the former things have passed away' (21: 4).

Jesus is conqueror over opposition. Nobody enjoys it, least of all from his friends. Jesus showed us how to take it without bitterness or retaliation. The Lion of Judah turned out to be the Lamb. He was the non-violent conqueror over violent opposition and flagrant injustices. And he lives, and is with his beleaguered servants as they face the hatred and cruelty of a hard world.

Jesus is conqueror over the world. To each of the Seven Churches he, the conqueror, promises to recognise those who in his strength overcome the world. The pressures deriving from social conformity, political persuasion, economic boycott, financial stringency, and the general climate of a society which leaves God out of account can be overcome. Jesus did it. And he lives on in his followers.

Jesus is conqueror over evil. He faced every combination of wickedness on the cross, and he overcame. He achieved the defeat of every evil power ranged against him by absorbing their venom into himself–and rising triumphant. The cross spelt the defeat of evil in God's world. That tree was for the healing of the nation (22: 2).

Jesus is conqueror over the devil. It is a shallow theology which dismisses Satan as unreal. The great anti-God force is very much in business still. But he is still a defeated foe. He met his match in Christ on Calvary. That victory presaged the final banishment of Satan to the bottomless pit (ch. 20). And it meant that, though hard beset, the followers of Jesus can join the host of heaven, and exult 'Now the salvation and the kingdom of our God and the authority of his Christ have come, for the accuser of our brethren has been thrown down, who accuses them day and night before our God. And they have conquered him by the blood of the Lamb, and by the word of their testimony, for they loved not their lives even unto death' (Rev. 12: 10f).

Jesus is conqueror over death itself. 'Fear not', he says to us,

'I am the first and the last, and the living one. I died, and behold I am alive for evermore, and I hold the keys of death and hades' (1. 18). That resurrection of his on the first Easter Day is the guarantee that 'death shall be no more' (21: 4).

What a conqueror! In his company we can face any problem, any circumstance, with joyful anticipation. Christians should be totally distinctive in this respect. 'In the world you shall have tribulation' he had told them. 'But be of good cheer. I have overcome the world'. If the church is to regain its credibility in society, its members must be helped to see that they have all power in heaven and earth available to them in Jesus Christ their Lord. They must celebrate his victory in every circumstance of life and death. That is both a challenge and a possibility for the disciples of Jesus the conqueror.

*Jesus the magnet*
In John 12: 20ff we meet some Greeks, precursors of millions after them, who were interested in Jesus and wanted to encounter him. It does not appear that they had their request granted at that time. The evangelist wants his readers to see that only after the passion could Gentiles be drawn to the Messiah. 'Unless a grain of wheat falls into the ground and dies, it remains alone' said Jesus. 'But if it dies, it bears much fruit'. He was thinking of his own death, and the fruit it would bear among those Greeks and many like them. '"I, when I am lifted up from the earth, will draw all men to myself". He said this to show by what death he was to die' (12: 32f). His death for their life would be the great magnet to draw people of all types and all ages to himself.

It is fitting to end with this aspect of the cross of Christ, because it is so central. The heart of man hungers for love. The love of God magnetises the human heart. All down the centuries many Christians have followed Abelard and stressed the magnetic power of the cross to evoke love in our cold hearts and bring us to God: while others have followed Anselm in stressing the perfect satisfaction and reparation which that cross displayed. Both are needed. Both are true. The preacher will proclaim the joyful news of a substitute for our sins, a representative forerunner into God's presence, a mighty victor over the power of evil. But he must never forget to allow the sheer grace of Christ crucified and risen to shine out from his preaching. God is love, and men see it when they look at Calvary. Christ draws to himself millions who have no idea about redemption and sacrifice. But if they begin to see that the Lord loved them enough to die for them; if he, risen and ascended bids them come–why, come they will, from all countries and backgrounds, magnetised by that amazing grace. The preacher needs to kneel before that cross of Christ until it calls forth tears of gratitude. Then he must proclaim it as a loving God's supreme gift to sinners, his arms outstretched to block the way to hell and welcome the returning prodigal. The Christian preacher must never get so taken up with a clinical study of the atonement that he cannot in all simplicity marvel with St. Paul that 'the Son of God loved me, and gave himself for me' (Gal. 2: 20).

Thanks be to God for his inexpressible gift!

# Chapter
## 13

The Empty Cross and the Counsellor

'Bread and circuses' was the prescription in the days of the impending collapse of the Roman Empire. The people were kept happy by the provision of material needs for their bodies and entertainment for their minds. One does not need particularly acute insight to perceive that something very similar may be happening in Western society at the end of the twentieth century. The threat of the bomb, the unashamed selfishness, the collapse of values, the disintegration of families, the growth of crime, the prevalence of abortion, the spread of permissiveness, the dependence on drugs by an enormous part of the population: all these factors, together with the sheer pace of life, tend towards a strain in our world which has never been paralleled. It is hardly surprising that an increasing number of people are cracking under the strain. There can be little doubt that this will continue, and that counselling will become a major industry as the fabric of society falls apart.

A great deal of modern counselling is non-directive. It encourages the client to make his or her own decisions in a mature way. The counsellor is anxious to avoid dependence, anxious, too, to avoid putting his or her own ideas into the mind of the client. All this is healthy. But there is, I fancy, another factor at work on the side of non-directional counselling, and from the Christian viewpoint this is less good. Modern counsellors abjure directional counselling because they no longer believe in norms and absolutes. This is the age of relativism run riot. Not only is it too crude, too legalistic to say 'I suggest that you do this: it seems the right course'. But the very word 'right' has ceased to have any absolute meaning. Right and wrong have become matters of convention. They depend on individual choice, the choice of individual or society, like whether you drive on the left or right.

There are some signs that non-directive counselling is less popular than it was. Dr. Spock, whose whole approach to the bringing up of children had been non-directional, has admitted publicly that he was utterly mistaken. But of course by that time the damage was done with millions of parents whose whole approach to bringing up their children had been moulded by Spock. At all events, Christians can never surrender entirely to non-directional counselling. They believe that the absolute has come into the world of the relative, and that his name is Jesus. They believe that there is a difference between right and wrong, however great the social conditioning we have been exposed to, however many allowances need to be made for the failures we have all made. The Christian counsellor will certainly not have a set of ready-made solutions to pastoral problems which will be dispensed like pills to the appropriate patients. He knows that in a fallen world the right thing to do necessarily means to choose the lighter of two shades of grey: choices are rarely black and white. He will be grateful that God does not treat any of us by the rule book, but by confrontation with the truth in human form, Jesus, whose life is the model and inspiration for all Christian discipleship, and whose death and resurrection give the power for change.

Let us look, then, at some of the pastoral situations which occur commonly enough in the experience of any parish priest. I believe that to one and all the empty cross of Jesus is the key.

### The handling of guilt
It was a shallow psychology that sought to explain away guilt. Guilt feelings are a very different matter. They are often not related to real guilt at all. But there is such a thing as real guilt:

being in the wrong with oneself, with others, with society, with God. And people are ravaged by it. It is very common indeed, and any pastor worth his salt is required to handle it frequently.

Two things must be avoided by the counsellor at all costs. One is indifferentism, telling the client that it does not matter: he knows it does matter. That is why he has come for help in the first place. The other is moralising, coming up with ethical remedial measures. These may in due course be needed, but what the client is crying out for is to have the past undone, the slate wiped clean. There is only one place where that is possible: it is face to face with the man of Calvary. As we saw in an earlier chapter, this is where the evangelical power of the cross is so mighty. Once a person sees that although his guilt is red, yet it is possible to be washed whiter than snow, because of what God himself has done about it–then the burden begins to roll from the aching shoulders. If Christ has burdened himself with my guilt, then I need carry it not one moment longer. This is where the value of Paul's juridical understanding of the atonement comes in. Forgiveness is one thing, and it has wonderful personal overtones, and the restoration of relationships. But it is also very important to know that I am judicially acquitted by the highest court in the world, that I can anticipate the eschatalogical judgment now, a judgment which God himself will never reverse: acquitted. Thus the full seriousness of sin is acknowledged. Repentance is no mere remorse for having done a horrible thing: it is repentance towards God (Acts 20: 21), a change of attitude towards the one against whom I rebelled, but who has sacrificed everything in order to secure my return. It brings a release which can be secured in no other way. And it tends to bring a hatred of sins and a love for the Saviour which is the greatest hope and motivation for changed behaviour in the future.

I remember on two occasions people coming to me with long lists of sins that were on their conscience. Neither was morbid: both were seriously burdened. On each occasion I took that list and without looking at it tore it to pieces, showing that this is exactly what God has done with it. Christ took the accusing list of our failures, written in our own hand, and put it out of the way for ever, nailing it to his cross (Col. 2: 14). When that gets through to a person, it changes him. I have often found these words of Isaiah full of comfort for the person burdened by guilt.

Come now, and let us reason together,
  says the Lord:
Though your sins are like scarlet,
  they shall be as white as snow;
though they are red like crimson,
  they shall become like wool. (Isa. 1: 18f).

There are two particular areas of guilt that are frequently met. One is, 'There is someone I can't forgive.' The answer to this, of course, is exposure to Calvary love. By themselves they may indeed be unable to forgive someone who has hurt them deeply. But under the gaze of the dying Saviour that resentment tends to melt away. 'If you forgive men their trespasses, your heavenly Father will also forgive you. But if you do not forgive men their trespasses, neither will your Father forgive your trespasses' (Matt. 6: 14f). There is nothing mean about this. It is simply that if my fist is clenched against someone else, it cannot at the same time be open to receive the gift of God. When I see how much it cost him to forgive me, my resentment against the other party that injured me is seen in its true light, and relinquished for the petty thing it is.

The other commonly felt problem in this area is 'I can never forgive myself for such and such.' Again, the cross of Jesus Christ, and his living, loving welcome, is the way to handle it. Once the person comes to see that whether he can forgive himself is immaterial: it may well depend on the upbringing he has had. But if God Almighty not only forgives him but affirms that his sins are cast into the depths of the sea, and will never be brought to mind, then that is what matters. And when that is fully assimilated, self-forgiveness normally follows.

## The handling of desolation

This is more common than might be supposed. Many people are utterly desolate. Their circumstances, their upbringing maybe, were so awful that they are, by my book, heroes to have retained their sanity. They include people who have been betrayed by their closest friends, or framed for a crime they did not commit, people who have been made the victims of appalling sexual crimes, or have been rejected from birth onward because they were not wanted or were the wrong sex. These things can consign a man or woman to a living hell. In our house we always have a box of tissues available when counselling. More often than not, in our increasingly fractured society, some agonising tale of desolation comes out and leads to uncontrollable weeping.

It is important for the counsellor to stay alongside, and to stay quiet. The client needs room. He or she needs the opportunity to work through the feelings of desolation which are so agonising. It is the height of folly to cry 'Peace, peace' where there is no peace. But when the paroxysm is over, then is the time to point to Calvary. For Jesus knew what it was to be utterly desolate. He tasted alienation and the horror of deep darkness. And for him, too, there had been no word of comfort, only silence as he too cried, 'My God, why?' He knew what it was to experience utter Godforsakenness. And it is this Jesus, no other, who is present in the counselling situation. He is present because he is risen and alive. He is present in the person of the Christian counsellor, whether or not he is recognised by the client. Indeed, the empathy of the counsellor underlines the empathy of the Saviour, and may well lead the client to put his trust in Christ if he has not done so already.

Certainly, I know of nothing else that can cure deep, chronic desolation but the empathy of Christ followed by the coming of his Spirit to fill the void within. The gospel of the empty cross is unfailing medicine for the desolate who will avail themselves of it.

This applies, also, to those who are suffering terrible

torment. They often feel that God must have forsaken them. The counsellor will be on hand to explain that Jesus felt that too, but that nevertheless 'God was in Christ, reconciling'. He will stress the cross of Christ as the surpassing proof of God's identification with suffering humanity, and its outcome in glorious resurrection. In a mysterious way the cross shows that suffering can be redemptive. As we enter positively into our suffering we can in some strange way 'fill up in our flesh what is lacking in Christ's afflictions, for his body's sake, the church' (Col. 1: 24), and can even, perhaps, not be surprised at the fiery trial which assays us, but rather rejoice in so far as we share Christ's sufferings, so that we may rejoice and be glad when his glory is revealed (1 Pet. 4: 13). Once again, it is the empty cross which is held before us as the antidote of suffering.

Martin Hengel puts this well.

The earliest message of the crucified messiah demonstrated the solidarity of the love of God with the unspeakable suffering of those who were tortured... In the person and fate of one man, Jesus of Nazareth, this saving solidarity of God with us is given its historical and physical form. In him, the 'Son of God', God himself took a slave's death on the tree of martyrdom (Phil. 2:8), given up to public shame (Heb. 12: 2), so that in the 'death of God' life might win victory over death (*Crucifixion*, pp. 88f).

*Handling the low self-image*

This is an increasingly common problem. Often it goes back to the earliest days of life when one or other parent had made the child feel unloved, unvalued, acceptable only if certain rules were kept, and so forth. Gradually that person grew up to feel 'I'm no good', even if superficially they happened to become very successful in their job. Crises such as unemployment and retirement, divorce and broken homes, all tend to reinforce this low self-image. It is useless for the counsellor to point to areas where the client *ought* to think highly of himself. The ache lies far deeper than the area of mere achievement. Instead, he needs to be taken to the cross of Jesus. He needs to see how greatly God Almighty valued him, what Christ was prepared to do and to suffer on his behalf.

A great many people these days are denied true, altruistic love. They are 'loved' only when they achieve what is expected of them, only when they keep the rules, whatever the rules may be. 'I love you so long as . . .' is the message that gets through to them, though it is generally unspoken. Robbed of unconditional love, the sunshine in which the plant of human life is meant to grow, is it surprising that they develop a low self-image? They find it almost impossible to conceive of one who loves them irrespective of their deserts, who sacrifices himself for them when they have broken all the rules. But gradually the message gets home, particularly if it is embodied in the approach of the counsellor. 'The Son of God loved me, and gave himself for me' is the cry of one who, for all his achievements, activism and bravado, seems to have had a very low self-image (1 Cor. 15: 9; Eph. 3: 8; 1 Tim. 1: 13-15). But once the unconditional love of the Saviour pierced his defences and melted the icicles of fear in his heart, he began to stand high. He began to see that he was justified, accepted in the Beloved; that neither life nor death nor anything else in all creation could separate him from the love of God in Christ Jesus his Lord. And modern Sauls begin to stand high and lift their drooping heads once it dawns on them that God believes in them. They come to see that they are not nobodies: they are so valuable that the Son of God came to Calvary in their pursuit, that he deigns to enter and inhabit their very lives in the power of his resurrection. To find that the Lord himself loves and values them tremendously brings an enormous sense of a proper self-love. They are sons and daughters of the Almighty, princes and princesses with God. Of what should they be afraid?

A friend of mine led two condemned murderers to Christian faith in a Canadian jail. He visited them, again the next day, and found that this truth was bringing enormous encouragement to one of the men. 'Yeah, man, *God believes in me!*' was the amazed exclamation of this man in whom society emphatically did not believe. It was the beginning of his reclamation.

## The handling of loneliness

Loneliness is one of the most common attitudes to be found anywhere in the world today, but particularly in the West. We have lost the real appreciation of the family, except perhaps the small nuclear family; and it is only a tiny minority of those which offer much fulfilling and lasting companionship. Our individualism turns sour, and loneliness sets in. It is the prime cause of suicides among students in the United States. Very likely it is in Britain as well. It very frequently brings a person for counsel.

What have we to say to such a person? Tell them to get back among their friends? But they have few friends, in all probability, and may well have commitment-anxiety into the bargain. Arrange visits from well-meaning colleagues? But that would not solve inner loneliness. It is all too possible to be lonely in a crowd. Indeed, any human companion suffers from two serious disabilities. In the first place he cannot always be with us. In the second, he might well jettison us if he really knew what we were like. So we have to hide some aspects of our lives, and even the best relationships inevitably disappoint. What, then, can the Christian counsellor advise?

He can show that God offers to meet us in our loneliness in two very specific ways. The incarnation shows that God is like that. He cares. He takes the initiative. His very name is companionship: 'Emmanuel, God is with us'. But even in the days of his flesh the companionship of Jesus was strictly limited, if only because when he was in one place talking with one person he could not be elsewhere to provide companionship for somebody different. But since the passion all is changed. The destruction of the temple of his body resulted in the building of a very different sort of temple for the Spirit to indwell (Eph. 2: 21f). This was made up of men and women from every conceivable background, Jews and Gentiles,

Scythians, barbarians, bond and free. Together they constituted a dwelling place for God, through the Spirit of the risen and ascended Christ. That community is still available. It is the Christian church. Alas, the church is often a very long way from the intention of its Founder in this as in other respects. But millions of believers the world over would bear testimony to the quality of love and welcome, of fellowship and caring they receive in the Christian family. It is part of God's answer to loneliness, particularly when the individual is not merely left to join the worshipping community, but is made part of a small cell group within the church where he or she may experience in ordinary weekday life the fellowship of other members of the Body of Christ, and the cure for loneliness which that provides.

The other way in which Christ comes to meet us in our loneliness is no less rooted in the passion. The Jesus who died and rose comes by his Spirit to indwell the lives of Christians the world over. 'Lo, I am with you always', he says, 'to the close of the age'. It is very moving to see people of all ages and races coming to discover this for themselves, once they surrender to the Crucified. They begin to find an undreamed-of blessing, the presence of his Spirit within them which nothing in all the world can efface or diminish. The end of Romans 8 is seen no longer as a purple passage from an enthusiast, but as sober truth.

As I write I think of a senior officer's widow. She had attended a mission at which I was preaching. She came to see me personally next day, and this led to her conversion. I still have some of the letters she wrote to me in the months that followed. Greatly to her surprise these twin answers to her loneliness began to take shape. She found that the Lord had entered her life as he promised he would (Rev. 3: 20), and that he did in fact stay with her through thick and thin. Here was the friend who stuck closer than a brother. Here was a friend who knew the worst about her and still loved her just the same. And she also found herself drawn to the Christian church. She discovered brothers and sisters in that family which she had entered through Christ. And instead of bemoaning her loneliness she opened her flat to the young singles and marrieds who were plentiful in that church. She was amazed that they wanted to come. Amazed that they were interested in someone forty years their senior. Amazed . . . and thrilled. In the Christ and in the Church she discovered the answer to loneliness.

### Handling defeat

Everybody knows the force of temptation. Everybody knows what it is to fall to it persistently. And Christians are no exception. The church is riddled by habitual sins, so it is not in the least surprising that the Christian counsellor is asked to handle the problem of moral defeat a great deal.

He does so as a fellow sinner. He does so as one himself torn between the 'already' and the 'not yet'. He will have no glib message of 'complete victory' if only certain regulations are kept, if only the client is 'filled with the Holy Spirit' if only he or she receives the 'second blessing'. There is no short cut to holiness. It comes from years of companionship with the Holy One, and by no other path.

Nevertheless the Christian counsellor can do a good deal to clarify the situation, and put the client in the way of receiving the grace of God for holy living. He will pay attention to the devotional life of the one seeking his advice. He will explore areas of unconfessed sin, which effectively insulate us from the power of God. But having done that, it is to the empty cross of Jesus that he will want to take his friend. For it was on that cross that Jesus endured all the assaults of the evil one–and overcame.

Supremely it is the place of victory. And the victor is alive and present with the believer. As we shall see in the next chapter, the cross and resurrection of Jesus need to have a counterpart in our own lives. It is as we die with Christ to the temptations of the world, the flesh and the devil that we rise with him into newness of life, and the *imago dei* in us, so sadly marred, begins to become recognisable once again. This is the message of Romans 6. It is also the message of Colossians 3, and there the apostle applies the principle specifically to the failings of his church members. They must realise that they have died to the old earthly life: accordingly, they must be willing to put to death such failings as fornication, greed, idolatry, malice, slander, filthy talk and the rest. These things are to be discarded, one by one, like soiled clothes into the dirty linen basket of the cross. It will require a deliberate act of will and identification with the Crucified. Then they are to put on a wonderful array of new clothes, made available to them in Christ: kindness, mutual forgiveness, love, the peace which Jesus gives, his word to guide them, his joy to cheer them; and their guiding star will be the pleasing of their Lord. All sides of life are brought under those two simple injunctions: 'put off' . . . 'put on'. These were two headings of early Christian catechesis. It would be well if they figured in our own teaching rather more prominently. The Colossians, Paul reminds them, must depend no longer on legalistic regulations, 'Do not touch this . . . do not taste that'. Have they not died with Christ to all that? They have been raised with Jesus, and must set their minds on things that are above (3:1).

Years ago an old pioneer from the mid-West of America gave a young colleague some good advice on what to do if and when he found a prairie fire bearing down upon him, and there was no escape. He said 'Start another fire downwind at your feet, and when it has consumed the corn or stubble, stand on the burnt ground. The prairie fire will swirl about you, but will have nothing to burn up. You will be safe on the burnt ground.' That is precisely what the Christian in fear of defeat by temptation's wall of fire must do. He must stand on the burnt ground. Calvary is that burnt ground. If he takes his stand there in solidarity with Christ, he cannot be defeated (Gal. 2: 20; Phil. 3: 10, 4: 13).

The only answer for defeated Christians is Christ the conqueror. He can conquer in us because he conquered on the cross (Col. 2: 15). He can conquer in us because he is risen and present. We can know, therefore

the immeasurable greatness of his power in us who believe,

according to the working of his great might which he accomplished in Christ when he raised him from the dead and made him sit at his right hand in the heavenly places, far above all rule and dominion, and above every name which is named not only in this age, but also in that which is to come (Eph.1: 19ff).

History is full of examples which show that this is no pious talk by the apostle. Men like Augustine and John Newton, deeply sunk in vice, became in due time models of Christian living as they put to death their own sinful proclivities, identifying them with Christ crucified, and experienced in their mortal bodies the power of his resurrection. I can only say that in years of counselling others in this area, I have seen particular sins broken at once, and gradual reformation of character follow. However great the temptations to which we are exposed God does not allow us to be tested more than we can endure, and he does provide a way of escape (the way of looking to him for the power we lack) so that we are able to bear them, and to find that we are indeed more than conquerors through him who loved us (1 Cor. 10: 13; Rom. 8: 37).

*Handling death*
Death has replaced sex as the forbidden topic of conversation in polite society. In an age which has learned more than any other about the meaning of life, we still seem unable to contemplate the enigma of death. When we do mention it, we wrap it up. The mortuary is a 'chapel of rest'. The cemetery is a 'garden of repose'. We short-sightedly continue to live as if we did not have to die; we enjoy the present and leave the future to look after itself. And in wealthy and sophisticated America 'morticians endeavour to transform the dead, with lipstick and rouge, into horizontal members of a perennial cocktail party' as Arthur Koestler sardonically observed.

Yet death refuses to be brushed aside. It catches up with all of us. It is therefore not surprising that counselling in the face of death is of paramount importance because it is so widespread a need. Moreover, the very extent of our repression of the thought of death drives it deep underground in our personalities, and there it is apt to fester.

There are two main areas where the counsellor needs to be able to handle death. The first is bereavement, the second fear of dying.

Bereavement is a complicated process, in which shock, anger, bitterness, regret, self-pity and loneliness oscillate. Counselling the bereaved requires the ability to get alongside and stay there, the ability to listen, and to allow the story of the death to be retold time and again. It requires much practical help and caring, the provision of companionship, the suggesting of new directions, and a host of other things. But at its heart, effective counselling of the bereaved at a deep level comes back to the empty cross of Jesus. Here the mourner can see that the Lord himself tasted the bitter fruit of death. Here he drew the poisonous sting of death, sin's guilt and entail. Here he overcame death itself, and demonstrated as much by the resurrection.

It is as the bereaved are drawn back to Good Friday and Easter Day that it becomes possible for them to gain a wider frame of reference for their personal tragedy, and a solid hope to sustain them. This world is not all there is. The dead in Christ are safe with him. 'Since we believe that Jesus died and rose again, even so, through Jesus, God will bring with him those who have fallen asleep' (1 Thess. 4: 14). We have not seen the end of our loved ones. At the last day 'the dead in Christ shall rise first; then we who are left shall be caught up together with them to meet the Lord ... And so we shall always be with the Lord' (v. 7). No wonder he begins this piece of teaching by bidding his readers grieve over their dead (how could they not?) but not as those grieve who have no hope (v. 13). No wonder he ends it with the injunction 'Therefore comfort one another with these words' (v. 18). They are in fact the only words that do any good. All else is shifting sand. But on the solid rock of the death and resurrection of Jesus Christ all man's hope is founded both in this world and the next. That is why people often derive so much comfort from the words of a funeral service. That service enshrines so much teaching from scripture about the one who has gone before through death to fullness of life. And where the head has gone, the members of the body can follow.

Christian confidence in the face of the last enemy has long been one of the most notable aspects of the faith. It has made a great impression on observers down the centuries. It still does. I shall not soon forget a couple whose only daughter had been killed by a careless motorist shortly after she had gone to Oxford to train as an occupational therapist. My friends were full of grief, but also of hope–the living Christ was a great reality in their lives. We had a lunch in my house for the funeral party after the service, and the father spoke to the assembled guests and told what the resurrection faith meant to him and his wife. They were amazed–and so was an agnostic undergraduate who had come to see me, arrived early, and had been brought into the tail-end of the lunch party. Somehow her list of objections to the Christian faith with which she had come armed faded into irrelevance. She had seen something of what the empty cross of Jesus can mean in bereavement, and it was one of the major factors which brought her soon afterwards to faith.

But there is another aspect to counselling in the face of death, no less important because it is generally hidden. Bertrand Russell once said robustly 'I should scorn to shiver with terror at the thought of annihilation' but many men are more like Rousseau: 'He who pretends to face death without fear is a liar.' That fear is very widespread. I remember once meeting a very lively undergraduate in an overseas university during the course of a mission. She was a healthy extrovert, one would have thought, without a care in the world. But in point of fact she was haunted by the fear of death. I showed her how the death of Christ had drawn death's sting. I explained to her about the resurrection of Christ and the difference this can make to those who know him. As a result of this conversation she put her own faith in Christ, and it was not long afterwards that she wrote to me about the tremendous joy of knowing the risen Christ, and the way in which his coming into her life had banished the fear of death. Many could echo the truth of that. I know of nobody but Jesus, crucified and risen, who can bring about that transformation. For the writer to the Hebrews this is one of the main reasons why Jesus came to share our flesh and blood: 'that through death he might destroy him who had the power of death, that is the devil, and deliver all those who through fear of death were subject to lifelong bondage' (2: 14f).

*Handling the occult*
An increasing number of people these days are involving themselves in the occult. As with drink and drugs, people often start out of curiosity but they can all too easily get enmeshed. There must be few parish priests closely in touch with young people (and older people for that matter) who have not been called on to minister the deliverance of Christ to those who have got into occult bondage.

In recent years I have been called on to do a good deal of this sort of ministry–and that in the heart of one of the most sophisticated cities in the world, Oxford, where one might imagine that these things do not happen! We find ourselves being called to help those in haunted houses, those who have been cursed while back in the womb, those on whom death spells have been cast, those involved in astrology, black magic, spiritism and downright Satan worship. Often it began with nothing more serious than attempts at levitation, tea leaf reading, tarot cards or the ouija board. Often, too, these people have sought medical or psychiatric help, but have not found release. That release is to be found in Jesus Christ, and in him alone. He is the victor over Satan and all his devices. His cross bruised the serpent's head. His resurrection sealed for ever his triumph over evil in all its forms. Therefore though one always shrinks from this sort of ministry, knowing it will be intensely demanding, there is no doubt about the ultimate outcome. Christ cannot but be conqueror.

I do not want to write much on this subject. I have explored it in *I Believe in Satan's Downfall.* Suffice it to say that the key to deliverance in these situations is to claim the power of Christ's sacrificial blood upon the cross, and to exalt the risen Lord with praise and prayerful dependence. The sign of the cross itself is mighty. I have been attacked by someone with their bare hands, by another person with a knife and with a broken glass, and I have made the sign of the cross in the air and found that the person has been unable to come beyond it. Another strange thing is that someone under strong occult influence can often not look a Christian in the face: the eyelids become firmly closed over the eyes. But when the person can be induced to look at any representation of the cross he quickly discovers release. For as the living Christ applies to those in bondage the fruits of Calvary, they do in practice discover the freedom which the gospel promises. It derives from no other source.

*Marriage counselling*
Surprising though it may seem, even counselling before marriage takes us back to the empty cross of Jesus. A clergyman will count such interviews among the greatest privileges of his ministry. But he will know very well that the bright-eyed and totally sincere couple before him have a statistically low chance of being together in fifteen years' time. 'Feeling in love' will wear off. Solemn promises may not be strong enough. The bonding of children may not suffice, either. Marriage is an increasingly risky institution if it is lived without self-sacrifice. And the supreme example of self-sacrifice is Christ. What is more, if he is a reality to both partners it will provide a power to keep them together in his love. 'A threefold cord is not quickly broken.'

This lies at the heart of the teaching on marriage in Ephesians 5: 21-32. Paul compares the bond between Christ and the church to that between married partners. The secret of both relationships is submission. Christ submitted. He loved the church, he cherished it. He gave himself for it in order to be its Saviour. The husband is called to that sort of submission:

marriage is no place for the selfish. He must love his wife, cherish her, sacrifice himself for her and protect her. Equally, both the church and the wife must submit. That means pleasing him, respecting him and cleaving to him. And where did this pattern of submission come from? Clearly from Jesus Christ, culminating in his cross.

That is the pattern for the Christian, and more specifically, for Christian couples. But how are they to cope with the pressures towards self-indulgence and separation which are part of the modern air they breathe? Only by availing themselves of the power of the risen Christ. Their prayers together, their worship, their joint honouring of the Lord will prove a marvellous cement in their marriage. The way of self-surrender is in fact the way of self-fulfilment. It is the pattern of dying and rising supremely exemplified on Calvary. But in marriage, too, it is all too true that 'whoever would save his life shall lose it; and whoever loses his life for my sake . . . will save it'. And that is the direction, the direction of the empty cross, in which the counsellor is privileged to point the couple at their marriage. The extent to which they are able to follow it will have enormous repercussions not only for their own marriage but for the whole fabric of society.

*Handling agnosticism*
As a final example of the centrality of the empty cross in the counsellor's armoury I would like to take the matter of the scepticism about spiritual things which corrodes the Western world. It is fashionable to be agnostic about the most important things in life (whether there is a God, whether life has a purpose, whether we live after death), though, curiously, it is not fashionable to be agnostic on matters of less moment. Christians are often content to leave the agnostic or the atheist to his own devices, and are reluctant to embark on discussions in which they might be worsted or might become argumentative. This is a pity, because although agnosticism cannot be dislodged if the atheist account of mankind is correct, yet if the theist account is true, agnosticism can most certainly be

overturned. There is no possible reason why, if God exists, he should not be able to disclose himself to his creatures. And the Christian claim is that this is precisely what he has done. In the incarnation, the cross and resurrection of Jesus of Nazareth God has given a palpable, historical answer to agnosticism. We date our era by it–and so do the agnostics and atheists!

It is the privilege, therefore, of the Christian counsellor to point the enquirer to the one place where the claim is made (and believed by a third of the human race) that God came to our rescue. The events of Christmas, Good Friday and Easter are the focus of that claim. And I find that when men and women are prepared to read the first hand evidence, provided by the New Testament witness, to the person, the death and resurrection of Jesus, they become fascinated. They realise that if this is true, then so much else falls into place: the existence of God, life after death, the purpose of life, the enigma of suffering, the source of values–all this and much more receives a lot of illumination if Jesus Christ did in fact come from God, if he did in fact die on the cross for our sins, and if, risen from the tomb, he is alive today.

I spend a good deal of time counselling those who are very unsure of the truth of these phenomenal claims, as well as they should be. Nobody ought to believe them unless he had looked long and hard at the evidence. But I find that time after time intelligent young men and women are prepared to expose themselves to the evidence provided by the New Testament and see where it leads them. They are not expected to regard it as inspired. They are expected to regard it as an honest attempt to make sense of the greatest person who ever lived, by the circle most closely in touch with him. But what adds a note of challenge as well as possible discovery to the quest is the fact which most of them intuitively if dimly grasp from the outset, that if they are convinced, it is going to mean the end of a brash atheism or an easy-going agnosticism. It is going to lead to discipleship. The question of who runs their life is dependent on the answer they give to that enquiry about Jesus.

Time after time they will come back some months later,

convinced by an honest appraisal of the evidence, and ready at length to commit themselves to Christ. And what is it that has convinced them? Nearly always it is three things. First, the quality of his life coupled with the authority of his claims. Second, the appeal of his cross, and his life given for his enemies. Third, the powerful evidence for his resurrection from the tomb. In other words, it is the person of Jesus, crucified and risen, who shines through the written page and beckons them into discipleship. They have come, as is natural for members of a society so greatly influenced by science, using the inductive method of enquiry. They have begun with the evidence and seen where it leads them. It has led them to the empty cross of Jesus, and there they make the most important discovery of their lives, and thank God for allowing them access to the hard facts of the cross and resurrection on which to base the voyage of discovery. It is the wise counsellor who keeps these central factors before the eyes of serious enquirers. Of such stuff disciples are made.

# Chapter
# 14

## The Empty Cross and the Disciple

'When Jesus calls a man, he bids him come and die.' So wrote Dietrich Bonhoeffer. In his own pilgrimage he had to die to family, to fame, to success, to patriotism. In the end he was led out to suffer physical execution. And as he left his colleagues in the cells he said, 'This is the end–but for me the beginning of life.' He knew that the way of the cross and the way of the resurrection were interlaced for the believer as they were for his Lord.

Jesus had made it very plain from the moment he was acclaimed as 'Messiah' by Peter, that such triumphalist notions needed translating into a different language, the language of suffering and vindication. He had not come to be a political or religious Messiah. He had come to give his life for others, and to take it again. He taught the amazed disciples that 'the Son of man must suffer many things, and be rejected by the elders and the chief priests and the scribes, and be killed, and after three days rise again. And he said this plainly. And Peter took him and began to rebuke him. But turning and seeing his disciples he rebuked Peter and said, "Get behind me Satan! For you are not on the side of God but of men"' (Mark 8: 31f). Peter had a great shock when he learnt that his beloved Master was not going to bring in the kingdom by storm but was going to die. He was given another shock when Jesus continued, and showed that the cross was not going to be unique to the Master but was the way of life and death for the disciple too. 'If any man would come after me, let him deny himself and take up his cross and follow me. For whoever would save his life will lose it; and whoever loses his life for my sake and the gospel's will save it.'

This teaching was reinforced on other occasions. Once when Jesus had been teaching the free gift of entry into the kingdom, he turned and began to spell out the cost of discipleship. Among the aspects of that cost the most far-reaching was this: 'Whoever does not bear his own cross and come after me, cannot be my disciple' (Luke 14: 27). Time and again he taught the lesson of dying and rising as a pattern for the disciple as well as for himself. It was the pruned vine which brought forth fruit, the grain of wheat that fell into the ground and died which produced a crop.

*Following Christ's self-denying life*
Jesus was offering something radically new in leadership. He was providing a pattern for self-giving. He who washed his disciples' feet, was introducing them to a quite new dimension of thought and action. Relentlessly he pressed home the lesson of greatness measured in terms of service. 'Do you know what I have done to you? You call me Teacher and Lord; and you are right, for so I am. If I then, your Lord and Teacher, have washed your feet, you also ought to wash one another's feet. For I have given you an example, that you also should do as I have done to you. Truly, truly, I say to you, a servant is not greater than his master; nor is he who is sent greater than he who sent him. If you know these things, blessed are you if you do them' (John 13: 12-17). What a contrast to secular ideals of leadership! 'The kings of the Gentiles exercise lordship over them ... but not so with you; rather let the greatest among you become the youngest, and the leader as one who serves' (Luke 22: 25, 26).

Painful and revolutionary though this teaching was, it began to take root in the hearts and lives of the disciples. They learnt to give and not to count the cost. They learnt to serve one another in love. They learnt to deny themselves and follow Jesus; so much so that their lives reminded people of him (Acts

11: 26; 4: 13). Peter himself came to terms with this teaching, after what struggle we can only imagine. In his first Letter, we find him constantly advocating the way of self-denial, of suffering service: 'Servants, be submissive to your masters with all respect, not only to the kind and gentle but also to the overbearing... If you do right and suffer for it, you have God's approval... Likewise you wives be submissive... Likewise you husbands, live considerately with your wives... For it is better to suffer for doing right, if that should be the will of God...' and so on. John, the disciple who wanted to call down fire upon the Samaritan village that was reluctant to give Jesus and his followers accommodation, becomes the supreme advocate of love: 'Beloved, let us love one another, for love is of God... He who does not love abides in death... He laid down his life for us, and we ought to lay down our lives for the brethren' (1 John 4: 7; 3: 14, 16).

There can be no doubt that this gentleness of spirit, this willingness to serve rather than to be served, made a profound impression on the tough Roman world. They could not understand it. Christians like Ignatius at the turn of the first century went with joy–almost enthusiasm–to their martyrdom. Clement of Alexandria tells how the man whose denunciation of the apostle James had led to his arrest by Herod Agrippa, was so impressed by his testimony to Christ in court that he himself became a believer, and was led to execution along with James. 'On the way he asked James for forgiveness. And James looked at him for a moment and said "Peace be to you" and kissed him. So both were beheaded at the same time' (Eusebius, *H.E.* 2.8).

The self-sacrifice of the Christians under persecution has long been a powerful witness to the reality of their faith. In A.D. 203 a 22-year-old African girl, Perpetua, with a baby at her breast, was martyred for her faith at Carthage. Before her death she managed to write down her impressions. Her father had tried everything to make her recant. First he was rough with her, but found that distressed her to no effect. Then he turned to appeals: his grey hairs, her mother, and her own tiny son who would not be able to survive her. All of these were thrown into the scale to induce her to change her mind and deny Christ. But she knew the pattern of denying herself, taking up the cross, and following Christ. She went to her death with dignity and courage. Twenty-five years earlier a Gallic slave girl, Blandina, showed the same spirit of unimaginable courage under persecution. She was a recent convert and totally dedicated to Christ. Quietly, she maintained, 'I am a Christian woman, and nothing wicked happens among us.' She was forced to watch the murder of her Christian companions, then was heated on a gridiron, thrown to wild beasts in the arena, and finally impaled on a stake. Totally in Christian character, she died praying for her persecutors with love and fervency: her death nerved a 15-year-old lad, Ponticus, to follow her example. (Eusebius, *H.E.* 5. 1-61). There was no trace of triumphalism in early Christianity, nor is there today where the faith is strong and pure. There is a sober recognition that to follow Christ can be exceedingly costly, even to death; but death itself cannot separate the believer from Christ, and therefore the cause grows. 'The oftener we are mowed down by you', wrote Tertullian, 'the more we grow in number. The blood of Christians is seed' (*Apologeticus*, 50). He spoke from much personal experience.

This pattern of willingly undertaking the cross as the path to union with Christ and resurrection with him has continued down the centuries. The annals of the faith are red with the blood of martyrs who have not counted their lives dear to themselves. In the twentieth century probably more Christians have been martyred for their Lord than in all the other nineteen centuries put together, and still the blood of the martyrs is seed. Still the way of self-sacrifice rather than self-assertion is seen to be the Jesus way, and remains the only hope for the world. What other way can break the demonic forces at work in South Africa or Russia? Without this self-giving spirit of Jesus and his people, the lust for power becomes all-consuming, the exercise of power becomes selfish, and when arrogance induces revolution, yesterday's oppressed become tomorrow's oppressors. Heroes like Martin Luther King and Alexander Solzhenitsyn, Festo Kivengere, Richard Wurmbrand and Janani Luwum abundantly validate the Jesus way of life through death, and victory for love through the endurance of evil.

*Sharing Christ's dying and rising life*
But there is an even more profound aspect to the dying and rising theme in the New Testament. We are called to share in the death and resurrection of Christ. There is, if you like, a cross and a throne in every life. Either Christ is still on the cross and our own self is on the throne; or else he is enthroned, and our selfish nature is put in the place of death. This principle is often associated with the suffering for Christ which we have just been considering. But it is even more radical. It goes to the heart of man's motivation and ambition. And it is expected of us all.

So Paul can write of baptism in these profound terms: 'All of us who have been baptised into Christ Jesus were baptised into his death. We were buried therefore with him by baptism into death, so that as Christ was raised from the dead by the glory of the Father, we too might walk in newness of life' (Rom. 6: 3, 4). In other words, the baptismal life is one of dying and rising. This is no prerogative of a select circle of high-powered Christians, but it is the mark of being a Christian at all. The death and resurrection of Jesus lie at the heart of the Christian life. Our baptism was a union with Jesus both in death and resurrection. Paul continues: 'For if we have been united with him in a death like his, we shall certainly be united with him in a resurrection like his'. The dying is proleptic: it will only be finalised when we die physically. Equally, the rising to newness of life is also proleptic. The best is still to be–at the last day, when we shall be united with him in a resurrection like his. But in the meantime, dying and rising is the secret of holy living.

Paul's teaching in the verses that follow can conveniently be summarised under three imperatives. Know... reckon... yield. We know, says Paul, 'that our old self was crucified with him, so that the sinful body might be destroyed, and we might no longer be enslaved to sin' (v. 6). Difficult teaching, but the thrust of it is not too obscure. He is saying that the death and resurrection of Jesus have a representative capacity. When Christ died on that cross, it was the death-knell of selfish humanity. It was the supreme victory over self-centredness in all its forms. It was the destruction of the sin-infected 'self' which plagues us all. Christians are meant to know that a cosmic battle was won on that cross. The last Adam succeeded where the first Adam fell. His victory involves us all.

It is one thing to know this. It is quite another to consider or 'reckon on' it (v. 11). If I do not reckon on it, I shall not enjoy the victory he has made possible. I need to face the pressures arising from my base desires, confident that Christ has dealt them their death blow on Calvary, and that I need not succumb to them unless I wish to. I have therefore to consider myself dead to the temptations which appeal to the self-life. There is no make-believe about this. I am not pretending that the attractions of sin are unattractive. It is simply that I am called to face the temptation head-on and say, 'You have no rights over me, and you shall have no power over me. Christ defeated you on Calvary. I consider myself dead to your blandishments. I am now living for the Lord, and in the power of his cross and resurrection I confront you.'

Third, I must yield (v. 13). There is no need for sin to go on reigning in my life, though it will never be totally expelled this side of the grave. There is no reason why I should be forced, Paul says, against my will, to obey sin's passions. Do not, he urges, go on yielding your members as instruments for sin to use: but make an act of unconditional surrender to God as those he has rescued from death. And put your members at his disposal. Of course, that attitude of surrender will need daily and hourly to be renewed. But without the radical act of abnegation, without the unconditional surrender, the hourly and daily surrender will never happen. If, however, that total surrender to Christ is my aim and direction, then sin will not hold tyranny in my life. I shall never be quite free of it in this life. But it will no longer dominate; and progressively its forces will be driven back as I abide in Christ, and in his dying and rising life.

And all this is the outworking of the baptismal life! 'The baptism of Christ can never be repeated' wrote Bonhoeffer.

> By baptism we were made partakers in the death of Christ. Through our baptismal death we have been condemned to death and have died just as Christ died once for all. There can be no repetition of his sacrifice. Therefore the baptised person dies in Christ once and for all. Now he is dead. The daily dying of the Christian life is merely the consequence of the one baptismal death, just as the tree dies after its roots have been cut away... From now on the baptised can know themselves only as dead men, in whom everything necessary for salvation has already been accomplished. The baptised live, not by a literal repetition of this death, but by a constant renewal of their faith in the death of Christ as his act of grace in us. The source of their faith lies in the once-for-allness of Christ's death, which they have experienced in their baptism (*The Cost of Discipleship*, p. 210).

*Living out this dying and rising principle*
How is this dying and rising life to be worked out? It covers all aspects of our lives. Let Bonhoeffer furnish an example.

> 'I shall have no right' he wrote to Niebuhr, 'to participate in the reconstruction of Christian life in Germany after the war if I do not share the trials of this time with my people. Christians in Germany will face the terrible alternative of either willing the defeat of their nation in order that Christian civilisation may survive, or willing the victory of their nation and thereby destroying our civilisation. I know which of these alternatives I must choose.'

And choose he did. Great patriot though he was, he knew his patriotism had to die if Christ's resurrection life was to be seen in his beloved land. That courageous decision cost him his life, as he knew it would. But the power of the resurrection is manifest through his example and writings.

Archbishop Janani Luwum was equally aware of the supremacy of his Christian allegiance over his personal safety. Clerics do not generally take on the leaders of their country. They are often mute in the face of injustice. They act as if they were part of the establishment. But Luwum told General Amin repeatedly that his reign of terror was evil in the sight of God; and he paid the penalty for his integrity with his life. He, too, knew this would happen. He quite deliberately chose death rather than his natural desire for safety, and to allow the Lord to rise through his death. That happened very speedily and very wonderfully. The authorities would not release his body for the funeral. It took place round an empty grave in the grounds of the Namirembe cathedral. And the retired Archbishop, Erica Sabiti, preached to scores of thousands, who defied the government's ban in order to be present, on the text. 'He is not here: he is risen.'

That principle can be applied across the board. We are to die to all claims of the self-indulgent life. Ambition, love of ease and comfort, wealth, employment, marriage, family, self-will must all be offered to Jesus. We must ask him to nail to the cross all that is unworthy of him, so that his life can be seen in our mortal bodies. For the disciple, as for the Lord, the crown is unattainable without the cross.

In Colossians Paul makes further use of this dying and rising motif.

> Put to death, therefore, what is earthly in you: fornication, impurity, passion, evil desires, and covetousness, which is idolatry... Put them all away: anger, wrath, malice, slander, and foul talk from your mouth. Do not lie to one another, seeing you have put off the old nature with its practices, and have put on the new nature, which is being renewed in knowledge after the image of the creator (Col. 3: 5ff).

As the old nature is done to death, as 'I am crucified with Christ' (Gal. 2: 20), so the image of God is renewed in his fallen creatures, by the agency of the Holy Spirit within him. But there is a corresponding duty to this 'putting to death'. 'If you, then, have been raised with Christ, seek the things that are above, where Christ is' (3: 1). The risen life with Christ needs to be actively pursued. And it is very practical.

It means self-giving for husbands and wives, for children and parents, for masters and servants. It means forgiving others, putting up with difficult people, cultivating kindness and meekness, doing one's job wholeheartedly to please Christ, not just to get by. It means prayerfulness, a life dominated by the peace of Christ and informed by the word of Christ, a life of joy in all circumstances, and of seeking to please Christ in everything. Those are the ways in which the rest of Colossians 3 spells out the risen life of Jesus which longs to see growing in his followers. The dying and the rising are inextricable. 'We always carry in the body the dying of the Lord Jesus,' wrote Paul, 'so that the life of Jesus may also be manifested in our bodies. For while we live we are always being given up to death for Jesus' sake, so that the life of Jesus may be manifested in our mortal flesh. So death is at work in us, but life in you' (2 Cor. 4: 10ff). Much the same thought is to be found in 1 Peter 4: 1ff. Dying and rising is the heart of the Christian life.

And what does Christ offer the disciple who is prepared to come and die with him? He offers a daily walk in newness of life (Rom. 6: 4). He offers the certainty of future resurrection with him (6: 5). He offers emancipation from bondage to evil habit (6: 7). He offers the manifest indwelling of the risen Christ as the believer accepts crucifixion with him (Ga. 2: 20). He offers the inalienable promise of his presence throughout all imaginable trials (Rom. 8: 36-9). He offers the joy of his risen life (Acts 13: 52). He offers his moral power (Rom. 8: 11). He offers membership of a society which will always suffer hardships, but against which the gates of hell shall not ultimately prevail (Matt. 16: 18).

*Avoiding the dying and the rising life*
The dying and rising life which is at the heart of discipleship is very difficult. It is hardly surprising therefore that there have been constant efforts throughout human history to find some other way for the church to live.

The most common over the centuries has been simply deliberate forgetfulness. The church has chosen to take no notice of what Jesus said about taking up the cross and following him. It has taken up an establishment role and lived in the shadow of that. The church, like Rome in the Middle Ages, has so often either become a political power, wielding all the weapons of the world in establishing its own position, or else a prop of the existing establishment as was the Orthodox Church in Russia before the Revolution. Moreover, there has been a singularly complete amnesia about Jesus' teaching that Christian leadership is to be marked by the pattern of the Servant. Instead, it has almost universally adopted the mode and manners of autocratic secular leadership. The dying and rising life has not been seen. The beauty of Jesus has, accordingly, not been portrayed.

From time to time anther denial of the dying and rising life emerges. This is one of the many forms of triumphalism. The crown is separated from the cross. Success is lionised, and the path of suffering despised or repudiated. This seems to have been the situation in first-century Corinth. The Corinthians were already full, had already entered on their reign, while the poor apostles remained the offscourings of the pot, suffering contumely and persecution throughout the Roman world (1 Cor. 4: 8-13). Perhaps that is why in those letters Paul gives such emphasis to the cross, and wears his sufferings and hardships like medals (1 Cor. 2: 2; 2 Cor. 11: 21f). Triumphalism is a perennial danger for the church. When it overcomes the morbid, lack-lustre image of the kill-joy, it tends to swing to the other extreme and claim for now what belongs to heaven. Healing, prosperity, victorious living, church growth are all suffused in the glow of the resurrection, while the shadow of the cross is carefully expunged.

As I write, one such triumphalist movement is sweeping both America and South Africa. It is a type of prosperity doctrine. If you have faith–and join their membership–you can be assured of God's prosperity, his healing, his victory and his success in your life. 'Anything you ask' is the slogan of these soldiers of the resurrection who have forgotten that they follow a crucified Jesus, and that they are bidden to 'share in suffering as a good soldier of Jesus Christ' (2 Tim. 2: 3). Forgetting that they remain 'in Adam' as well as 'in Christ' they teach that their spirit is perfect, and that temptation comes to them only through a fallen soul and body. 'The spiritual nature of man is a fallen nature. A satanic nature. No man can change his own nature. *But God can!*' writes Kenneth E. Hagin, leader of the Rhema Church. 'At your new birth something went on *inside* you. Instantaneously! Out from you went that old satanic nature. And into you came the very life and nature of God. God created you a brand new creature. A new creation. The man on the inside–the real you, which is a spirit man–*has already* become a new man in Christ' (*Faith Food*, January 3rd, 1979).

There is truth there, but unbalanced truth. The man on the inside is both 'in Adam' and 'in Christ'. The old nature has, alas, not gone out: nor will it before we see him as he is. Then, and not till then, shall we be like him (1 John 3: 2). In the meantime, there is a constant battle, as passages like Galatians 5 and Romans 7 (not to mention our own experience!) make plain. We are far from perfect in our present state. But we are on the winning side. And dying and rising with Christ daily is the only way to grow in holiness: not by repeatedly 'confessing' as Hagin calls it, that we have already arrived. Here are some of the 'confessions' he urges on his followers:

'I' bring my body into subjection to 'me'.
I refuse to walk as mere men. I am changed. I will walk as a spiritual man. 'I' (the man on the inside) will dominate my being.
Now I have what God says I have. Now!

The Name of Jesus belongs to me. Whatever I demand in the Name of Jesus, he will do it.
I will release the Love nature within me.
I am a Love person. I am of good cheer.

The trouble I have with such statements is that they give us only one half of the picture. They are resurrection oriented, and they do not touch the sacrifice, the pain, the cross-bearing of the Christian life. They are not conducive to repentance. There is in them more than a touch of auto-suggestion. There is a lot of similarity to the quite secular 'power of positive thinking' advocated by Norman Vincent Peale.

Such prayers are poles apart from the 'Jesus Prayer' of the Orthodox Church. That too is meant to be repeated many times, in relaxation, faith and humility. 'Lord Jesus Christ, have mercy on me a sinner.' Such a prayer combines the humility of the sinner with the sacrifice of 'Jesus' (Yahweh saves) and deep trust in the One who is 'Lord'. It has a balance not to be found in Rhema confessions of 'fullness now'. That way lay the Gnosticism of the early centuries. No amount of effort can identify it with the full-orbed incarnation, crucifixion and resurrection theology of Catholic Christianity.

*Misunderstanding the dying and rising life*
There is another very popular misunderstanding of the dying and rising life of the disciple. It is found in many of the holiness movements of evangelical Christianity. I have heard it taught at the Keswick Convention. It has been given widespread circulation through the writings of the saintly Chinaman, Watchman Nee.

It is all based on Romans 6, and assumes that whereas chapters 1-5 were concerned with justification, how a person gets into Christ, chapters 6ff are all about sanctification, how a person lives in Christ. The commands to 'know . . . reckon . . . yield' are the gateway to sanctification, to a different quality of Christian life, entered by faith. We are told that as we believed for our justification, so we must believe for our santification; that as we accept in faith that Christ took our sins to the cross, so we must accept that he took our sinful nature to the cross as well. 'The self you loathe is on the cross with Christ. And he that is dead is freed from sin [v. 7]. This is the Gospel for Christians' (Watchman Nee, *The Normal Christian Life*, p. 38). The inference is then drawn that our sinful nature has been given its death blow through the cross, and that Christians can by faith live 'the overcoming life', something perilously near sinless perfection. And it comes by virtue of a deep spiritual experience, a 'second blessing'.

But is this what St. Paul is teaching by his command to 'know... reckon... yield'? Surely not. In the first place, Paul does not use *dikaioō*, the word for 'justify', exclusively for anticipating God's final verdict through Christ: he also uses the *dikaios* root for practical holy living (e.g. Rom. 6: 13, 18; Eph: 5: 9). Equally, the *hagiazō* root is not exclusively used for what Reformation theology has called 'sanctification', that is to say the working out of the divine life in the believer. It is also used of our initial entry into Christ (Eph. 5: 26ff), or to describe Christians generally (1 Cor. 1: 2) and even of those who are not themselves Christians but are linked by kinship (7: 14). It is therefore by no means a word reserved for advanced Christian holiness. It is simply a cultic, possession word in contrast to the 'justification' root, which is a forensic, position word. Both words share the tension of New Testament eschatology, the 'already' and the 'not yet'.

Words apart, does Romans 6 teach the continuously victorious life of Christians, and entered by faith? No, it does not. It is talking about the implications of baptism, the most basic Christian experience. It is speaking of something that should apply to all Christians, not to a group of Christians who claim deep faith and a second experience.

Baptism is the sacrament of Christian initiation, of entering into union with Christ through his death and resurrection (6: 1-5). It is this union with Christ which renders deliberate sinning as a policy unthinkable. Dr. John Stott, in his *Men Made New,* is properly critical of the second blessing theology based on Romans 6, and argues that 'dying to sin' means only that the Christian is involved as a beneficiary in Christ's bearing of sin's penalty on the cross. 'We have died to sin in the sense that in Christ we have borne its penalty. Consequently our old life has finished: a new life has begun' (p. 43). But that surely underestimates the tension in Paul's words. He is not simply asserting that 'by faith and baptism we were united to Christ in his death'. The death he died to sin became our death; its benefits were transferred to us. So, having died to sin with Christ, we have been justified from our sin (v. 7) and having risen with Christ we are alive, justified, to God (v. 8, 9). Our old life finished with the death it deserved. Our new life began with a resurrection' (*op. cit.*, p. 48). True, but inadequate. It evades the eschatological tension of the Christian in this world. It imports into the text the notions of 'penalty' and 'benefits'. It sees the death of Christ too much as substitute and not enough as representative.

For Christ is both representative and substitute, as we saw in chapter 12. I am indeed 'in Christ' (Paul's most favoured description of what it means to be a Christian), but I am also, alas, in Adam, incorporate in the fallen humanity, prone to weakness and death, of which he was the progenitor. And in Adam I stay throughout my life. There is no way I can escape the entail of his mortality and sinfulness. But I am also, thank God, in Christ. Incorporate in him I share in the sonship, the perfect standing, the power and the victory of which he is the progenitor. I am a citizen of two worlds, a child in two families, and I always remain such as long as I live.

There is no stage in this life when I shall be able to say 'I have arrived'. Always there is the tension between the two backgrounds I inherit, between the two natures I share, between the life of the 'old man' and the 'new man'. Both remain active. My baptism signifies to me both my election (proceeding from God's grace, grounded in Christ's atonement, incorporating me in his body) and my calling (to become empirically in my behaviour what I already am in Christ). Paul is saying that far from being free to sin as we please after becoming Christians, we are free from the obligation to sin, because we belong to the crucified and risen Saviour, Jesus Christ.

Paul is not teaching sinless perfection here, let alone a second blessing. The imperative of verse 11 ('reckon yourselves dead to sin and alive to God') is grounded in the indicative of verse 6 ('we know that our old self was crucified with him so that ... we might no longer be enslaved to sin'). We are free from sin, but not sinless. In driving Christ to the cross sin overreached itself, overplayed its hand, and lost the war (cf. 1 Cor. 2: 8). And so the Christian's relation to sin has been decisively broken by the death of Jesus. We are no longer under its tyranny.

Indeed, one can look at chapters 5-8 of Romans as four aspects of what it means to be put in the right with God. We find four tyrannical giants whose prisons have suffered earthquake through the death of Christ. To be justified means to be freed from the clutches of the Giant Wrath (ch. 5), the Ogre Sin (ch. 6), the Tyrant Law (ch. 7) and the Despot Death (ch. 8). In each case we are taken from the grasp of these enemies *and released so that we can fight them*! Nevertheless the tension remains. Freed from Wrath, we still have to face the consequences of our actions. Freed from Sin, we can (and still do) fail every day. Freed from Law we remain under the law to Christ (1 Cor. 9: 21). Freed from Death, we still have to die. Christian deliverance is inaugurated in Christ *now*: it will be consummated in Christ *then*.

So St. Paul is not in these crucial doctrinal chapters talking about second blessings, sinless perfection and the like. But neither must we water his teaching down into relativism. He is being totally realistic. He is talking about rescue from our pre-conversion plight. He is not thinking moralistically of sin as wrongdoing: but dynamically of sin as a power from whose bondage we have been liberated in order that we might fight it. There is no contradiction between verse 6 ('our old self was crucified with him') and verse 12 ('do not let sin reign in your mortal bodies'). There is no mixture of pietism and activism here, as in so much Christian teaching on 'victory'. It is plain common sense. You cannot enter the lists against sin's army until you have been set free from sin's dungeon. That Christ has done! We share his life: we are called to wear his colours in the fight.

We have only one 'Lord' – more is impossible. We did have Sin as our Lord, but now we acknowledge Christ as our Lord. Sin therefore shall no longer – can no longer – be boss (*kurieusei,* v. 14) in our lives. It is not removed from us, but it is dethroned in us. It is as if we have deserted from the ranks of the rebel duke and rallied to the standard of the heir to the throne. Now we recognise one legitimate authority, his: the orders of our old captain leave us cold. But this does not mean that we may not at times fall in with enemy intentions, and it certainly does not mean we cannot be wounded by enemy attacks.

That this is the meaning of Romans 6 is backed up by the two closing analogies, that of a change of master and a change of marriage partner. The slave of sin has exchanged one set of obligations and ties for another, since the day of his emancipation. It is the same with the marriage partner. When emancipated (through death) the partner says goodbye to one set of ties as he or she forges a new set. It is a contrast of two states, before and after deliverance. But it is also an emphatic pointer to a new way of life befitting the change. As slaves of Christ, that must be righteous behaviour (6: 18): as brides of Christ, that must be 'godly offspring' (7: 4) in contrast to the old days when the offspring of man and Law was Death.

There will always be distortions of Christian doctrine. We have looked at some of them in this chapter as they bear on the discipleship of the Christian. But whether they come from antinomian, triumphalist, legalist or perfectionist sources, the antidote is the same. It lies in the dying and rising of Jesus, which is both the pattern and the power for the disciple to follow his Lord. This and this alone is authentic Christianity. Our baptism indicates its centrality. Whatever our station in life, our situation, our nationality, it remains true that the disciple must be as his Lord. 'If anyone will come after me, let him deny himself and take up his cross and follow me. For whoever would save his life shall lose it, and whoever loses his life for my sake and the gospel's will save it' (Mark 8: 34ff). Only a Christian life stamped with that hallmark is genuine.

# Chapter
# 15

The Empty Cross and the Destiny of Man

In 1974 Professor Robert Heilbroner, one of the leading
economists in the U.S.A., published his book *An Enquiry into
the Human Prospect*. His opening sentence concluded with the
question, 'Is there a hope for man?' His conclusion was that in
the light of the enormous problems facing mankind and our
extreme reluctance to make the necessary changes in our way
of life to face them, there could be little hope. The book had a
great deal of influence, and created a sharp division of opinion
in the Western World. In 1980 it was republished, updated and
reconsidered. The main thesis remains unaltered. Heilbroner
takes no joy in predicting the collapse of industrial civilisation.
'Am I not a child and beneficiary of that civilisation? Can I
discuss its death-throes unaware that I am talking about my
own decease?' (p. 174). A similar conclusion is reached by
Ronald Higgins in his book *The Seventh Enemy*, which has
also had an enormous influence. Behind six appalling threats
which overhang mankind there is a seventh: the combination
of short term political pragmatism and personal inertia, arising
from the conviction that the problems are too overwhelming,
and nothing can be done. Men like Heilbroner and Higgins are
not doom-watchers. They are very acute and widely read. They
are trying to read the signs of the time. And what they read is
not comforting. Is there a future for *homo sapiens*?

*The basis for Christian optimism*
The Christian, like the economist and political theorist, is

deeply concerned about the future of man and his world. And from the earliest days, when believers dated martyrdoms *regnante Jesu Christo*, 'in the reign of Jesus Christ' and Augustine wrote his *City of God* while the civilised world was crumbling round his ears, Christians have been optimistic about the ultimate future. Why? Because of the empty cross of Jesus.

It is rather like a game of chess. At some time in the game there comes a move which is absolutely critical and determinative of the outcome. The game goes on, but struggle as he may, one player is doomed since that critical move was played by his opponent. The cross and resurrection of Jesus are that move. Since then the game goes on: the problems remain, the suffering continues and the outlook seems black. But the outcome is assured. Because of that cross and resurrection we can be confident of the final destiny of mankind and the world. It is not bound for destruction and chaos, but for the omega point of God's purpose. That phrase from Teilhard de Chardin must not be taken to imply, as I think he implied, an evolutionary optimism based on Darwinian parallels. Such is not the Christian hope for the future. That would be to treat with insufficient seriousness the fallen nature of man. There is nothing in the human prospect that gives ground for ultimate optimism. But then the New Testament never encourages us to suppose that all will gradually improve in this, the best of all possible worlds. On the contrary, Jesus warns his followers that all will get worse before the climactic return of the Son of Man at the end of history (Mark 13; Matt. 24). Christians *must* strive for better conditions on earth, if the spirit of their Master really indwells them; to heal, to teach, to care, to love–this is his way. And yet Christians must never succumb to the liberal myth of building 'Jerusalem in England's green and pleasant land'. The 'Jerusalem that is above, which is the mother of us all', is not ours to build. God will bring it about in his time and in his way. The consummation of the kingdom will be as much God's sovereign work as was its inauguration through the coming and dying and rising of the Messiah. The Christian hope for the future has nothing whatever to do with such concepts as the perfectibility of man, the evolution of morals, or the eradication of ills in society. It depends simply and solely on God. And God has pledged his future by means of his decisive action in the past: the dying and rising of Jesus. As Jack Clemo puts it in his book *The Invading Gospel*, 'Truth did not for ever remain on the scaffold. Truth came down from the scaffold, walked out of the tomb and ate boiled fish'. The assurance about God's final outcome has been given already. That is the ground for true Christian optimism. There is nothing either shallow or anthropocentric about it. It does not fail to take seriously the appalling problems in our world to which people like Heilbroner and Higgins draw attention. It simply stakes all on the God who raises the dead. He has done it at the mid-point of time in one very special person, Jesus. He is the last Adam, the head of the new race, and his people's future is wrapped up in his own. Flesh and blood cannot inherit the kingdom of God. There is no way in which mortal man can win immortality. But 'just as we have borne the image of the man of dust, so we shall also bear the image of the man of heaven'. Just as we all share by our common humanity in the lot of the first Adam who became a living being; so we shall all share, by our common faith and baptism, in the lot of the last Adam who became a life-giving spirit (1 Cor. 15: 45-50).

What, then, has the New Testament to say about this final hope based on the resurrection of the crucified Messiah?

## The Release of the Spirit

The New Testament teaches that the release of the Holy Spirit in the life of believers is dependent upon the death and resurrection of Jesus (John 7: 39). The Paraclete could not come to the disciples unless Jesus 'went away' (John 16: 7). But once Jesus had died and risen the Spirit was poured out into the lives of the waiting disciples, as the Acts records and as the whole history of earliest Christianity makes abundantly plain. 'This Jesus God raised up' Peter is recorded as saying on the Day of Pentecost, 'and of that we are all witnesses. Being therefore exalted at the right hand of God, and having received from the Father the promised Holy Spirit, he has poured out this which you see and hear' (Acts 2: 32ff). The Holy Spirit is made available through the death and resurrection of Jesus, and he is the pledge, the *aparche* of God's new creation (Rom. 8: 22f; 1 Cor. 15: 20). He is that part of the future which we have now in the present. And the function of the Spirit in the lives of believers before the final curtain of God's drama, is clearly defined in the New Testament. This is to be no barren period of waiting, no time to kill before the Lord returns at the end of history to bring it to a climax. God has given us his Spirit for a threefold purpose.

First, the Holy Spirit is given in order to make disciples resemble Jesus. He is given into the lives of believers in order to transform them from one degree of *doxa*, 'glory', to another (2 Cor. 3: 18). His fruit is love, joy, peace, longsuffering and the like, in contrast to the works of self which are ugly–fornication, impurity, idolatry, enmity and so forth (Gal. 5: 16-26). Individual transformation of sinners is part of the reason for the gift of the Spirit.

But that is far from all. The Holy Spirit came, secondly, to form believers into the Community of the Resurrection: not only giving personal allegiance to the risen Jesus, but corporately celebrating his victory and praising his name. The whole life of worship in the church is the concern of the Holy Spirit. He longs to forge Christians into a corporate temple which he can inhabit, and which we all too easily ruin by our divisions (1 Cor. 3: 16ff). He longs to control the worship (14: 26f), as he did at Antioch (Acts 11: 27f; 13: 2), not to be organised out of the possibility of all intervention. He has gifts for his people: words of wisdom and knowledge, tongues and interpretations, gifts of healing and faith, gifts of prophecy and deliverance (1 Cor. 12: 8ff). Some he wants to make teachers, some leaders, some administrators in Christ's body (12: 27ff). He inspires the love and zeal, the hospitality and service, the hope and patience of different members of the Body (Rom. 12: 3-13). In all this he is seeking to equip the Christian community to be, here and now in the present brutal world, a 'colony of heaven' (Phil. 3: 20). The life and behaviour, the love and mutual service of Christians is all the work of the Spirit. Jesus is the chief cornerstone in the building, and 'in him the whole structure is joined together and grows into a holy temple in the Lord: in whom you also are built into it for a dwelling place of God in the Spirit' (Eph. 2: 21f).

Supremely at each eucharist the Church demonstrates that life of the age to come. It unambiguously declares that the cross and resurrection stand together as the central redemptive act of God. It embodies the polarity in which all Christians live. On the one hand we look back to that empty cross and the redemption achieved once for all through it. On the other we cry '*Marantha*' (1 Cor. 16: 22) and strain towards that future salvation, that perfect healing and salvation, of which the Lord's Supper is the pledge (11: 26). And now as the church celebrates the eucharist 'between the times', in the overlap of the ages, the Spirit of the risen Lord nourishes us, unites us and makes us willing and able to lay down our lives in sacrifice even as we draw on the power of Christ's resurrection. Certainly, the Spirit is given to disciples to make them the Body of Christ in and for a needy world.

And that leads into the third purpose for the giving of the Spirit. It is to equip the church for mission. Christians would never embark on the difficult task of evangelism were it not for the leading of the Holy Spirit. It is he who thrusts the church out in mission, he who provides the words to say (Mark 13: 10f). God intends the time before the End not to be empty but full of the church, full of the Spirit, full of mission. It is the Spirit who convicts of sin, who glorifies Christ in a person's eyes and makes him attractive. It is the Spirit who enables him to make the baptismal confession 'Jesus is Lord', who baptises him into Christ, who makes a new creature of him and gives him the assurance of belonging to the family of God, so that he can call God as Jesus did, *Abba*, Father (John 16: 8, 14; 1 Cor. 12: 1, 13; John 3: 5; Rom. 8: 15-17). At every point the initiative lies with the Holy Spirit. For in the economy of God his purpose is to make Christians holy, to make the church credible as the worshipping and loving Body of Christ, and to win others into the allegiance of the crucified and risen Jesus. The Spirit is the first instalment of God's future for us. He is the demonstration to us that God has a future for his world. In the Spirit we have a taste of that future.

*The security of dead believers*
Very early in the history of the church the problem of death reared its head. It may well be that the disciples expected Jesus to culminate his victory over death by bringing in the kingdom of God then and there. The puzzle caused by delay in the parousia is to be seen in many parts of the New Testament. But the remarkable thing is the confidence Christians had from the very beginning that their dead were safe in the company of Jesus. The resurrection showed Jesus to be the Messiah. And the Messiah was never without his people. The famous promise of John 14: 3 'When I go to prepare a place for you I will come again and take you to myself' is the heart of Jewish expectation about the Messiah. He and the Messianic people belong together. Jesus himself made use of much the same argument when rebuking the Sadducees about their unwillingness to believe in the resurrection and the power of God. His insistence that God *is*, not *was* the God of Abraham, Isaac and Jacob is actually the essence of all proper assurance about life after death. It depends totally on the grace and faithfulness of the God who will not scrap one who has trusted in him: instead, he calls him by his name. And that assurance has been underlined by the resurrection of Jesus.

Thus when the first Christians die off at Thessalonica or at Corinth, there is no gloom in the Christian camp. Confusion, maybe. But not gloom. For however much they may have expected the return of Christ first, they had no misgivings about their situation. Their dead were safe with Christ. They were 'with Christ, which is far better' (Phil. 1: 23). They were 'asleep', a lovely word from which we derive our 'cemetery'. It is based, as a description of the dead, on the words of Jesus to describe Jairus' little girl who had died: 'behold, she is not dead but asleep' (Mark 5: 39). The words speaks of suspended consciousness and animation, but of continuing life. There is no shallow euphemism in all this. The Gospels make very plain that death is a real enemy, the final enemy. We have already seen the contrast between the death of Jesus and the death of Socrates. Socrates saw death as a friend which would liberate his immortal soul. Jesus knew death was the ultimate and terrible enemy. It is death, and not the body, that must be conquered by the resurrection. Only when we take seriously the horror, the stench, the utter finality of death can we begin to appreciate the Easter exultation of the early church. 'Death before Easter is really the death's head surrounded by the odour of decay' wrote Cullmann. 'Whoever has not grasped the horror of death cannot join Paul in the hymn of victory: "Death is swallowed up in victory!"' (*Immortality of the Soul*, p. 27). There is nothing beautiful about the death inflicted on Jesus. He underwent death in all its most stringent horror, and he overcame. Those who love him are with the victor in that supreme battle. Such was the Christian confidence, and it was based fairly and squarely on the resurrection of Christ from the most awesome of deaths.

Thus Paul can say 'If Christ has not been raised, those who have fallen asleep in Christ have perished ... But in fact Christ *has* been raised from the dead' (1 Cor. 15: 17f). Their security lies in their union with him, who died for them and rose again. When, therefore, the Thessalonians plied Paul with questions about life after death, he was able to point them to an objective consideration which would rid them of the inconsolable grief and anguish of a Judaism or a paganism which had very little hope. 'We would not have you ignorant, brethren, concerning those who are asleep, that you may not grieve as others who have no hope. For since we believe that Jesus died and rose again, even so, through Jesus, God will bring with him those who have fallen asleep' (1 Thess. 4: 13f). He goes on to assert that the believers who are living at the end of history will not get the better of those who are asleep. No! The dead in Christ will rise first, and then there will be a wonderful reunion with each other and the Lord for ever. 'Therefore comfort one another with these words'. I am sure they did!

The resurrection was one of the most basic elements in Christian teaching (Heb.6: 1, 2). It was the basis not only of the Christian gospel but of the Christian hope. It changed the whole attitude to mourning and bereavement among Christians. The departed had gone to be with the Lord! Despite uncertainties about whether the dead Christian was conscious (as seems to be indicated by Heb. 12: 1; Phil. 1: 23) or asleep (as seems to be indicated by Rev. 14: 13; 1Thess. 4: 13), Christians had the deep assurance that the believing dead were *sun Christō*, 'with Christ'. That phrase is used characteristically in the New Testament to describe the position of the believing dead. *En Christō*, 'in Christ' is the common way, particularly in Paul, of describing the situation of the Christian living. *Sun Christō* seems to denote a particularly close intimacy of the departed with their risen Lord. The state is not described in any detail. It is simply *with Christ*. And that is sufficient guarantee of their total security.

Such confidence about the future, born from the atoning death and resurrection of Jesus, has beautiful results. It grows the fruit of peace instead of gnawing worry about the future: 'Have no anxiety about anything', writes the apostle Paul from prison. 'Let your requests be made known to God, and the peace of God which passes all understanding will guard your hearts and minds in Christ Jesus' (Phil. 4: 6, 7). That attitude was superbly exemplified by Peter in prison, the night before he was due for execution: he was, we are told, 'sleeping between two soldiers' (Acts 12: 6), peacefully dreaming!

If you have that serene confidence about the future, you can face any hardship with confidence. The worst that can happen is that you get killed. But even that will usher you into the closer presence of your Lord, so it is to be welcomed when the time comes. Romans 8: 37-9 is the classic expression of that confidence, but 2 Corinthians 1: 9 runs it close. Paul had been through some terrible hardship which brought him to the edge of death. He was 'unbearably crushed, so that he despaired of life itself'. But that, he observed, was intended to make him rely not on himself but on God who raises the dead. 'He delivered us from so deadly a peril, and he will deliver us; on him we have set our hope that he will deliver us again' (2 Cor. 1: 10).

This ability to face anything in the knowledge that even death could not separate from Christ, meant that the Christians, at their best, had a proper indifference to whether they lived or died. The important thing was to fulfil God's purpose for them (Acts 20: 24). Therefore Paul can quite coolly consider the pros and cons of living on for further ministry, and going to be with Christ, which seemed to him preferable (Phil. 1: 21-4). 'To me to live is Christ and to die is gain' he could say: and he lived that way. Time and again he was on the very edge of death, and it did nothing to deter him from his course (2 Cor. 11: 23ff). That explains how he and Silas could lie in a stinking inner prison singing at midnight! (Acts 16: 25). They knew the believing dead were not worse off than the living, but better: they knew they were secure with the Christ who had died for their sins and was raised for their justification.

## Third Day and Last Day

We cannot go further into the future hope unless we concentrate on the return of Jesus Christ. The unified eschatological expectation of the Old Testament was radically transformed by Jesus. He taught that with him the Kingdom of God had come, but yet that it was still future. There was an 'already' and a 'not yet' in the last days which he inaugurated. The coming of Jesus had split the *eschaton*. The ultimate revelation of God had come. The ultimate redeemer of God had acted. Yet there still remained a consummation to the Kingdom. And at the end mankind would be face to face with the Jesus who had already come. The great New Testament hope is the public appearance and public coronation of the Jesus who is even now on the throne of the universe.[1]

---

[1] See S.H. Travis, *I Believe in the Second Coming of Jesus.*

The one who rose on the third day will return at the last day
(Acts 1: 11; 3: 20; 17: 31; Phil. 1: 6; 3: 20; 1 Thess. 4: 16; 5: 2;
Heb. 10: 25; 2 Pet. 3: 10). *This same Jesus* will return at the
climax of history. And although the expectation is developed
in a multitude of ways in the New Testament, the overall
emphasis is that Jesus in person is the one with whom we will
have to do in the end. This is by no means a shallow happy
ending, or an anthropocentric myth. It answers the most
profound questions we could pose about the future. Is the
world going anywhere or not? Yes, it is. History is neither
circular nor aimless. It is essentially *his story*, and it is leading
to the return of the King. Is human nature worth anything in
this increasingly impersonal world? Yes, it is worth everything.
For in the end it is by the man Jesus that we shall be saved–and
judged. Is there any meaning in the universe? Yes, there is. The
ultimate reason, *logos*, in the universe has taken human form,
has died for us and risen again, and in the last day will take us to
himself. Is it, then, just a matter of waiting for his return? By no
means. We meet him incognito along the daily paths of life: by
our response to the poor and needy, the prisoners and the
hungry. Thus we either do or do not build up a faculty of
recognising him: we shall know him when we see him face to
face (Matt. 25: 31-46; 1 John 2: 28). Gradually this practice in
discerning him will change us into his likeness (1 John 3: 2, 3).

One of the New Testament's favourite words for the ultimate
disclosure of Christ at the end of time, is *parousia*. It can mean
both 'presence' and 'coming', and often there may well be a
deliberate ambivalence in its use (1 Cor. 15: 23; 1 Thess. 2: 19; 4:
15; 5: 23; 2 Thess. 2: 1, 8; James 5: 7f; 2 Pet. 3: 4; 2 Cor. 10: 10; 1
John 2: 28). For the one who is to come is also the one who has
come, and who is already present with us through his Spirit.
*This same Jesus* shall return . . . In this way the New Testament
maintains the continuity between the incarnate, risen and
coming Jesus. They are inseparable. And that is how we can
have confidence for God's purposes for our world. In the end it
will be a transformation of this world, not something entirely

different. Jesus is the one who holds that continuity together in his own person.

Another key word for the return of Christ loved by the writers of the New Testament is *apokalupsis* or *epiphaneia*, 'unveiling' or 'manifestation' (1 Cor. 1: 7; 2 Thess. 1: 7; 2: 8; 1 Tim. 6: 14; 2 Tim. 4: 1, 8; 1 Pet. 1: 7, 13; 1 John 3: 2). The Jesus who came on the first day, and rose on the third day, is even now King, albeit hidden. One day the veil will be ripped aside and all men will see him as he is (Luke 17: 24; Rev. 1: 7). What is now clear to the eye of faith will be made universally manifest in the last day.

Such is the heart of the Christian hope about the future. It is not utopian nonsense, for it is based on the resurrection of Jesus. *This same Jesus* shall return.

And when he does, he will not return alone. Already the people of the Messiah are risen with Christ in a provisional sense (Col. 3: 1). At the end, dead Christians will come with Christ. The Messiah is never separated from his people. At the parousia 'God will bring with him those who have fallen asleep', when he comes, not in solitary glory, but 'to be glorified in his saints' (2 Thess. 1: 10). So the goal of all history is not even 'the blessed hope, the appearing of the glory of our great God and Saviour Jesus Christ' (Tit. 2: 13) but the parousia of the whole Christ, head and members, Saviour and saved together. That is why the New Testament lays such stress on the importance of the last day. Final salvation will be corporate.

*The resurrection of the body*
Intimately associated with the last day is the resurrection of the body. It is this which is the final Christian hope for all believers. It is this which is indicated by the resurrection of the body of Jesus.

Let us be clear what is not meant by the resurrection of the body in Christian teaching.

It is not the temporary resuscitation of a corpse. That happened to Lazarus, the widow of Nain's son, Jairus'

daughter and perhaps a few others in the time of Jesus. It has
happened through the kiss of life and life support systems in
our own day, very often. But all such people die again. That is
not the Christian hope.

It is not the reconstitution of our present body. Many Jews
clearly expected resurrection at the last day (John 11: 24) to be
an exact replica of the present body, warts and all. In the time
of the Maccabees men looked for the reassembling and
restoration of the tortured limbs of the martyrs (2 Macc. 7: 14-
38; 14: 46). Baruch asks God 'In what shape will those live who
live in thy day?' and the answer is 'The earth will then assuredly
restore the dead, which it now receives, in order to preserve
them, making no change in their form, but as it has received, so
it will restore them, and as I delivered them unto it, so also will
it raise them' (2 Baruch 49: 2-4). Thus many dying rabbis gave
detailed instructions as to how they were to be buried and how
their corpse was to be clothed, for the *Tractate Sanhedrin* held
that a man would be raised in the same clothes in which he was
laid in the tomb (*Sanhedrin*, 90b). Naturally Jewish speculation was not entirely crass. 2 Esdras 7: 97 strikes the note of
transformation 'how their face is destined to shine like the sun,
and how they are destined to be made like the light of the stars,
henceforth uncorruptible'. 2 Baruch, too, anticipates transformation into the splendour of angels, suffused with
loveliness and light (51: 5, 10). But none of this is more than a
development of the two passages in the Old Testament which
speak specifically of the resurrection life to come (Isa. 26: 19
and Dan. 12: 2, 3). Here we find a general resurrection ('many'
in Dan. 12: 2 being a Hebraism for 'all'), a physical
resurrection, two destinies, and the transformation of
believers. O'Collins is wrong in his claim that there were many
contradictory resurrection doctrines in first century Judaism
(*The Easter Jesus*, p. 105). There were certainly variations in
detailed expectations, but with the possible exception of the
*Book of Wisdom*, which sold out to Greek views of the
immortality of the soul because it was seeking to commend
Judaism to those versed in Greek philosophy, all Jewish

expectations of life after death looked for an embodied life on a renewed earth. For to the Hebrew mind, man does not have a body: he is a body, a psychosomatic unity.

If the Christian hope is neither resuscitation nor reassembly, it is certainly not the immortality of the soul. Man is not inherently immortal. Life, whether now or hereafter, is never seen as a possession of man, but as a gift of God. That is why, to the Hebrew, the body is not a 'tomb' as it was to many Greek thinkers like Socrates and Plato: it was an essential form of expression for the person. Again, death was not a 'friend', liberating the immortal soul from the earthly confines of the body: it was the last enemy, it was utterly final–unless there is indeed a God who raises the dead.

No. The Christian hope of resurrection is none of these things. The Old Testament sees man as 'flesh', *basar*. It is a word that speaks of our frailty and creatureliness. It lies behind two Greek words which must at least be glanced at, *sarx* and *soma*, both sometimes translated 'flesh' and 'body', but actually quite distinct.

I do not have *sarx* (flesh). I am *sarx*. It means an earthly being, a weak and fallen being, a mortal being compared with the living God who creates and sustains all life. But a sinister note is introduced into *sarx*: it becomes the seat of sin and rebellion, for that, too, is part of fallen man (Rom. 8: 6ff).

Equally, I do not have a *sōma* (body). I am *soma*. For many of their wide range of meanings *sōma* and *sarx* would be interchangeable. But there is a difference. While *sarx* speaks of man in his frailty and alienation from the Creator, the sinful, fallen mankind, *soma* on the other hand, may denote all that, but sees us as made by God for him. To be sure, the *sōma* is captive, like the *sarx*, to sin and death (Rom. 6: 12; 8: 11; 7: 24; 8: 10; Col. 2: 11) but there is a fundamental difference. The fate of the *sarx* is to be destroyed: *sarx* can never inherit the kingdom of God (1 Cor. 15: 50). But the marvellous good news of the gospel is that our *sōma* can be raised with Christ (Rom. 8:11; 1 Cor. 6: 13f).

Now we are in a position to understand the argument of Paul

in 1 Corinthians 15. Whether his opponents at Corinth were maintaining that the only life after death is the immortality of the soul, or whether they believed that for such enthusiastic believers as themselves 'the resurrection was past already' (2 Tim. 2: 18) is of secondary importance. Paul was asserting that Christ had risen bodily, as the Jews expected would happen at the last day. But he had risen on the third day! In Jesus alone, the destiny of the righteous at the end had been anticipated. Even his resurrection bespoke no inherent quality of his own: God had given him a body as he chose. The flesh of Christ had been totally transformed and taken up in the resurrection. He was sown a mortal body: he was raised a spiritual body. That does not mean that his body was any the less body. It does mean that it was dominated by the Spirit. The key words are indeed, as O'Collins has seen (*The Easter Jesus*, p. 112) 'continuity' and 'transformation', just as they were in the best Jewish thought about the resurrection. But now through the resurrection of Jesus, as Paul realised on the Damascus road, there is in existence an actual example of the spiritual body, the risen Jesus. And the apostle is clear that the people of the risen Messiah will share his type of risen body.[1]

Continuity and transformation: that is precisely the message of the seed and the ear, which is the only analogy Paul produces. What a marvellous one it is. How could we guess at the glory of a complete ear of corn, waving in full ripeness in the field, if we had never seen one? We could not even hazard a guess, as we looked at the shrivelled little grain in our hand. But put that grain in the ground, and the principles of transformation and continuity hold good: the miracle takes place.

But it is just at this point, as we saw in chapter 8, that Professor Lampe makes his objection (*The Resurrection*, p.

---

[1]Augustine has a shrewd comment on the resurrection body. It will be, he says, a spiritual body in the sense that 'the spiritual flesh shall become subject to the spirit, yet shall it be flesh still, as the carnal spirit before was subject to the flesh and yet a spirit still' (*City of God*, 22).

59). When Christians die they do not immediately rise like Christ, he points out–very properly. His conclusion is that Paul did not believe in the empty tomb and that Jesus was not physically raised. But he misses the essential point. Paul does not believe that dead Christians share the condition of the risen Christ *now*: but that in the last day they *will*. At present Jesus is the only resurrected body in existence. He is the firstfruits. The full harvest will come at the end, when all will rise with their full resurrection body, given by God as it pleases him (1 Cor. 15: 38). He is the prototype of us all. But only the prototype is in existence hitherto. Dr. C.F.D. Moule most sensitively picks up Lampe's objection and gives a most illuminating answer to it.

> Perhaps it is permissible to speculate, very tentatively, along the following lines. Literal belief in the empty tomb would mean that the material of which the body was composed was somehow transformed into a different mode of existence... it would mean that it was actually taken up into and superseded by the new mode, rather as fuel is used up into energy.

That is, of course, precisely not what happens to the bodies of Christians. They decompose: they are not transformed. Professor Moule continues:

> But is it possible that the total matter of this space-time existence is destined by the Creator not to be scrapped, but to be used up into some other existence?

This would certainly be congruous with the idea of a God who never creates anything without a purpose. He goes on:

> If so, is it inconceivable that in just the area of the body of Jesus, which alone had been surrendered to death in total, absolute obedience to the will of God, this transformation and using up was anticipated; while with the rest of mankind the 'material' returns to the collective reservoir of the totality

of matter one way or another, by decomposition slow or sudden, until this totality of things is ultimately used as the material of a new existence in which they, by the grace of God, will share? (*The Significance of the Message of the Resurrection,* ed. C.F.D. Moule, p. 10)

In other words, the resurrection body of Jesus is the pledge and the pattern for that of believers at the last day.

And the last day needs to be stressed. For the New Testament makes it plain that believers who have died are not now already in the final bliss, even though they are with the Lord. In 2 Corinthians 5: 1-10 Paul wrestles with the notion of nakedness, disembodiedness, which he knows he may have to face if he dies before the parousia. He wants to have the 'clothing' of his heavenly house, the resurrection body, put on over this earthly tent in which he lives, without having to undergo death and have that tent struck. But he knows that such may not be God's purpose for him. He knows that 'nakedness' is a possibility. And in a moving passage in Revelation 6:9, where the souls of the martyrs cry out 'Lord, how long?', it is plain that the Christian dead are like us, between the times. They too have waited.

Final bliss will not be for any of God's redeemed until it is for all. But the cross and resurrection have been the great turning point. It is through them that the martyrs can face death unafraid. They are with Christ. They are asleep. They are at peace. They rest from their labours. To be sure, they remain in the interim state; but while in it, they have a special intimacy and union with their risen Lord. The teeth of death have been drawn through that representative death and resurrection of the Head of the race. Therefore believers are not abandoned in death: they have the Spirit of the risen One within them, and they are already blessed in death ('from now on' in Rev. 14: 13). Even now 'death is swallowed up in victory' (1 Cor. 15: 54). Although the full realisation of the new body and the new creation belong to God's future, believers can say with joy and confidence, 'whether we live or die we belong to the Lord'. For 'Christ is Lord of the living and the dead' (Rom. 14: 8, 9).

## The Kingdom of God

All through the Bible, and most notably in the teaching of Jesus, the Kingdom of God has a very prominent place. Jesus came to proclaim that Kingdom, indeed in one sense to inaugurate it. The Christian hope is that at the end of history he will consummate it.

Plato at the end of *The Republic* maintained that it was not possible to speak meaningfully of the start and close of the existence of the world without resort to myth, picture language. This does not at all impugn the reality of the event; it merely recognises that if we seek to describe the beyond in the terms of the present we can at best do so only figuratively. And so the golden streets of the heavenly Jerusalem, the casting of crowns before the throne of God, the heavenly Jerusalem foursquare like a cube (the perfect shape), and radiant with jewels (the most precious things man possesses)–all such language is *evocative* rather than *descriptive*. It is meant to take the most wonderful conceptions we are capable of and say to us 'There, God's future is like that, only infinitely more wonderful. Lift up your eyes! Strengthen your drooping limbs! God has promised to bring in his final salvation, and he can be trusted.'

The Bible closes with two of the most marvellous pictures of God's Kingdom in its fulfilment.

Then I saw a new heaven and a new earth; for the first heaven and the first earth had passed away, and there was no more sea. And I saw the holy city, new Jerusalem, coming down out of heaven from God, prepared as a bride adorned for her husband; and I heard a loud voice from the throne saying 'Behold, the dwelling of God is with men. He will dwell with them, and they shall be his people, and God himself shall be with them; he will wipe away every tear from their eyes, and death shall be no more, neither shall there be mourning nor crying nor pain any more. For the former things have passed away.

And he who sat on the throne said 'Behold I make all things new'... and he said 'I am the Alpha and the Omega, the beginning and the end. To the thirsty I will give of the water of life without payment. He who conquers shall have this heritage, and I will be his God and he shall be my son.' (Rev. 21: 1-7).

It is all there: the marriage relationship between the Messiah and his people; the cessation of the restless ebb and flow of the sea of life (Jews were convinced landlubbers!); the church-holy, prepared, waiting; God's removal of pain and sorrow, of suffering and even death; and finally, his indissoluble joining to all his people. We are brought face to face with the God who acts, who makes all things new, who is both Alpha and Omega in his universe. It is he, and he alone who brings about the Messianic marriage, who brings in the heavenly Jerusalem. And to the end he remains a giver. He offers the unfailing fountain of his life to all: only those are excluded who reject his clemency and generosity, who rush past the arms of love extended to them on the cross, and away from the Risen One whose love pursues them (21: 27).

As if this were not enough, the very last chapter of the Bible takes the picture a little further.

Then he showed me the river of the water of life, bright as crystal, flowing from the throne of God and of the Lamb through the middle of the street of the city; also, on either side of the river, the tree of life with its twelve kinds of fruit, yielding its fruit every month; and the leaves of the tree were for the healing of the nations. There shall be no more any-thing accursed, but the throne of God and of the Lamb shall be in it, and his servants shall worship him; they shall see his face, and his name shall be on their foreheads. And night shall be no more; they need no light of lamp or sun, for the

Lord God will be their light, and they shall reign for ever and ever (22: 1-5).

It is God who produces the water of eternal life; to turn away from him means ultimate self-destruction: there is no way in which this element can be removed from the teaching of the Bible or of the empty cross. But for those who allow Christ to reconcile them, what riches are allusively set forth here! Constant fruitfulness; complete healing for all the nations of the redeemed; where the mark of Cain had once marred the forehead, the mark of God's Spirit and possession is seen instead; no more night, no more sin, no more curse. Total victory at last for all God's ransomed creation. Paradise Lost has become Paradise Regained. And the only possible response of redeemed humanity is to worship the God who conceived such cosmic salvation, and the Lamb who has stepped from his empty cross to the throne of the universe.

What a vision this new creation of new heavens and new earth presents to us with, full of renewed people! How different from the eschatology of Communism which sees the fulfilment state on this earth with all the failures of sinful men and women disfiguring it; with only one class, the proletariat, sharing in it: and only those who are alive at the end, not those whose labours built the Revolution and its sequel. How different from some humanist assumptions, taken from Aristotle, that human life on this earth would go on for ever! What a shallow thought that is in these days of bristling nuclear armaments. Christian thought, for all its diversity, has never anticipated an unchanged eternal life of man on this earth, but always has stretched out towards God's completion of what he has inaugurated in the incarnation, death and resurrection of Jesus. This Jesus is already reigning. He is already at the right hand of God. He is already on the throne of the universe. But his reign is hidden and his enemies rampant. Oscar Cullmann has helpfully distinguished the reign of Christ (hidden but real all the time between the Advents) from the reign of God, when at the parousia Jesus will submit himself as the head of the new humanity and renewed universe to his Father, God, who is blessed for ever (1 Cor. 15: 24-8).

> Then comes the end, when Christ delivers the kingdom to God the Father after destroying every rule and every authority and power. For Christ must rule until he has put all his enemies under his feet. The last enemy to be destroyed is death. When all things are subjected to him, then the Son himself will also be subjected to him who put all things under him, that God may be everything to everyone.

We are now in the *regnum Christi*: at the end it will be the *regnum Dei*. That is the event towards which all creation strives. For the created order is subject to frustration and decay, just like its human inhabitants. But one day

> the creation itself will be set free from its bondage to decay and obtain the glorious liberty of the children of God. We know that the whole creation has been groaning in travail until now; and not only the creation, but we ourselves, who have the firstfruits of the Spirit, groan inwardly as we wait for adoption as sons, the redemption of our bodies. For in this hope we were saved (Rom. 8: 21ff).

Majestic, breathtaking hope. Hope that soars beyond what man could conceive. 'Eye has not seen nor ear heard nor the heart of man conceived the things that God has prepared for those who love him. But God has revealed them to us by his Spirit' (1 Cor. 2: 9).

But is it all pie in the sky? Are we to agree with Troeltsch that 'there is far more certainty about the advent of the last man cooking the last potato with the last fire of coals, than . . . of the Second Coming of Christ'? Alas, in a nuclear holocaust there will be only seconds of warning, if that. The last man will not have time to cook his last potato before mankind is wiped out on this earth.

Or are we to oscillate between despair and hope, like Jean-

Paul Sartre at the end of his life? He wrote in a journal in 1980:

> With this third world war which might break out one day, with this wretched gathering which our planet now is, despair returns to tempt me. The idea that there is no purpose, only petty personal ends for which we fight! We make little revolutions, but there is no goal for mankind. One cannot think such things. They tempt you incessantly, especially if you are old and think 'Oh well, I'll be dead in five years at the most.' In fact, I think ten, but it might well be five. In any case the world seems ugly, bad, and without hope. There, that's the cry of despair of an old man who will die in despair. But that's exactly what I resist. I know I shall die in hope. But that hope needs a foundation.

It does indeed: Sartre was dead within a month. That foundation he needed is the empty cross of Jesus Christ. That is the sign, given to us in the midst of history, that life on earth will not go out like a light, and that history is not a tale told by an idiot, full of sound and fury, signifying nothing. It is the story of God's comprehensive salvation for his rebel world. And the pledge of the validity of that future hope is the bitter cross and empty tomb. Karl Barth was strong in insisting on the physical resurrection and empty tomb of Jesus: not because the empty tomb is the Easter faith. It is not. But it is the necessary precondition of it. It is the *sign* that, in the midst of our suffering and death, God has acted decisively. He has shown us what he is going to do for the world. He will not scrap it. He will take the constituent elements within it and make something new.

Dr. Roger Pilkington in his book *World Without End* gives these reflections on the resurrection body of Jesus:

> If matter is no more than an arrangement of energy, then it is perfectly conceivable (if surprising), that where the sheer essence of the whole creation was poured into human form, the body could dissociate into sheer energy and redistil, as it

were, outside the tomb, in a state which was, on the whole, more energy than matter, but definitely material enough to have some shape and substance.

Long before him, Augustine, though innocent of physics, had envisaged something similar. An image maker, he points out, can melt down a statue and remodel it without its former unshapeliness, while at the same time using every particle again (*City of God*, 22.20). Cannot God, he asks, do the same?

Cannot God do the same–and more? Christians believe he can, and they are not credulous: they are persuaded by the empty cross. It tells them that God cares so very much about us in our alienation that he is willing to come and bear it. It tells them that he has shared our human life and we belong to him. It tells them that he has conquered sin and death and is the final victor. It tells them that there is nothing in the whole wide world which is stronger or more durable than sacrificial love. That love is on the throne of the universe. It is hardly surprising, then, that the note of worship predominates in the Apocalypse, that book which constantly holds in counterpoint the ghastly mess in the world and the glorious victory of the empty cross. John sees the redeemed in heaven, numbering 'myriads of myriads and thousands and thousands, saying with a loud voice "Worthy is the Lamb who was slain to receive power and wealth and wisdom and might and honour and glory and blessing".' And every creature in heaven fell down and said 'Amen'. And just as the empty cross in history, so the bread and wine in worship constitute the sign of God's Kingdom, inaugurated by Christ, and one day to be consummated by him.[1] It is on the Lord's day, and especially in the eucharist, that we are most powerfully made aware of the

---

[1]Moltmann in *Theology of Hope* p. 228 shows that Barth is wrong in talking of Christ's parousia as only unveiling his kingly rule and not adding anything. 'The Christian hope expects from the future of Christ not only unveiling but also final fulfilment'. Moltmann's book has a valuable, if speculative, final section on the outworking of Christian understanding of eschatology in modern society.

indissoluble link between the third day and the last day. Never in our highest experience of worship, never in the furthest extent of heaven, will God's people cease to pour out love and worship for that empty cross of Jesus.

# Select Bibliography

Writing on this subject is immense, but the following are a few books I have found helpful.

J.N.D. Anderson, *A Lawyer among the Theologians*, Hodder.
G. Aulén, *Christus Victor*, S.P.C.K.
D.M. Baillie, *God was in Christ*, Faber.
W. Barclay, *Crucified and Crowned*, S.C.M.
C.K. Barrett, 'The Background of Mark 10.45' in *New Testament Essays*, ed. A.J.B. Higgins, Black.
F.R. Barry, *The Atonement*, Hodder.
K. Barth, *Dogmatics in Outline*, S.C.M.
D. Bonhoeffer, *The Cost of Discipleship*, S.C.M.
E. Brunner, *The Mediator,* Lutterworth.
N. Clarke, *Interpreting the Resurrection*, S.C.M.
O. Cullmann, *Immortality of the Soul or Resurrection of the Body?*, Epworth.
R.W. Dale, *The Atonement*, Hodder.
R.J. Daly, *The Origins of the Christian Doctrine of Sacrifice*, D.L.T.
J. Denney, *The Death of Christ*, IVP.
*The Christian Doctrine of Reconciliation*, Hodder.
F.W. Dillistone, *The Significance of the Cross*, Lutterworth.
*The Atonement*, Nisbet.
C.F. Evans, *Resurrection and the New Testament*, S.C.M.
L. Evely, *The Gospels without Myth*, New York.
P.T. Forsyth, *The Justification of God*, Independent Press.
*The Cruciality of the Cross*, Independent Press.
*The Work of Christ*, Independent Press.
L. Geering, *Resurrection, a Symbol of Hope*, Hodder.

M. Green, *The Day Death Died*, IVP.
H.E. Guillebaud, *Why the Cross?* IVP.
M. Hengel, *The Crucifixion*, S.C.M.
*The Atonement*, S.C.M.
F.C.N. Hicks, *The Fulness of Sacrifice*, S.P.C.K.
M.D. Hooker, *Jesus and the Servant*, Epworth.
*Jesus and the Son of Man*, Epworth.
L. Hodgson, *The Doctrine of the Atonement*, Scribners.
T.H. Hughes, *The Atonement: Modern Theories of the Doctrine*, Allen & Unwin.
J.F. Jansen, *The Resurrection of Jesus Christ in New Testament Theology*, Westminster.
J. Jeremias, *The Eucharistic Words of Jesus*, S.C.M.
W. Künneth, *The Theology of the Resurrection*, S.C.M.
G.E. Ladd, *I Believe in the Resurrection of Jesus*, Hodder.
G.W.H. Lampe and D.M. McKinnon, *The Resurrection*, Mowbrays.
W. Marxsen, *The Resurrection of Jesus of Nazareth*, S.C.M.
R.C. Moberley, *Atonement and Personality*, Murray.
J. Moltmann, *The Crucified God*, S.C.M.
*Theology of Hope*, S.C.M.
L. Morris, *The Apostolic Preaching of the Cross*, Tyndale.
*The Cross in the New Testament*, Paternoster.
'The Meaning of "hilasterion" in Romans 3.25', *New Testament Studies*, ii, 1955.
C.F.D. Moule (ed), *The Significance of the Message of the Resurrection for Faith in Jesus*, S.C.M.
L. Newbigin, *Sin and Salvation*, S.C.M.
G. O'Collins, *The Easter Jesus*, D.L.T.
W. Pannenberg, *Jesus, God and Man*, S.C.M.
R.S. Paul, *The Atonement and the Sacraments*, Abingdon.
O.C. Quick, *The Gospel of the New World*, Nisbet.
A.M. Ramsey, *The Resurrection of Christ*, Bles.
H. Rashdall, *The Idea of the Atonement in Christian Theology*, Macmillan.
P. Stuhlmacher, 'Das Bekenntnis zur Auferweckung Jesu von

den Toten und die Biblische Theologie', *Zeitschrift für Theologie und Kirche,* 70, 1973.

V. Taylor, *The Atonement in New Testament Teaching,* Epworth.

*Jesus and his Sacrifice,* Epworth.

*Forgiveness and Reconciliation,* Epworth.

*The Cross of Christ,* Epworth.

G.W.C. Thomas, Article in *Church Quarterly Review,* April-June 1957.

K.C. Thompson, *Once for All,* Faith.

H.E.W. Turner, *The Patristic Doctrine of Redemption,* Mowbrays.

G. Vermes, *Jesus the Jew,* Collins.

J. Wenham, *Easter Enigma,* Paternoster.

B.F. Westcott, *The Victory of the Cross,* Macmillan.

D.E.W. Whiteley, 'St. Paul's Thoughts on the Atonement', *Journal of Theological Studies,* ii, 1957.

H.A. Williams, *True Resurrection,* Mitchell Beazley.

*Jesus and the Resurrection,* Mitchell Beazley.

F.M. Young, *Sacrifice and the Death of Christ,* S.P.C.K.

U. Wilckens, *Resurrection,* St. Andrew.